BARRON'S
BILINGUAL BUSINESS GUIDES

TALKING BUSINESS IN ITALIAN

Dictionary and Reference for International Business

Phrases and Words You Need to Know

by Frank G. Rakas
Director, Exhibition Center/Market Research
Italian Trade Commission
New York City

P9-CSG-495

BARRON'S

BARRON'S EDUCATIONAL SERIES, INC.
New York • London • Toronto • Sydney

650.03
RAK

© Copyright 1987 by Barron's Educational Series, Inc.

All rights reserved.
No part of this book may be reproduced in any form, by photostat, microfilm, xerography, or any other means, or incorporated into any information retrieval system, electronic or mechanical, without the written permission of the copyright owner.

All inquires should be addressed to:
Barron's Educational Series, Inc.
113 Crossways Park Drive
Woodbury, New York 11797

Library of Congress Catalog Card No. 86-14645
International Standard Book No. 0-8120-3754-5

Library of Congress Cataloging-in-Publication Data
Rakas, Frank G.
Talking business in Italian.

1. Business—Dictionaries. 2. Commerce—Dictionaries. 3. Business—Dictionaries—Italian. 4. Commerce—Dictionaries—Italian. 5. English language—Dictionaries—Italian. 6. Italian language—Dictionaries—English. I. Barron's Educational Series, inc. II. Title.
HF1001.R35 1987 650′.03′51 86-14645
ISBN 0-8120-3754-5

PRINTED IN THE UNITED STATES OF AMERICA

789 969 987654321

CONTENTS

Preface and Acknowledgments v

Pronunciation Guide 1

Introduction
Doing Business in Italian-speaking Countries 3

Before You Go... 6

BASIC WORDS AND PHRASES 9

General words and phrases for getting by, including amenities, answers to standard questions, and other essential expressions.

BUSINESS DICTIONARY 41

English to Italian 41
Italian to English 130
Key Words for Key Industries 213

GENERAL INFORMATION 235

Abbreviations 235
Weights and Measures 239
Temperature and Climate 240
Communications Codes 241
Postal Services 242
Time Zones 242
Major Holidays 244
Currency Information 244
Major Periodicals 245
Annual Trade Fairs 246
Travel Times 248
Travel Tips 249
Major Hotels 252
Major Restaurants 254
Useful Addresses 256
Maps 258

PREFACE

It is the nature of business to seek out new markets for its products, to find more efficient ways to bring its goods to more people. In the global marketplace, this often means travel to foreign countries, where language and customs are different. Even when a businessperson knows the language of the host country, the specific and often idiosyncratic terminology of the business world can be an obstacle to successful negotiations in a second language. Pocket phrase books barely scratch the surface of these problems, while standard business dictionaries prove too cumbersome.

Now there is a solution—Barron's *Talking Business in Italian.* Here is the essential pocket reference for all international business travelers. Whether your business be manufacturing or finance, communications or sales, this three-part guide will put the right words in your mouth and the best expressions in your correspondence. It is a book you'll carry with you on every trip and take to every meeting. But it is also the reference you'll keep on your desk in the office. This is the business dictionary for people who do business.

Barron's *Talking Business in Italian* offers you the following features:

- a 6,000-entry list of basic business terms, dealing with accounting, advertising and sales, banking, computers, export/import, finance and investment, labor relations, management, manufacturing, marketing, retail and wholesale sales, and more.
- a quick guide to basic terms and expressions for getting by when you don't know the language.
- a pronunciation guide for speaking the language.
- a comprehensive list of common business abbreviations.
- reference words for numbers and amounts, days of the week, months and seasons of the year.
- conversion tables for metric and customary measurements.
- lists of major holidays, annual trade fairs, travel times between cities, average temperatures throughout the year.
- information on international currencies, country and city telephone codes, useful addresses in the foreign countries.

This book is one of a new series of business dictionaries. We welcome your comments on additional phrases that could be included in future editions.

Acknowledgments

We would like to thank the following individuals and organizations for their assistance on this project:

John Downes, Business Development Consultant, Office for Economic Development, New York, New York; Gianfranco Paone of Long Island Trust; Luciana Silvers of the Ital Trade USA Corporation; Warren T. Schimmel, Senior Vice-President, Academic Affairs, The Berkeley Schools; the Commercial Office of the Embassy of Italy in the United States for their assistance in preparing the Introduction; and Dolores Maggiore and Viera Morse, for their detailed and careful attention to the manuscript.

Portions of Part I of this book are reprinted with permissions from *Italian at a Glance,* by Mario Costantino, published by Barron's Educational Series, Inc. The information about Switzerland in the Introduction is reprinted with permission from Pierre Weil's Introduction to *Talking Business in French,* also published by Barron's.

PRONUNCIATION GUIDE

This book assumes you are already somewhat familiar with the basic pronunciation rules of Italian, but for those whose knowledge is a little rusty, here are some tips. Many vowels and consonants in Italian are pronounced as they would be in English. There are some exceptions, however, which are given below. Since these sounds don't usually vary, you can follow these guidelines in pronouncing all Italian words. Note: When pronouncing the words in the following examples, stress the vowels that appear in CAPITAL letters.

ITALIAN LETTER(S)	SOUND IN ENGLISH	EXAMPLE
	Vowels	
a	ah (yacht)	casa (kAH-sah), house
è	eh (net)	leggere (lEH-jeh-reh), to read
e	ay (hay)	mela (mAY-lah), apple
i	ee (feet)	libri (lEE-bree), books
o	oh (rope)	boccone (boh-kOH-neh), mouthful
u	oo (cool)	tutto (tOOt-toh), everything
	Consonants	
ci	chee (cheese)	cinema (chEE-nay-mah), movies
ce	chay (chair)	piacere (pee-ah-chAY-reh), pleasure
ca	kah (cot)	casa (kAH-sah), house
co	koh (cold)	cotto (kOHt-toh), cooked
che	kay (kent)	perchè (pehr-kAY), because
chi	key (key)	pochi (pOH-key), few
gi	jee (jeep)	giro (jEE-roh), turn
ge	jay (general)	generale (jay-nay-rAH-leh), general
gh	gh (spaghetti)	spaghetti (spah-ghAY-tee)
gli	ll (million)	egli (AY-ly-ee), he bottiglia (boht-tEE-ly-ee-ah), bottle

ITALIAN LETTER(S)	SOUND IN ENGLISH	EXAMPLE
gn	ny (can<u>y</u>on)	magnifico (mah-ny-EE-fee-koh), magnificent
qu	koo (<u>qu</u>iet)	aquila (AH-koo-ee-lah), eagle
sce sci	sh (fi<u>sh</u>)	pesce (pAY-sheh), fish sciopero (shee-OH-peh-roh), strike
z or zz	ts (ea<u>ts</u>)	pizza (pEE-tsah), pizza zero (tsEH-roh), zero

INTRODUCTION

DOING BUSINESS IN ITALIAN

by Stephanie Siciarz, Cultural Office, Embassy of Italy in the United States

Doing business with another culture and in another language can be a difficult and mystifying experience. Customs and procedures may be quite different from what is perceived as the "normal" way of conducting oneself in a business circumstance.

In this introduction, some important cultural and economic aspects of Italy and Switzerland are outlined. Basic knowledge of these facts will assist you in effectively conducting business in the Italian speaking world.

Usual Hours of Operation

Italy	Mon to Fri 8:30 or 9:00 AM – 12:30 & 3:00 PM – 5:30 or 6:00 PM
Switzerland	Mon to Fri 7:30 AM – 5:30 PM with 1 – 2 hours lunch

Business Customs

Italy: Italian business people tend to be quite formal. For instance, when the title of an Italian executive is unknown, he/she should be addressed as *Dottore/Dottoressa.* This title generally denotes one who has earned the equivalent of an American bachelor's degree. Also, at the beginning of a business meeting, casual conversation is appropriate. The aggressive "strictly business" attitude of some American businessmen is not common in the Italian business world, and this American aggressiveness could be mistaken for rudeness or coldness. It is advisable, however, to avoid addressing current political events, as Italians are very politically aware and opinionated; a discussion of politics could lead to heated debate and awkwardness for the American executive.

Switzerland: Discretion is highly valued in all circumstances. Punctuality is important for any occasion, business or social. Refrain from first-name basis also.

General Government Policy and Economic Situation

Italy: The Italian Republic is subdivided into twenty regions, each of which is to a large extent an autonomous entity. Each region is governed by a regional Council within the guidelines set by the Constitution and the laws of the State. Each region is also responsible for its own police, markets, sanitation, tourism, museums and libraries, and education, among others. These legislative functions must not conflict in any way, however, with the national interest or with the interest of other regions.

Although Italy is among the seven most industrialized democracies in the world, agriculture continues to play an important role in the Italian economy. Agricultural production, which has remained extremely stable, engages approximately 12% of Italy's work force. The major crops are wheat, grapes, sugar beets, olives, and fruits. Current improvements in mechanization, fertilization, and irrigation should increase the efficiency of production.

Industry, which accounts for approximately 33% of Italy's labor force, is very diverse, encompassing production of iron and steel, chemicals and fuel oils, electrical machinery, and textiles.

The production of iron and steel is of particular importance, despite the fact that it must rely on the fluctuation of the automobile and building industries. Italy is the fourth world producer of steel and machine tools.

The chemical industry accounts for a major portion of the Italian economy as well. Italy is one of the biggest world producers of such chemical products as fertilizers, dyes, plastics, fuel oils, and pharmaceuticals.

In the field of electrical machinery and appliances, Italy has become the first world producer of electric motors, the second world producer of sewing machines and motorcycles, and the third world producer of household appliances.

The textile industry has a long history and accounts for a generous portion of Italy's foreign trade profit. Italy is the first world producer of leather apparel and ranks third in the world for the production of fabrics after the United States and Japan. Italian clothing and footwear have enjoyed especially strong demand in the foreign market.

The remainder of Italy's work force is divided into the service sector, which accounts for 40% of the labor force and includes such fields as commerce, transportation, and communication; and the field of public administration, which accounts for 15% of those employed.

Italy is largely a free economy, though governmental participation does play an important role particularly in the industrial sector. Through the large holding companies of the State, such as the IRI (Institute for Industrial Reconstruction), the ENI (National Hydrocarbons Agency), and others, the government is able to exercise power in order to further develop this important sector of the economy.

Main imports: Consumer goods, raw materials, fuels, machinery.

Main exports: Automobiles, wines, petroleum derivatives, organic chemical products, textiles, steel and metal products, motors and machinery, industrial equipment, office machinery, furniture, clothing, footwear, jewelry.

Principal trading partners: Countries with which Italy conducts the most business include, the United States, Belgium, Luxembourg, France, Federal Republic of Germany, United Kingdom, Austria, Switzerland, Netherlands, USSR, Saudi Arabia, Libya, and Iran. Italy, which conducts a major portion of its trade activity with other European nations, is a member of the European Economic Community (EEC). In 1984 Italy's trade balance showed a deficit of $6 million.

Inflation rate: Slightly over 8%*.

Population: 56.6 million.

Language: The principal language of Italy is Italian. Accents and dialects vary from region to region, with the purest Italian considered that of the Toscana region (Tuscany). In the Valle d'Aosta region on the French border, French is spoken as well as Italian. Similarly, in the Friuli-Venezia Giulia region bordering Yugoslavia there is a Slovakian language spoken, and in the Alto Adige region bordering Austria and Switzerland one is likely to hear some German. In addition, in the regions of Puglia, Calabria, and Sicily, there are small Greek-speaking and Albanian-speaking communities.

Religion: Roman Catholic.

GNP: $360 billion.

GNP per inhabitant: $6,400.

Unemployment rate: 10.4%.

Switzerland: The Swiss Confederation is made up of about 3,000 communes that have a great deal of local autonomy. The 26 cantons (or states) each have their own constitution and their own method of choosing representatives to the federal level. The Italian-speaking area of Switzerland is in the canton of Ticino. Bellinzona is its capital and Lugano is its principal city.

Switzerland is a highly industrialized country based on a free market economy.

Major industries: Machinery, machine tools, precision instruments, chemicals, pharmaceuticals, textiles.

Main imports: Foodstuffs, agricultural and forestry products, coal, oil, textiles, clothing, paper, leather goods, construction materials, metal products, motor vehicles, raw materials.

Main exports: Precision instruments, watches, machinery, chemicals, pharmaceuticals, electronics, textiles.

Principal trading partners: West Germany, France, the United States, Italy, the United Kingdom.

Inflation rate: 4% (1983).*

Population: 6.6 million.

Languages: German 65%, French 18%, Italian 10%, Romansch 1%, others 6%.

Religion: Roman Catholic 48%, Protestant 44%, others 8%.

GNP: $96.1 billion.

GNP per inhabitant: $14,773.

Unemployment rate: 1.2%.

In all Italian-speaking countries, during negotiations the pace is usually slower and it would be advisable not to use the hard-sell method. As elsewhere, an appointment is preferred and it is recommended to telephone if detained. Courtesy goes a long way to smooth the relationship.

* Statistics given in this section are generally accurate for the mid-1980s period.

BEFORE YOU GO . . .

Passports

All permanent U.S. residents must carry a valid passport. Application should be made by mail or in person at least eight (and preferably twelve) weeks in advance to either (1) a U.S. Passport Agency office located in twelve major cities and Washington, D.C.; (2) designated U.S. post offices throughout the country; or, (3) State and Federal courthouses. You may also consult your travel agent or international airline office. All of these offices will let you know what documents you need and the proper procedures to follow.

Requirements for citizens and non-citizens differ somewhat. No international travel tickets will be issued by an airline or travel agent to persons without valid passports.

Visas

No visas are required for Italy, Malta, or Switzerland for travelers with U.S. passports whose stay does not exceed three months.

Immunizations

There are no immunization requirements for smallpox or other diseases for entry into these countries or upon return to the United States. If you plan to include travel outside Europe to Asia, Africa or the Middle East, consult your doctor or the nearest U.S. Public Health Service office.

Customs and Currency Regulations

In general, travelers with U.S. passports are allowed to bring in fairly generous amounts of duty-free items for their own *personal* use. These items include tobacco, alcohol and perfumes and are typically allowed in the following quantities (despite local variation):

400 cigarettes *or* 100 cigars *or* 500 grams of tobacco (about 1 lb.)
2 liters of wine or ¾ liters of liquor
2 ounces of perfume

If you are not well in excess of these amounts, a simple statement of "nothing to declare" will be respected by most customs officials.

For gifts whose final destination is the country you are entering, the rules are a bit stricter. It would be wise to check on the duty-free limits beforehand and to declare whatever is in excess.

For personal valuables like jewelry or furs and foreign-made items like watches, cameras, typewriters, or tape recorders (acquired before your trip) you should have proof of possession or register with U.S. Customs before departure. This will ensure that they are not subject to duty either by the United States upon return or by any country you visit.

Upon returning to the United States, each person has a duty-free allowance of $400, including 100 cigars and 1 carton of cigarettes. Each adult may bring in only 1 liter of wine *or* other liquor duty-free. Gifts worth $50 or less may be sent home subject to certain restrictions. For further up-to-date details, ask your travel agent or airline to provide a copy of U.S. Customs regulations.

There are usually no restrictions on the amounts of *foreign currency* (or checks) which foreign nationals may bring *into* these countries. However, in Italy the equivalent of L1,000,000 or more must be declared on entry or exit; and in Malta all foreign currency must be declared. If in doubt, consult a travel agent.

Traveler's Checks, Credit Cards, Foreign Exchange

All major international traveler's checks and credit cards are accepted by most hotels, restaurants and shops. However, it is always best to inquire at each establishment beforehand. The checks most recognized are: American Express, Barclays, Visa, CitiBank, and Bank of America. The cards most acceptable are: American Express, MasterCard, Visa, and Diners Club.

However, be advised that the exchange rate on dollar traveler's checks is almost always disadvantageous. If you want, you can buy foreign currency checks and/or actual currency in the United States before leaving at rates equivalent to or better than the bank rate you will get over there. Currency or checks may be purchased from retail foreign currency dealers. The largest of these, Deak-Perera, will send information if you contact them at: 29 Broadway, New York, NY 10006, 212-757-6915.

A warning to credit card users: When charging, make sure that the following information appears on the original and all copies of your bill: the correct date; the type of currency being charged (*francs, marks, kroner,* etc.); the official exchange rate for that currency on that date (if possible); and, the total amount of the bill. Without this information, you may end up paying at an exchange rate less favorable to you and more favorable to your European host, and for a larger bill than you thought!

Driver's License

A valid American (state) license is usually respected. However, if you have time, and want to avoid language problems on the road, it is a good idea to get an international drivers' document through the AAA or a local automobile club.

Electrical Appliances

If you plan to bring along any small electrical appliances for use without batteries, be aware that Europe's system of electric current and voltage differs from ours. If your appliance has no special internal adapters or converters made especially for use in Europe, you will have to supply your own. For most appliances, you will need *plug adapters* (one for continental Europe and one for Great Britain) that provide the proper number and shape prongs for European outlets.

For further information on foreign electricity, contact Franzus Company, 352 Park Avenue South, New York, NY 10010, 212-889-5850.

BASIC WORDS AND PHRASES

Fundamental Expressions

Yes.	Sì. (see)
No.	No. (noh)
Maybe.	Forse. (fOHr-seh)
Please.	Per piacere. (pEHr pee-ah-chAY-reh)
Thank you very much.	Mille grazie. (mEEl-leh grAH-tsee-eh)
You're welcome.	Prego. (prEH-goh)
Excuse me.	Mi scusi. (mee-skOO-see)
I'm sorry.	Mi dispiace. (mee dee-spee-AH-cheh)
Just a second.	Un momento. (OOn-moh-mEHn-toh)
That's all right/okay.	Va bene. (vah bEH-neh)
It doesn't matter.	Non importa. (nohn eem-pOHr-tah)
Sir	Signore (see-nyOH-reh)
Madame	Signora (see-ny-OH-rah)
Miss	Signorina (see-ny-oh-rEE-nah)
Good morning/afternoon.	Buon giorno (boo-OHn jee-OHr-noh)
Good evening/night.	Buona sera/notte. (boo-Oh-nah sAY-rah/nOH-teh)
Good-bye.	Arrivederci. (ahr-ree-veh-dAYr-chee)
See you later.	A più tardi. (ah pee-OO tAHr-dee)
So long.	Ciao. (chee-AH-oh)
See you tomorrow.	A domani. (ah doh-mAH-nee)

NOTE: Generally, **buon giorno** is used throughout the day until about 4–6 P.M. The expression **buon pomeriggio** ("good afternoon") is generally not used in conversation. **Buona sera** is used when meeting people in the late afternoon and throughout the evening. **Buena notte** is used when leaving at the end of the evening. The casual expression **ciao** ("hello", "bye", "so long") is used only with friends and family.

Glad to make your acquaintance.	Molto lièto[a]. (mohl-toh lee-AY-toh [ah])
How are you?	Come sta? (kOH-meh stah)
Very well, thank you.	Bene, grazie.(beh-neh grAH-tse-eh)
And you?	E lei? (ay lEH-ee)
Fine.	Bene. (beh-neh)
What is your name?	Come si chiama? (kOH-meh see key-AH-meh)
My name is ____.	Mi chiamo ____. (mEE-eh key-AH-moh)
How do you do?	Come sta? (kOH-meh stah)
Glad to meet you.	Lièto[a] di conoscérla. (lee-EH-toh [ah] dee koh-nOH-shehr-lah)
The pleasure is mine.	Il piacere è stato mio.(eel pee-ah-chAY-reh EH stAH-toh MEE-oh)
Where are you from?	Lei di dov'è? (lEH-ee dee doh-vEH)
How long will you be staying?	Quanto tempo resterà qui? (koo-AHn-toh tEHm-po reh-steh-rAH koo-EE)
What hotel are you staying at?	In quale hotel sta? (een koo-AH-leh oh-tEHl stAH)
Here's my address and my telephone number.	Ecco il mio indirizzo e il mio numero. (EHk-koh eel mEE-oh een-dee-rEE-tsoh ay eel mEE-OH nOO-meh-roh)
See you tomorrow.	A domani.(ah doh-mAH-nee)
See you later.	A più tardi/ciao. (ah pee-OO tAHr-dee/chee-AH-oh)

Communication

Do you speak English?	Parla inglese? (pAHr-lah een-glAY-seh)
I don't speak Italian.	Io non parlo italiano. (EE-oh nohn pAHr-loh ee-tah-lee-AH-noh)
I speak a little Italian.	Parlo poco l'italiano. (pAHr-loh pOH-koh lee-tah-lee-AH-noh)

Is there anyone here who speaks English?	C'è qualcuno qui chi parla inglese? (chEH koo-ahl-kOO-noh koo-EE key pAHr-lah een-gLAY-seh)
Please speak more slowly.	Parli più piano, per favore. (pAHr-lee peeOO pee-AH-noh pehr fah-vOH-reh)
Please repeat that.	Ripeta questo, per favore. (ree-pEH-tah koo-AYs-toh pehr fah-vOH-reh)
How do you say ____ in Italian?	Come si dice ____ in italiano? (kOH-meh see dEE-cheh een ee tah-lee-AH-noh)
What do you call this in Italian?	Come si chiama questo in italiano? (kOH-meh see key-AH-mah koo-AYS-toh een ee-tah-lee-AH-noh)

Common Questions and Phrases

Where is ____?	Dov'è ____? (doh-vEH)
When?	Quando? (koo-AHn-doh)
How?	Come? (kOH-meh)
How much?	Quanto? (koo-AHn-toh)
Who?	Chi? (key)
Why?	Perchè? (pehr-kAY)
Which?	Quale? (koo-AH-leh)
Here is ____.	Ecco ____. (EHk-koh)
There is ____.	C'è ____. (chEH)
There are ____.	Ci sono ____. (chee sOH-noh)
That is ____.	Quello[a] è ____. (koo-AYl-loh[ah] EH)
It is ____.	E ____. (EH)

Useful Nouns

address	l'indirizzo (leen-dee-rEE-tsoh)
amount	quantità, il prezzo (koo-AHn-tee-tah, eel prEH-tsoh)
appointment	l'appuntamento (lahp-poon-tah-mEHN-toh)
bill	il conto (eel-kOHn-toh)
business	l'affare (lahf fAH-reh)
car	la macchina, l'auto (lah MAH-key-nah, lAH-oo-toh)
cashier	il cassiere (eel kahs-see-AY-reh)
check	l'assegno (lahs-sAY-ny-oh)
city	la città (lah cheet-tAH)
customs	la dogana (lah doh-gAH-nah)
date	la data (lah dAH-tah)
document	il documento (eel doh-koo-mEHn-toh)

elevator	l'ascensore (lah-shayn-sOH-reh)
flight	il volo (eel vOH-loh)
friend	l'amico[a] (lah-mEE-koh[a])
hanger	l'attaccapanni (laht-tAH-kah-pAHn-nee)
highway	autostrada (lah-oo-toh-strAH-dah)
key	la chiave (lah key-AH-veh)
list	la lista (lah lEEs-tah)
luggage	il bagaglio (eel bah-gAH-ly-e-oh)
maid	la cameriera (lah kah-meh-reeEH-rah)
mail	la posta (lah pOHs-tah)
magazine	la rivista (lah ree-vEEs-tah)
manager	il direttore (eel-dee-reht-tOH-reh)
map	la carta, cartina (lah kAHr-tah, lah-kahr-tEE-nah)
mistake	lo sbaglio (loh-sbAH-ly-ee-oh)
money	il denaro (eel day-nAH-roh)
name	il nome (eel nOH-meh)
newspaper	il giornale (eel jee-ohr-nAH-leh)
office	l'ufficio (loof-fEE-chee-oh)
package	il collo, il pacco, il pacchetto (eel kOH-loh, eel pAH-koh, eel pah-kAY-toh)
paper	la carta (lah kAHr-tah)
passport	il passaporto (eel-pahs-sah-pOHr-toh)
pen	la penna (lah pAYn-nah)
pencil	la matita (lah mah-tEE-tah)
porter	il portabagagli (eel pOHr-tah-bah-gAH-ly-ee)
post office	l'ufficio postale (loof-fEE-chee-oh pohs-tAH-leh)
postage stamp	il francobollo (eel frahn-koh-bOHl-loh)
price	il prezzo (eel prEH-tsoh)
raincoat	l'impermeabile (leem-pehr-mayAH-bee-leh)
reservation	la prenotazione (lah preh-noh-tah-tsee-OH-neh)
rest room	il gabinetto (eel gah-bee-nAYt-toh)
restaurant	il ristorante (eel rEEs-toh-rAHn-teh)
road	la strada (lah strAH-dah)
room	la camera (lah kAH-meh-rah)
shirt	la camicia (lah kah-mEE-chee-ah)
shoes	le scarpe (leh skAHr-peh)

shower	la doccia (lah dOH-chee-ah)
store	il negozio (eel nay-gOH-tsee-oh)
street	la via, la strada (lah vEE-ah, lah strAH-dah)
suit	l'abito (lAH-bee-toh)
suitcase	la valigia (lah vah-lEE-jee-ah)
taxi	il tassì (eel tahs-sEE)
telegram	il telegramma (eel teh-leh-grAHm-mah)
telephone	il telefono (eel teh-lEH-foh-noh)
terminal	il capolinea (eel kah-poh-lEE-neh-ah)
ticket	il biglietto (eel bee-ly-AYt-toh)
time	l'ora, il tempo (lOH-rah, eel tEHm-poh)
tip	la mancia (lah mAHn-chee-ah)
train	il treno (eel trEH-noh)
trip	il viaggio (eel vee-AH-jee-oh)
umbrella	l'ombrello (lohm-brEH-loh)
waiter	il cameriere (eel kah-meh-ree-EH-reh)
watch	l'orologio (loh-roh-lOH-jee-oh)
water	l'acqua (lAH-koo-ah)

Useful Verbs (Infinitive Forms)

accept	accettare (ah-cheht-tAH-reh)
answer	rispondere (rees-pOHn-day-reh)
arrive	arrivare (ahr-ree-vAH-reh)
ask	domandare, chiedere (doh-mahn-dAHr-reh, key-AY-day-reh)
assist	aiutare (ah-ee-oo-tAH-reh)
begin	cominciare (koh-meen-chee-AH-reh)
bring	portare (pohr-tAH-reh)
buy	comprare (kohm-prAH-reh)
call	chiamare (key-ah-mAH-reh)
carry	portare (pohr-tAH-reh)
change	cambiare (kahm-bee-AH-reh)
close	chiudere (key-OO-deh-reh)
come	venire (vay-nEE-reh)
confirm	confermare (kohn-fayr-mAH-reh)
continue	continuare (kohn-tee-noo-AH-reh)
cost	costare (kohs-tAH-reh)
deliver	consegnare (kohn-say-ny-AH-reh)
direct	indicare (een-dee-kAH-reh)
do	fare (fAH-reh)

eat	mangiare (mahn-jee-AH-reh)
end	finire (fee-nEE-reh)
enter	entrare (ayn-trAH-reh)
examine	esaminare (ay-sah-mee-nAH-reh)
exchange	scambiare (skahm-bee-AH-reh)
feel	sentire (sayn-tEE-reh)
finish	finire (fee-nEE-reh)
fix	riparare (repair) (ree-pah-rAH-reh)
follow	seguire (say-goo-EE-reh)
forget	non-ricordare, dimenticare (nohn-ree-kohr-dAH-reh, dee-mehn-tee-kAH-reh)
forward	spedire (spay-dEE-reh)
get	ottenere (oht-teh-nAY-reh)
give	dare (dAH-reh)
go	andare (ahn-dAH-reh)
hear	sentire (sayn-tEE-reh)
help	aiutare (ah-ee-oo-tAH-reh)
keep	tenere (tay-nAY-reh)
know	sapere (fact) (sah-pAY-reh) conoscere (someone, something) (koh-nOH-shay-reh)
learn	apprendere (ahp-prAYn-deh-reh)
leave	partire (go out) (pahr-tEE-reh)
listen	ascoltare (ah-skohl-tAH-reh)
look	guardare (gooAHr-dAH-reh)
lose	perdere (pEHr-deh-reh)
make	fare (fAH-reh)
mean	significare (see-ny-ee-fee-kAH-reh)
meet	incontrare (een-kohn-trAH-reh)
miss	mancare (mahn-kAH-reh)
need	avere bisogno di (ah-vAY-reh bee-sOH-ny-oh dee)
open	aprire (ah-prEE-reh)
order	ordinare (ohr-dee-nAH-reh)
park	parcheggiare (pahr-kay-jee-AH-reh)
pay	pagare (pah-gAH-reh)
prefer	preferire (preh-fay-rEE-reh)
prepare	preparare (preh-pah-rAH-reh)
present	presentare (preh-sayn-tAH-reh)
prove	provare (pro-vAH-reh)
pull	tirare (tee-rAH-reh)
purchase	comprare (kohm-prAH-reh)
put	mettere (mAYt-tay-reh)
read	leggere (lEH-jeh-reh)
receive	ricevere (ree-chAY-vay-reh)

recommend	raccomandare (rAH-koh-mahn-dAH-reh)
remain	restare (rays-tAH-reh)
repair	riparare (ree-pah-rAH-reh)
repeat	ripetere (ree-pEH-teh-reh)
rest	riposare (ree-poh-sAH-reh)
return	ritornare (ree-tohr-nAH-reh)
run	correre (kOHr-ray-reh)
say	dire (dEE-reh)
see	vedere (vay-dAY-reh)
send	mandare (mahn-dAH-reh)
show	mostrare, indicare (mohst-rAH-reh, een-dee-kAH-reh)
sit	sedersi (say-dAYr-see)
speak	parlare (pahr-lAH-reh)
stand	alzarsi (ahl-tsAr-see)
start	cominciare (koh-meen-chee-AH-reh)
stop	fermare (fayr-mAH-reh)
take	prendere (prayn-dAY-reh)
talk	parlare (pahr-lAH-reh)
tell	dire (dEE-reh)
think	pensare (pehn-sAH-reh)
try	provare (proh-vAH-reh)
turn	girare (jee-rAH-reh)
use	utilizzare, servirsi di, usare (oo-teel-ee-tsAH-reh, sehr-vEEr-see dee, oo-sAH-reh)
visit	visitare (vee-see-tAH-reh)
wait	aspettare (ahs-peht-tAH-reh)
walk	camminare (kahm-mee-nAH-reh)
want	volere, desiderare, (voh-lAY-reh, day-see-day-rAH-reh)
wear	portare (pohr-tAH-reh)
work	lavorare (lah-voh-rAH-reh)
write	scrivere (skrEE-veh-reh)

Useful Adjectives and Adverbs

above/below	sopra/sotto (sOH-prah/sOHt-toh)
best/worst	migliore/peggiore (mee-ly-ee-OH-reh/peh-jee-OH-reh)
big/small	grande/piccolo[a] (grAHn-deh/pEE-koh-loh[ah])
early/late	presto/tardi (prEHs-toh/tAHr-dee)
easy/difficult	facile/difficile (fAH-chee-leh/deef-fEE-chee-leh)

few/many	pochi/molti (pOH-kee/mOHl-tee)
first/last	primo[a]/ultimo[a] (prEE-moh[ah]/OOl-tee-moh[ah])
front/back	anteriore/posteriore (ahn-teh-ree-OH-reh/pohs-teh-ree-OH-reh)
full/empty	pieno[a]/vuoto[a] (pee-AY-noh[ah]/voo-OH-toh[ah])
good/bad	buono[a]/cattivo[a] (boo-OH-noh[ah]/kaht-tEE-voh[ah])
hot/cold	caldo[a]/freddo[a] (kAHl-doh[ah]/frAYd-doh[ah])
high/low	alto[a]/basso[a] (AHl-toh[ah]/bAHs-soh[ah])
in front/in back	davanti/indietro (dah-vAHn-tee/een-dee-EH-troh)
inside/outside	dentro/fuori (dAYn-troh/fooOH-ree)
large/small	grande/piccolo[a] (grAHn-deh/pEE-koh-loh[ah])
more/less	più/meno (peeOO/mAY-noh)
near/far	vicino[a], prossimo[a]/lontano[a] (vee-chEE-noh[nah], prOH-see-moh[mah]/lohn-tAH-noh[nah])
old/new	vecchio[a]/nuovo[a] (vEHk-kee-oh/noo-OH-voh)
open/shut	aperto[ah]/chiuso[a] ([ah]-pEHr-toh[ah]/key-OO-soh[ah])
right/wrong	giusto[a]/sbagliato[a] (jee-OOs-toh[tah]/sbah-ly-AH-toh[tah])
slow/fast (adj.)	lento[a]/rapido[a] (lEHn-toh[tah]/rAH-pee-doh[dah])
slow/fast (adv.)	piano/presto (pee-AH-noh/prEHs-toh)
thin/thick	magro[a], fine/grosso[a], denso[a] (mAH-groh[grah], fEE-neh/grAH-soh[sah], dEHn-soh[sah])
to be right/wrong	avere ragione/avere torto (ah-vEH-reh rah-jee-OH-neh/ah/vEH-reh tOHr-teh)

Other Useful Words

a, an	un, uno, una (oon, OO-noh, OO-nah)
about	intorno (een-tOHr-noh)
across	attraverso (aht-trah-vEHr-soh)
after	dopo (dOH-poh)

again	un'altra volta, di nuovo (oon-AHl-trah vOHl-tah, dee noo-OH-voh)
all	tutto[a], tutti[e], (tOOt-toh[ah], tOO-tee[teh])
almost	quasi (kwAH-zee)
also	anche (AHn-keh)
always	sempre (sEHm-preh)
among	tra (trAH)
and	e (ay)
any	qualche (koo-AHl-keh)
another	un altro, un'altra (oon-AHl-troh, oon-AHl-trah)
around	intorno (een-tOHr-noh)
at	a, al, alla, etc. (ah, ahl, ahl-lah)
away	via (vEE-ah)
because	perchè (pehr-kAY)
before	prima di, davanti a (prEE-mah dee, dah-vAHn-tee ah)
behind	dietro a (dee-AY-troh)
between	fra (frAH)
both	tutti e due (toot-tee ay dOO-eh)
but	ma (mah)
down	giù (jee-OO)
each	ogni (OH-ny-ee)
enough	basta (bAHs-tah)
even if	anche se (AHn-keh seh)
every	ogni (OH-ny-ee)
except	eccetto (ay-chEH-toh)
few	pochi[e] (pOH-kee[keh])
for	per (pehr)
from	da, dal, dalla, etc. (dah, dahl, dahl-lah)
however	però (peh-rOH)
if	se (seh)
in	in, nel, nello, nella, etc. (een, nehl, nEHl-loh, nEH-lah)
instead	invece (een-vAY-cheh)
maybe	forse (fOHr-seh)
more	più (peeOO)
much	molto (mOHl-toh)
next to	vicino[a] (vee-chEE-noh[nah])
not	no, non (noh, nohn)
now	adesso/ora (ad-dEHs-soh/OH-rah)
of	di, dell, dello, della, etc. (dee, dehl, dEHl-loh, dEHl-lah)
often	spesso (spAYs-soh)
only	solamente (soh-lah-mEHn-teh)
or	o (oh)
other	altro[a] (AHl-troh[ah])

perhaps	forse (fOHr-seh)
same	stesso[a] (stAY-soh[ah])
since	poichè (poh-ee-kEH)
some	qualche (koo-AHl-keh)
still	ancora (ahn-kOH-rah)
that	che (kay)
these	questi[e] (koo-AYs-tee[ay])
this	questo[a] (koo-AYs-toh[ah])
to	a, al, alla, etc. (ah, ahl, AHl-lah)
unless	a meno che (ah mAY-noh keh)
until	fino a (fEE-noh ah)
very	molto (mohl-toh)
with	con (kohn)

Directions

North	il nord (eel nord)
South	il sud (eel sud)
East	l'est (lehst)
West	l'ovest (lOH-vehst)
Straight ahead	tutto diritto (tOO-toh dee-rEE-toh)
Left	sinistra (see-nEEs-trah)
Right	destra (dEHs-trah)
In the middle	in mezzo (een mEH-tsoh)

Days of the Week

Sunday	domenica (doh-mAY-nee-kah)
Monday	lunedì (loo-neh-dEE)
Tuesday	martedì (mahr-teh-dEE)
Wednesday	mercoledì (mehr-kok-leh-dEE)
Thursday	giovedì (jee-oh-veh-dEE)
Friday	venerdì (veh-nehr-dEE)
Saturday	sabato (sAH-bah-toh)
Today	oggi (OH-jee)
Yesterday	ieri (ee-EH-ree)
Tomorrow	domani (doh-mAH-nee)
Tonight	questa notte/stanotte (koo-AY-stah-nOHt-teh/stah-nOHt-teh)
Next week	la settimana prossima (lah seht-tee-mAH-nah prOH-see-mah)
Last week	la settimana passata (lah seht-tee-mAH-nah pahs-sAH-tah)
Next month	il mese prossimo (eel mAY-seh prOH-see-moh)
The day after tomorrow	dopodomani (dOH-poh-doh-mAH-nee)
This weekend	questa fine di settimana (koo-AYs-tah fEE-neh dee sayt-tee-mAH-nah)

What day is it today?	Che giorno è oggi? (kAY jee-OHr-noh EH OH-jee)
Today is _____.	Oggi è _____. (OH-jee EH)

Months of the Year

January	gennaio (jehn-nAH-ee-oh)
February	febbraio (fehb-brAH-ee-oh)
March	marzo (mAHr-tsoh)
April	aprile (ah-prEE-leh)
May	maggio (mAH-jee-oh)
June	giugno (jee-OO-ny-ee-oh)
July	luglio (lOO-ly-ee-oh)
August	agosto (ah-gOH-stoh)
September	settembre (seht-tEHm-breh)
October	ottobre (oht-tOH-breh)
November	novembre (noh-vEHm-breh)
December	dicembre (dee-chEHm-breh)
What's today's date?	Che data è oggi? (kay dAH-ta EH OH-jee)

The first of the month is *il primo* (an ordinal number). All other dates are expressed with *cardinal* numbers.

Today is August first.	Oggi è il primo di agosto. (OH-jee EH eel prEE-moh dee ah-gOH-stoh)
• fourth	• il quattro (eel koo-AHt-troh)
• 25th	• il venticinque (eel vayn-tee-chEEn-koo-eh)
This month	Questo mese (koo-AY-stoh mAY-seh)
Last month	Il mese scorso (eel mAY-seh skOHr-soh)
Next month	Il mese prossimo (eel mAY-seh prOHs-see-moh)
Last year	L'anno scorso (lAHn-noh skOHr-soh)
Next year	L'anno prossimo (lAHn-noh prOHs-see-moh)
May 1, 1876	Il primo maggio, mille ottocento settanta sei (EEl prEE-moh mAH-jee-oh mEEl-leh oht-toh-chEHn-toh seht-tAHn-tah-sEH-ee)
July 4, 1984	Il quattro luglio, mille novecento ottanta quattro (eel koo-AHt-troh lOO-ly-ee-oh mEEl-leh noh-veh-chEHn-toh oht-tAHn-tah koo-AHt-troh)

The Four Seasons

Spring	la primavera (lah pree-mah-vEH-rah)
Summer	l'estate (leh-stAH-teh)
Fall	l'autunno (lah-oo-tOOn-noh)
Winter	l'inverno (leen-vEHr-noh)
How is the weather today?	Che tempo fa oggi? (kay tEHm-poh fAH OH-jee)
It's good (bad) weather.	Fa bel/cattivo tempo.(fah behl/kaht-tEE-voh tEHm-poh)
It's hot.	Fa caldo.(fah kAHl-doh)
• cold	• freddo (frAYd-doh)
• cool	• fresco (frAY-skoh)
It's windy.	Tira vento. (tEE-rah vEEn-toh)
It's sunny.	C'è il sole. (chEH eel sOH-leh)
It's raining.	Piove. (pee-OH-veh)
It's snowing.	Nevica. (nAY-vee-kah)
It's drizzling.	Pioviggina. (pee-oh-vEE-jee-nah

Time

What time is it?	Che ora è? (kay OH-rah EH)

When telling time in Italian, *it is* is expressed by **è** for 1:00, noon, and midnight, **sono** is used for all other numbers.

It's 1:00	È l'una. (eh lOO-nah)
It's 12 o'clock (noon).	È mezzogiorno.(eh meh-tsoh-jee-OHr-noh)
It's midnight.	È mezzanotte. (eh meh-tsah-nOHt-teh)
It's early/late.	È presto/tardi.(eh prEH-stoh/tAHr-dee)
It's 2:00.	Sono le due. (sOH-noh leh dOO-eh)
It's 3:00, etc.	Sono le tre. (sOH-noh leh trAY)

The number of minutes after the hour is expressed by adding **e** ("and"), followed by the number of minutes.

It's 4:10.	Sono le quattro e dieci.(sOH-noh leh koo-AHt-roh ay dee-EH-chee)
It's 5:20	Sono le cinque e venti. (sOH-noh leh chEEn-koo-eh ay vAYn-tee)

Fifteen minutes after the hour and half past the hour are expressed by placing *e un quarto* and *e mezzo* after the hour.

It's 6:15.	Sono le sei e un quarto. (sOH-noh leh sEH-ee ay oon koo-AHr-toh)
It's 7:30.	Sono le sette e mezzo. (sOH-noh leh sEHt-teh ay mEH-tsoh)

After passing the half-hour point on the clock, time is expressed in Italian by *subtracting* the number of minutes to the *next* hour.

It's 7:40.	Sono le otto meno venti. (sOH-noh leh OHt-toh mEH-noh vAYn-tee)
It's 8:50.	Sono le nove meno dieci. (sOH-noh leh nOH-veh mAY-noh dee-EH-chee)
At what time?	A che ora? (ah kay OH-rah)
At 1:00.	All'una (ahl-lOO-nah)
At 2:00/3:00, etc.	Alle due/tre (AHl-leh dOO-eh/trAY)
A.M. (in the morning)	del mattino (dAYl-maht-tEE-noh)
P.M. (in the afternoon)	del pomeriggio (dAYl poh-meh-rEE-jee-oh)
At night.	Della notte. (dAYl-lah nOHt-teh)

Official time is based on the 24-hour clock. You will find train schedules and other such times expressed in terms of a point within a 24-hour sequence.

The train leaves at 15.30.	Il treno parte alle quindici a trenta. (eel trEH-noh pAHr-teh ahl-leh koo-EEn-dee-chee ay trEHn-tah)

Arrival/Hotel

My name is ____.	Mi chiamo ____. (mEE-eh keyAH-moh)
I'm American/British, Australian/Canadian.	Sono americano[a]/inglese/australiano[a]/canadese. (sOH-noh ah-mehr-ree-KAh-noh[ah]/een-glAY-seh/ah-oo-strah-lee-AN-noh[ah]/kan-nah-dAY-seh).

I'm staying at ____.	Sto abitando a ____. (stOH ah-bee- tAHn-doh ah)
Here is my ____.	Ecco il mio ____. (EHk-oh eel mEE-oh)
• passport	• passaporto (pahs-sah-pOHr-toh)
• business card	• la mia carta (la mEE-ah kAHr-tah)
I'm on a business trip.	Faccio un viaggio d'affari. (fAH-chee-oh oon vee-AH-jee-oh dahf-fAH-ree)
I'm just passing through.	Sono di passaggio. (sOH-noh dee pahs-sAH-jee-oh)
I'll be staying here for ____.	Ci sto abitando per ____. (chee stoh-ah-bee-tAHn-doh pehr)
• a few days	• qualche giorni (koo-AHl-keh jee-OHr-nee)
• a week	• una settimane (oo-nah seht-tee-mAH-neh)
• a few weeks	• qualche settimana (koo-AHl-keh seht-tee-mAH-nah)
• a month	• un mese (oon mAY-seh)
I'm traveling to ____.	Faccio il viaggio fino a ____. (fAH-chee-oh eel vee-AH-jee-oh FEE-noh ah)
I have nothing to declare.	Non ho niente da dichiarare. (nohn oh neeEHn-tay dah dee-key-ah-rAH-reh)
I'd like to go to the ____ Hotel.	Vorrei andare all'albergo ____. (vohr-rEH-ee ahn-dAH-reh ahl ahl-bEHr-goh)
Where can I get a taxi?	Dove si trova un tassì? (dOH-veh see trOH-va oon tahs-sEE)
I have a reservation.	Ho prenotazione. (OH preh-noh-tah-tsee-OH-neh)
I need a room for one night.	Ho bisogno di una camera per una notte. (OH bee-sOH-ny-oh dee OO-nah kAH-meh-rah pehr OO-nah nOHt-teh)
I want a double room with a bath.	Vorrei una camera doppia con bagno. (vohr-rEH-ee OO-nah kAH-meh-rah dOH-pee-eh kohn-bAH-ny-oh)
What is the rate per night?	Quant'è la camera? (koo-AHnt-ay lah kAH-meh-rah)
Does that include breakfast?	È compresa la colazione? (ay kohm-prEH-sah lah Koh-lah-tsee-OH-neh)
Where is the elevator?	Dov'è l'ascensore? (doh-vEH lah-shehn-sOH-reh)

Please send up some mineral water.	Mi mandi una bottiglia d'acqua minerale, per favore. (mee mAHn-dee OO-nah boht-tEE-ly-ee-ah dAH-koo-ah mee-neh-rAHl-leh pehr fah-vOH-reh)
Please wake me tomorrow at ____.	Per favore, mi svegli alle ____ domani. (pehr fah-vOH-reh mee svay-ly-ee AH-leh doh-mAH-nee)
Are there any messages for me?	Ci sono messaggi per me? (chee sOH-no mehs-sAH-jee pehr may)
I'd like to leave this in your safe.	Vorrei lasciare questo nella sua cassaforte. (vohr-rEH-ee lah-shee-AH-reh koo-AYs-toh nEH-lah soo-ah kAH-sa-fOHR-teh)
Please make this call for me.	Mi faccia questa telefonata. (mee fAH-chee-ah koo-AYs-tah teh-leh-fOH-nah-tah)
Would you please send someone up for my bags?	Mi faccia scendere il bagaglio, per favore? (mee fAH-chee-ah shAYn-day-reh eel bah-gAH-ly-ee-oh pehr fah-vOH-reh)
I'd like to check out.	Vorrei pagare il conto e partire. (vohr-rEH-ee pah-gAH-reh eel kOHn-to ay pahr-tEE-reh)

Transportation

bus	autobus (ah-oo-toh-bOOs)
train	treno (trEH-noh)
metro	metropolitana (meh-troh-poh-lee-tAH-nah)
ticket	biglietto (bee-ly-ee-AY-toh)
station	stazione (stah-tsee-OH-neh)
map	carting (kahr-tEE-nah)
stop	fermata (fehr-mAH-tah)
taxi	tassì (tahs-sEE)
Where can I rent a car?	Dove posso noleggiare una macchina? (dOH-veh POHs-soh noh-leh-jee-AH-reh OO-nah mAHk-kee-nah)
I want/I'd like ____.	Voglio/Vorrei ____. (vOH-lyee-oh/vohr-rEH-ee)
• a small car	• una macchina piccola (OO-nah mAHk-kee-nah pEE-koh-lah)

• a large car	• una macchina grande (OO-nah mAHk-kee-nah grAHn-deh)
• a sport car	• una macchina sportiva (OO-nah mAHk-kee-nah spohr-tEE-vah)
I prefer automatic transmission.	Preferisco il cambio automatico. (preh-feh-rEE-skoh eel kAHm-bee-oh ah-oo-toh-mAH-tee-koh)
How much does it cost ____?	Quanto costa ____? (koo-AHn-toh kOH-stah)
• per day	• al giorno (ahl jee-OHr-noh)
• per week	• alla settimana (AHl-lah seht-tee-mAH-nah)
• per kilometer	• per chilometro (pehr key-lOH-meh-troh)
• for unlimited mileage	• a chilometraggio illimitato (ah key-loh-meh-trAH-jee-oh eel-lee-mee-tAH-toh)
How much is the complete insurance?	Quant'è l'assicurazione completa? (koo-ahn-tEH las-see-koo-rah-tsee-OH-neh kohm-plEH-tah)
Is gas included?	E inclusa la benzina? (EH een-kloo-sah lah behn-tsEE-nah)
Do you accept credit cards?	Accetta carte di credito? (ah-chEHt-tah kAHr-teh dee krEH-dee-toh)
Here's my (international) driver's license.	Ecco la mia patente (internazionale) di guida. (EHk-koh lah mEE-ah-pah-tEHn-teh (een-tehr-nah-tsee-oh-nAH-leh) dee goo-EE-dah)
Do I have to leave a deposit?	Devo lasciare un acconto/un deposito? (dAY-voh lah-shee-AH-reh oon ahk-kOHn-toh/ oon day-pOH-see-toh)
Is there a drop-off charge?	C'è un supplemento per la consegna dell'auto? (chEH oon soo-pleh-mEHn-toh pehr lah kohn-seh-ny-ee-ah dayl-lAH-oo-toh)
I want to rent the car here and leave it in Turin.	Desidero noleggiare l'auto qui e consegnarla a Torino. (day-sEE-deh-roh noh-lay-jee-AH-reh lAH-oo-toh koo-EE ay kohn-say-ny-ee-AHr-lah ah toh-rEE-noh)

What kind of gasoline does it take?	Che tipo di carburante usa? (kay tEE-poh dee kahr-boo-rAHn-teh OO-sah)
Fill'er up with ____.	Faccia il pieno di ____. (fAH-chee-ah eel pee-AY-noh dee)
• diesel	• diesel (dEE-eh-sehl)
• regular (standard)	• normale (nohr-mAH-leh)
• super (premium)	• super (sOO-pehr)
Please check ____.	Per favore mi controlli ____. (pehr fah-vOH-reh mee kohn-trOHl-leh)
• the battery	• la batteria (lah baht-teh-rEE-ah)
• the carburetor	• il carburatore (eel kahr-boo-rah-tOH-reh)
• the oil	• l'olio (lOH-lee-oh)
• the spark plugs	• le candele (leh kahn-dAY-leh)
• the tires	• i pneumatici/le gomme (ee pnay-oo-mAH-tee-chee/leh gOHm-meh)
• the tire pressure	• la pressione delle gomme (lah prehs-see-OH-neh dAYl-leh gOHm-meh)
• the antifreeze	• l'acqua (lAH-koo-ah)
Change the oil (please).	Mi cambi l'olio, per favore. (mee kAHm-bee lOH-lee-oh pehr fah-vOH-reh)
Lubricate the car (please).	Mi lubrifichi la macchina, per favore. (mee loo-brEE-fee-key lah mAHk-kee-nah pehr fah-vOH-reh)
Charge the battery.	Mi carichi la batteria. (mee-kAH-ree-key lah baht-teh-rEE-ah)
Change this tire.	Mi cambi questa ruota. (mee kAHm-bee koo-AY-stah roo-OH-tah)
Wash the car.	Mi faccia il lavaggio alla macchina. (mee fAH-chee-ah eel lah-vAH-jee-oh AHl-lah mAHk-kee-nah)
Where are the restrooms?	Dove sono i gabinetti? (dOH-veh sOH-noh ee gah-bee-nAYt-tee)
Where is my hotel on this map?	Dov'è il mio albergo sulla cartina? (dov-vEH eel mEE-oh ahl-bEHr-goh sOO-lah khar-tEE-nah)

Drivers should be familiar with these universal road signs:

Guarded railroad crossing

Yield

Stop

Right of way

Dangerous intersection ahead

Gasoline (petrol) ahead

Parking

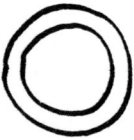

No vehicles allowed

Dangerous curve

Pedestrian crossing

Oncoming traffic has right of way

No bicycles allowed

No parking allowed

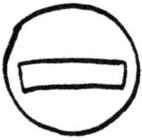

No entry

No left turn

No U-turn

No passing

Border crossing

Traffic signal ahead

Speed limit

Traffic circle (roundabout) ahead

Minimum speed limit

All traffic turns left

End of no passing zone

One-way street

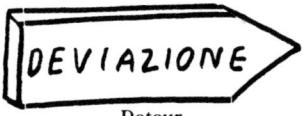

Detour

Danger ahead

Entrance to expressway

Expressway ends

Where is the bus stop?/the bus terminal?	Dov'è la fermata dell'autobus?/ il capolinea? (dov-vEH lah fehr-mAH-tah dayl-lAH-oo-toh-boos/eel kah-poh-lEE-neh-ah)
In which direction do I have to go?	In quale direzione devo andare? (een koo-AH-leh dee-reh-tsee-neh dAY-voh ahn-dAH- reh)
Where is the subway station?	Dov'è la stazione della metro-politana? (doh-vEH lah stah-tsee-OH-nee dAYl-lah meh-troh-poh-lee-tAH-nah)
How much is the fare?	Quanto costa il biglietto? (koo-AHn-toh kOH-stah eel bee-ly-ee-AYt-toh)
Where can I buy a ticket?	Dove posso comprare un biglietto? (dOH-veh pOHs-soh kohm-prAH-reh oon bee-ly-ee-AYt-toh)

Which is the train that goes to ____?	Qual è il treno che va a ____? (koo-ahl-lEH eel trEH-noh keh vah ah)
Does this train go to ____?	Questo treno va a ____? (koo-AYs-toh trEH-noh vAH ah)
Please tell me when we get there.	Può farmi sapere quando siamo arrivati. (poo-OH fAHr-mee sah-pAY-reh koo-AHn-doh see-AH-moh ahr-rEE-vah-tee)
Do I have to change trains?	Devo cambiare treno? (dAY-voh kahm-bee-AH-reh trEH-noh)
Is this seat taken?	È occupato questo postp? (EH oh-koo-pAH-toh koo-AYs-toh pOH-stoh)
Taxi! Are you free?	Tassì! È libero? (tahs-sEE EH lee-beh-roh)
Take me to this address.	Mi porti a questo indirizzo. (mee pOHr-tee ah koo-AYs-toh een-dee-rEE-tsoh)
How much is it?	Qual è la tariffa? (koo-ah-lEH lah tah-rEE-fah)
Faster. I'm in a hurry.	Più presto. Ho fretta.(pee-OO prEH-stoh. . .oh frAYt-tah)
Please drive slower.	Per cortesia guidi più piano. (pehr kohr-tay-sEE-ah goo-EE-dee pee-OO pee-AH- noh)
When is there a flight to ____?	Quando c'è un volo per ____? (koo-AHn-doh chEH oon vOH-loh pehr)
I would like ____.	Vorrei ____. (vohr-rEH-ee)
• a round trip/one-way ticket.	• un biglietto di andata e ritorno/di andata (oon bee-ly-ee-AYt-toh dee ahn-dAH-tah ay ree-tOHr-noh/dee ahn-dAH-tah)
• in tourist class	• in classe turistica (een klAHs-seh too-rEE-stee-kah)
• in first class	• in prima classe (een prEE-mah klAHs-seh)
I would like a seat ____.	Vorrei un posto ____. (vohr-rEH-ee OOn pOH-stoh)
• in the non/smoking section	• tra i non/fumatori (trAH ee nohn/foo-mah-tOH-ree)
• next to the window	• accanto al finestrino (ah-kAHn-toh ahl fee-neh-strEE-noh)
• on the aisle	• vicino al corridoio (vee-chEE-noh ahl kohr-ree-dOH-ee-oh)

What is the fare? Qual è il prezzo del biglietto? (koo-ah-lEH eel prEH-tsoh dAYl bee-ly-ee-EHt-toh)

Are meals served? Sono inclusi i pasti? (sOH-noh een-klOO-see ee pAH-stee)

When does the plane leave/arrive? A che ora parte/arriva l'aereo? (ah kay OH-rah pAHr-teh/ ahr-ree-vAH lah-EH-reh-oh)

When must I be at the airport? Quando dovrò trovarmi all'aeroporto? (koo-AHn-doh doh-vrOH troh-vAHr-mee ahl-lah-eh-roh-pOHr-toh)

What is my flight number? Qual è il [mio] numero di volo? (koo-AH-lEH eel [mEE-oh] nOO-meh-roh dee vOH-loh)

What gate do we leave from? Qual è la nostra porta d'uscita? (koo-ah-lEH lah nOH-strah pOHr-tah doo-shEE-tah)

I want to confirm/cancel my reservation for flight ____. Desidero confermare/cancellare la mia prenotazione per il volo ____. (day-sEE-deh-roh kohn-fayr-mAH-reh/kahn-chehl-lAH-reh lah mEE-ah preh-noh-tah-tsee-OH-neh pehr eel vOH-loh)

Leisure Time

Is there a discotheque here? C'è una discoteca qui? (chEE OO-nah dee-skoh-tEH-kah koo-EE)

Is there one at the hotel? C'è una in albergo? (chEE OO-nah een ahl-bEHr-goh)

I would like to make a reservation. Vorrei fare una prenotazione. (vohr-rEH-ee fAH-reh OO-nah preh-noh-tah-tsee-OH-neh)

Where is the check-room? Dov'è il guardaroba? (doh-vEH-eel goo-ahr-dah-rOH- bah)

Where can I find an English newspaper? Dove posso trovare un giornale in inglese? (dOH-veh pOHs-soh troh-vAH-reh oon jee-ohr-nAH-leh een een-glAY-seh)

I would like to see a soccer match. Vorrei vedere una partita di calcio. (vohr-rEH-ee veh-dAY-reh OO-nah pahr-tEE-tah dee kAHl-chee-oh)

Where can I buy the tickets? Dove posso comprare dei biglietti? (dOH-veh pOHs-soh kohm-prAH-reh dAY bee-ly-ee-AYt-tee)

Where is the stadium?	Dov'è lo stadio? (doh-vEH loh stAH-dee-oh)
What teams are going to play?	Quali squadre giocheranno? (koo-AH-lee skoo-AH-dreh jee-oh-keh-rAHn-noh)
Is there a pool near the hotel?	C'è una piscina nell'hotel? (chEE OO-nah pee-shEE-nah nAYl-loh-tEHl)
How far is ____?	Quanto dista ____? (koo-AHn-toh dEE-stah)

Restaurants

Breakfast	colazione (koh-lah-tsee-OH-neh)
Lunch	pranzo (prAHn-tsoh)
Dinner	cena (chEE-nah)
Excuse me, do you know a good restaurant?	Scusi, conosce un buon ristorante? (skOO-see koh-nOH-sheh OOn boo-OHN ree-stoh-rAHn-teh)
Is it very expensive?	È molto costoso? (eh mohl-toh koh-stOH-soh)
Waiter!	Cameriere! (kah-meh-ree-EH-reh)
We would like to have lunch.	Vorremmo pranzare. (vohr-rAYm-moh prahn-ts AH-reh)
The menu, please.	Il menu, per piacere. (eel may-noo pehr pee-ah-chAY-reh)
What's today's special?	Qual è il piatto del giorno? (koo-ah-lEH eel pee-AHt-toh dayl jee-OHr-noh)
What do you recommend?	Che cosa mi consiglia lei? (kay kOH-sah mee kohn-sEE-ly-ee-ah lEY-ee)
To begin with, bring us a cocktail.	Per cominciare, ci porti un cocktail. (pehr koh-meen-chee-AH-reh chee pOHr-tee oon kOHk-tayl)
A table for two, please.	Una tavola per due, per favore. (OO-nah tAH-voh-la pehr dOO-eh pehr feh-vOH-reh)
A bottle of • mineral water.	Una bottiglia d'acqua minerale • gassata. (oo-nah boht-tEE-ly-ee-ah dAH-koo-ah mee-neh-rAH-leh gahs-sAH-tah)
• a beer	• birra (bEEr-rah)
I would like to order now.	Vorrei ordinare adesso. (vohr-rEH-ee ohr-dee-nAH-reh ah-dEHs-soh)

Do you have a house wine?	Hanno il vino della casa? (AHn-noh eel vEE-noh dAYl-lah kAH-sah)
Waiter, we need ____.	Cameriere/a, abbiamo bisogno di ____. (kah-meh-ree-EH-reh/ah ahb-bee-AH-moh bee-sOH-ny-oh dee)
• a knife	• un coltello (oon kohl-tEHl-loh)
• a fork	• una forchetta (oo-nah fohr-kAYt-tah)
• a spoon	• un cucchiaio (oon koo-key-AH-ee-oh)
• a teaspoon	• un cucchiaino (oon koo-key-ah-EE-noh)
• a soup spoon	• un cucchiaio per la minestra/il brodo (oon koo-key-AH-ee-oh pehr lah mee-nEHs-trah/eel brOH-doh)
• a glass	• un bicchiere (oon bee-key-EH-reh)
• a cup	• una tazza (oo-nah tAH-tsah)
• a saucer	• un piattino (oon pee-aht-tEE-noh)
• a plate	• un piatto (oon pee-AHt-toh)
• a napkin	• un tovagliolo (oon tah-vah-ly-ee-OH-loh)
• toothpicks	• gli stuzzicadenti (ly-ee stOO-tsee-kah-dEHn-tee)
I would like an espresso, please.	Vorrei un espresso, per favore. (vohr-rEH-ee oon ehs-prEHs-soh pehr fah-vOH-reh)
Do you mind if I smoke?	Le dispiace se fumo? (leh dee-spee-ah-cheh sey fOO-moh)
Do you have a light/matches?	Ha un accendino/un fiammifero? (ah oon ah-chayn-dEE-noh/oon fee-ahm-mEE-feh-roh)
The check, please.	Il conto, per favore. (eel kOHn-toh pehr fah-vOH-reh)
Is the service included?	È incluso il servizio? (EH een-klOO-soh eel sehr-vEE-tsee-oh)
I don't think the bill is right.	Non penso che il conto sia corretto. (nohn pEHn-soh kay eel kOHn-toh sEE-ah kor-rEHt-toh)
Do you take credit cards?	Accettano carte di credito? (ah-chEHt-tah-noh kAHr-teh dee krEH-dee-toh)

Which ones?	Quale? (koo-AH-leh)
We're in a hurry.	Abbiamo fretta. (ahb-bee-AH-moh frAYt-tah)
Do you have American cigarettes?	Ha sigarette americane? (AH see-gah-rAY-teh ah-meh-ree-kAH-neh)
What brand?	Di che marca? (dee kay mAHr-kah)
Where are the restrooms?	Dove sono i gabinetti? (dOH-veh sOH-noh ee gah-bee-nAYt-tee)

Shopping

Where can I find ____?	Dove si trova ____? (dOH-veh see trOH-vah)
Can you help me?	Lei può aiutarmi? (lay poo-OH ah-ee-oo-tAHr-mee)
I need ____.	Ho bisogno di ____. (oh bee-sOH-ny-oh dee)
Do you have any others?	Ci sono altri ____? (chee sOH-noh AHl-tree)
Do you take credit cards?	Si accettano le carte di credito? (see ah-chEHt-tah-noh lay kAHr-teh dee krEH-dee-toh)
Can I pay with a traveler's check?	Posso pagare con un traveler's check? (pOHs-soh pah-gAH-reh kohn oon trAH-veh-lehs chEH-keh)
How much does ____ cost?	Quanto costa ____? (koo-AHn-toh kOHs-tah)
Do you have anything ____?	Ha qualche cosa ____? (AH koo-AHl-keh kOH-sah)
• smaller	• più piccolo (pee-OO pEE-koh-loh)
• larger	• più grande (pee-OO grAHn-deh)

Medical Care

Where is the nearest pharmacy?	Dov'è la farmacia più vicina? (doh-vEH lah fahr-mah-chEE-ah pee-OO vee-chEE-nah)
I need something for a ____.	Ho bisogno di qualche cosa per ____. (oh bee-sOH-ny-ee-oh dee koo-AHl-keh kOH-sah pehr)
• a cold	• il raffreddore (eel rah-frehd-dOH-reh)
• constipation	• la stitichezza (la stee-tee-kAY-tsah)
• a cough	• la tosse (lah tOH-seh)

• a headache	• il mal di testa (eel mAHl dee-tEH-stah)
• insomnia	• i'insonnia (leen-sOHn-nee-ah)
• a toothache	• il mal di denti (eel mAHl dee dEHn-tee)
• an upset stomach	• il mal di stomaco (eel mAHl dee-stOH-mah-koh)
I don't feel well.	Non mi sento bene. (nohn mee sEHn-toh bEH-neh)
I need a doctor right away.	Ho bisogno urgente del medico. (oh bee-sOH-ny-ee-oh oor-jEHn-teh dayl mEH-dee-koh)
Do you know a doctor who speaks English?	Conosce un dottore che parla inglese? (koh-nOH-sheh oon doht-tOH-reh kay pAHr-lah een-glAY-seh)
Where is his office/surgery?	Dov'è il suo ambulatorio? (doh-vEH eel sOO-oh ahm-boo-lah-tOH-ree-oh)
I have a pain in my chest.	Ho un dolore al petto. (oh oon doh-lOH-reh ahl pEHt-toh)
I had a heart attack.	Ho avuto un attacco cardiaco. (oh ah-vOO-toh oon ah-tAHk-koh kahr-dEE-ah-koh)
I am taking this medicine.	Sto prendendo questa medicina. (stOH prehn-dEHn-doh koo-AY-stah meh-dee-chEE-nah)
Do I have to go to the hospital?	Devo andare in ospedale? (dAY-voh ahn-dAH-reh een oh-speh-dAH-leh)
I have a toothache. Could you recommend a dentist?	Ho un mal di denti. Può raccomandarmi un dentista? (oh oon mAHl dee dEHn-tee. poo-OH rahk-koh-mahn-dAHr-mee oon dehn-tEE-stah)
I've broken these glasses.	Misi è rotta questi occhiali.
Can you replace them quickly?	Può darmene un'altro subito? (Mee see-EH rOHt-tah koo-AYs-tee oh-key-AH-lee.) (Poo-OH dAHr-meh-neh oon-nAHl-trah sOO-bee-toh)

Telephones

Where is ____?	Dov'è ____? (doh-vEH)
• a public telephone	• un telefono pubblico? (oon teh-lEH-foh-noh pOOb-blee-koh)

• a telephone booth	• una cabina telefonica? (OO-nah kah-bEE-nah teh-leh-fOH-nee-kah)
• a telephone directory	• un elenco telefonico? (oon eh-lEHn-koh teh-leh-fOH-nee-koh)
May I use your phone?	Posso usare il suo telefono? (pOHs-soh oo-sAH-reh eel sOO-oh teh-lEH-foh-noh)
Can I call direct?	Posso telefonare direttamente? (pOHs-soh teh-leh-foh-nAH-reh dee-reht-tah-mEHn-teh)
I want to reverse the charges.	Desidero fare una riversibile. (deh-sEE-deh-roh fAH-reh oo-nah ree-vehr-sEE-bee-leh)
Do I need tokens for the phone?	Occorrono i gettoni per il telefono? (ohk-kOHr-roh-noh ee jeht-tOH-nee pehr eel teh-lEH-foh-noh)
I want to make a ____ to ____.	Vorrei fare una ____ a ____. (vohr-rEH-ee fAH-reh OO-nah ah)
• local call	• telefonata urbana (teh-leh-foh-nAH-tah oor-bAH-nah)
• long-distance call	• una telefonata in teleselezione/interurbana, internazionale (OO-nah teh-leh-foh-nAH-tah een teh-leh-seh-leh-tsee-OH-neh/een-tehr-oor-bAH-nah, een-tehr-nah-tsee-oh-nAH-leh)
• person-to-person	• una telefonata diretta con preavviso (OO-nah teh-leh-foh-nAH-tah dee-rEHt-tah kohn preh-ahv-vEE-soh)
How do I get the operator?	Come si ottiene il centralino? (kOH-meh see oht-tee-EH-neh eel chehn-trah-lEE-noh)
Operator, can you give me ____?	Signorina (Signore) può darmi ____? (see-ny-oh-rEE-nah [see-ny-OH-reh] poo-OH dAHr-mee)
• number 23 345	• il ventitre trecentoquarantacinque (eel vayn-tee-trEH treh-chEHn-toh-koo-ah-rahn-tah-chEEn-koo-eh)
• extension 19	• interno diciannove (een-tEHr-noh dee-chee-ahn-nOH-veh)
• area code	• prefisso numero (preh-fEEs-soh nOO-meh-roh)

• country code	• prefisso internazionale (preh-fEEs-soh een-tehr-nah-tzee-oh-nAH-leh)
• city code	• prefisso interurbano (preh-fEEs-soh een-tehr-oor-bAH-noh)
My number is ____.	Il mio numero è ____. (eel mEE-oh nOO-meh-roh EH)
May I speak to ____?	Potrei parlare con ____? (poh-trEH-ee pahr-lAH-reh kohn)
I want to leave a message.	Vorrei lasciare un messagio. (vohr-rEH-ee lah-shee-AH-re oon mehs-sAH-jee-oh)
I was cut off.	È caduta la linea (ay kah-dOO-tah lah lEE-neh-ah)

Postal Service

Post Office	l'ufficio postale (loof-fEE-chee-oh poh-stAH-leh)
a post card	una cartolina postale (OO-nah kahr-toh-lEE-nah poh-stAl)
a letter	una lettera (OO-nah lAYt-teh-rah)
a telegram	un telegramma (oon teh-leh-grAHm-ah)
an airmail letter	una lettera via aerea (OO-nah lAYt-teh-rah vEE-ah ah-EH-reh-ah)
a registered letter	una lettera raccomandata (OO-nah lAYt-teh-rah rahk-koh-mahn-dAH-tah)
a package	un pacchetto (oon pah-kAYt-toh)
a special delivery letter	una lettera espresso (OO-nah lAYt-teh-rah ehs-prEHs-soh)
I would like to buy some stamps.	Vorrei comprare dei francobolli. (Vohr-rEH-ee kohm-prAH-reh day frahn-koh-bOHl-lee)
Which is the window?	Qual è lo sportello? (koo-ah-lEH loh spohr-tEHl-loh)
What is the postage to the United States/Canada/England/Australia?	Qual è l'affrancatura per gli Stati Uniti/Canada/Inghilterra/Australia? (koo-ah-lEH lahf-frahn-kah-tOO-rah per ly-ee stAH-tee oo-nEE-tee/kah-nah-dAH/een-gheel-tEHr-rah/ahoo-strAH-lee-ah)

I would like to mail a letter.	Vorrei spedire una lettera (vohr-rEH-ee spay-dEE-reh OO-nah lAYt-teh-rah)
Where is a letterbox?	Dov'è una cassetta postale? (doh-vEH oo-nah kas-sAYt-tah poh-stAH-leh)
I would like to send a telegram.	Vorrei mandare un telegramma. (vohr-rEH-ee mahn-dAH-reh oon teh-leh-grAMm-mah)
How late is the office open?	L'ufficio sta aperto fino a tardi? (loof-fEE-che-oh stah ah-pEHr-toh fEE-noh ah tAHr-dee)
How much is it per word?	Quanto costa la parola? (koo-AHn-toh kOH-stah lah pah-rOH-lah)

Signs

Acqua [non]potabile	(Not) potable water
Affito	For rent
Alt	Stop
Aperto	Open
Ascensore	Elevator (Lift)
Attenzione	Caution, watch out
Avanti	Enter (come in, go, walk [at the lights])
Caldo or "C"	Hot
Cassiere	Cashier
Chiuso	Closed
Divieto di sosta	No parking
Divieto di transito	No entrance, keep out
Donne Entrata	Ladies' Entrance
Freddo or "F"	Cold
Gabinetti (WC)	Toilets
Informazione	Information
Ingresso	Entrance
Libero	Vacant
Non calpestare le aiuole	Keep off the grass
Non Entrate	Do Not Enter
Non Fumate	No Smoking
Non ostruire l'ingresso	Don't block entrance
Non toccare	Hands off, don't touch
Occupato	Occupied
Pericolo	Danger
Privato	Private

Riservato	Reserved
Si affitta/si loca	For rent
Si vende	For sale
Signora	Women's room
Signore	Men's room
Spingere	Push
Strada privata	Private road
Tirare	Pull
Uomini	Men
Uscita	Exit
Vendite	For sale
Vietato fumare	No smoking
Vietato nuotare	No bathing
Vietato sputare	No spitting

Numbers

Cardinal Numbers

0	zero (tsEH-roh)
1	uno (OO-noh)
2	due (dOO-eh)
3	tre (trEH)
4	quattro (koo-AHt-troh)
5	cinque (chEEn-koo-eh)
6	sei (sEH-ee)
7	sette (sEHt-teh)
8	otto (OHt-to)
9	nove (nOH-veh)
10	dieci (dee-EH-chee)
11	undici (OOn-dee-chee)
12	dodici (dOH-dee-chee)
13	tredici (trEH-dee-chee)
14	quattordici (koo-aht-tOHr-dee-chee)
15	quindici (koo-EEn-dee-chee)
16	sedici (sAY-dee-chee)
17	diciassette (dee-chee-ahs-sEHt-teh)
18	diciotto (dee-chee-OHt-toh)
19	diciannove (dee-chee-ahn-nOH-veh)
20	venti (vAYn-tee)
21	ventuno (vayn-tOO-noh)
22	ventidue (vayn-tee-dOO-eh)
23	ventitrè (vayn-tee-trEH)
24	ventiquattro (vayn-tee-koo-AHt-troh)
25	venticinque (vayn-tee-chEEn-koo-eh)
26	ventisei (vayn-tee-sEH-ee)
27	ventisette (vayn-tee-sEHt-teh)

28	ventotto (vayn-tOHt-toh)
29	ventinove (vayn-tee-nOH-veh)
30	trenta (trEHn-tah)
40	quaranta (koo-ah-rAHn-tah)
50	cinquanta (cheen-koo-AHn-tah)
60	sessanta (sehs-sAHn-tah)
70	settanta (seht-tAHn-tah)
80	ottanta (oht-tAHn-tah)
90	novanta (noh-vAHn-tah)
100	cento (chEHn-toh)
101	centouno (chEHn-toh OO-noh)
102	centodue (chEHn-toh dOO-eh)
200	duecento (doo-eh-chEHn-toh)
300	trecento (treh-chEHn-toh)
400	quattrocento (koo-aht-troh-chEHn-toh)
500	cinquecento (cheen-koo-eh-chEHn-toh)
600	seicento (seh-ee-chEHn-toh)
700	settecento (seht-teh-chEHn-toh)
800	ottocento (oht-toh-chEHn-toh)
900	novecento (noh-veh-chEHn-toh)
1,000	mille (mEEl-leh)
2,000	duemila (dOO-eh mEE-lah)
3,000	tremila (trEH-mEE-lah)
4,000	quattromila (koo-AHt-troh-mEE-lah)
5,000	cinquemila (chEEn-koo-eh-mEE-lah)
6,000	seimila (sEH-ee-mEE-lah)
7,000	settemila (seHt-teh-mEE-lah)
8,000	ottomila (OHt-toh-mEE-lah)
9,000	novemila (nOH-veh-mEE-lah
10,000	diecimila (dee-EH-chee-mEE-lah)
20,000	ventimila (VAYn-tee-mEE-lah)
30,000	trentamila (trEHn-tah-mEE- lah)
40,000	quarantamila (koo-ah-rAHn-tah-mEE-lah)
50,000	cinquntamila (cheen-koo-AHn-tah-mEE-lah)
60,000	sessantamila (sehs-SAHn-tah-mEE-lah)
70,000	settantamila (seht-tAHn-tah-mEE-lah)
80,000	ottantamila (oht-tAHn-tah-mEE-lah)
90,000	novantamila (noh-vAHn-tah-mEE-lah)
100,000	centomila (chEHn-toh-mEE-lah)

200,000	duecentomila (doo-eh-cEHn-toh-mEE-lah)
300,000	trecentomila (treh-chEHn-toh-mEE-lah)
400,000	quatrocentomila (koo-aht-troh-chEHn-toh-mEE-lah)
500,000	cinquecentomila (cheen-koo-eh-chEHn-toh-mEE-lah)
600,000	seicentomila (seh-ee-chEHn-toh-mEE-lah)
700,000	settecentomila (seht-teh-chEHn-toh-mEE-lah)
800,000	ottocentomila (oht-toh-chEEn-toh-mEE-lah)
900,000	novecentomila (noh-veh-chEEn-toh-mEE-lah)
1,000,000	un milione (OOn mee-lee-OH-neh)
2,000,000	due milioni (dOO-eh mee-lee-OH-nee)
10,000,000	dieci milione (dee-EH-chee mee-lee-OH-neh)
100,000,000	cento milione (chEHn-toh mee-lee-OH-neh)
1,000,000,000	un miliardo (mee-lee-AHr-doh)

Ordinal Numbers

1°	primo (prEE-moh)
2°	secondo (seh-kOHn-doh)
3°	terzo (tEHr-tsoh)
4°	quarto (koo-AHr-toh)
5°	quinto (koo-EEn-toh)
6°	sesto (sEHs-toh)
7°	settimo (sEHt-tee-moh)
8°	ottavo (oht-tAH-voh)
9°	nono (nOH-noh)
10°	decimo (dEH-chee-moh)
the last one	l'ultimo (lOOl-tee-moh)
once	una volta (oo-nah vOHl-tah)
twice	due volte (dOO-eh vOHl-teh)
three times	tre volte (trEH-vOHl-teh)

Quantities

half of ____	la metà di ____ (lah meh-tAH dee)
half of the money	la metà dei soldi (lah meh-tAH day-ee sOHl-dee)
half a ____	mezzo ____ (mEH-tsoh)
half a kilo	mezzo chilo (mEH-tsoh kEE-loh)

a fourth (quarter)	un quarto (oon koo-AHr-toh)
a dozen	una dozzina (oo-nah doh-tsEE-nah)
a dozen oranges	una dozzina d'arance (oo-nah doh-tsEE-nah dah-rAHn-cheh)
100 grams	un etto (oon EHt-toh)
200 grams	due etti (dOO-eh EHt-tee)
350 grams	tre etti e mezzo (treh EHt-tee ay mEH-tsoh)
a pair/of	un paio/di (oon pAH-ee-oh/dee)
a pair of shoes	un paio di scarpe (oon pAH-ee-oh dee skAHr-peh)

Useful Italian Abbreviations

AA	Azienda Autonoma di Soggiorno e Turismo	Local Tourist Information Center
ACI	Automobile Club d'Italia	Automobile Club of Italy
Cap.	Capuluogo	Province
C.P.	Casetta Postale	Post Office Box
CAP	Codice Postale	Zip Code
ENIT	Ente Nazionale per il Turismo	Italian State Tourist Office
EPT	Ente Provinciale per il Turismo	Provincial Tourist Information Center Inc.
F.lli.	Fratelli	Brothers
FS	Ferrovie dello Stato	Italian State Railways
IVA	Imposte sul Valore Aggiunto	Italian State Tax
L.	Lire	Italian currency
N., n°	Numero	Number
Pro Loco	Ente Locale per il Turismo	Local Tourist Information Office
Prov.	Provincia	Province
P.za	Piazza	(City) Square
S.	San, Santo(a)	Saint
S.A.	Società Anonima	Inc.
Sig.	Signor	Mr.
Sig.na	Signorina	Miss
Sig.ra	Signora	Mrs.
TCI	Touring Club Italiano	Italian Touring Club
v.	Via	Street
v.le	Viale	Boulevard

BUSINESS DICTIONARY

ENGLISH TO ITALIAN

A

abandon (v) abbandonare

abandonment l'abbandono

abatement lo sconto, la riduzione

ability-to-pay concept il concetto di solvibilità

above par sopra la pari

above-mentioned il summenzionato, il succitato

above-the-line oltre la linea

absentee ownership il proprietario assente

absenteeism l'assenteismo

absorb (v) assorbire

absorb the loss (v) assorbire la perdita

absorption costing la capitalizzazione dei costi fissi nel costo dell'inventario

abstract of title il compendio del documento probatorio della titolarità di diritti

accelerated depreciation l'ammortamento accelerato

acceleration clause la clausola d'accelerazione

acceleration premium il premio d'accelerazione

accept (v) accettare

acceptable quality level il livello di qualità accettabile

acceptance l'accettazione

acceptance agreement l'accordo d'accettazione, la convenzione d'accettazione

acceptance bill l'accetazione cambiaria

acceptance credit il credito d'accettazione

acceptance house la casa di accettazione

acceptance sampling la campionatura per accettazione

acceptance test l'esame d'accettazione

acceptor l'accettante

accession rate il tasso d'adesione

accidental damage il danno accidentale

accommodation bill la cambiale di comodo

accommodation credit la facilitazione d'appoggio creditizio

accommodation endorsement la girata di comodo

accommodation paper la cambiale di comodo

accommodation parity la parità di comodo

accommodation platform la piattaforma di comodo

accompanied goods i beni accompagnati

accord and satisfaction l'accordo e la soddisfazione

account il conto

account balance il saldo contabile

account, current il conto corrente

account day il giorno di liquidazione

account executive la persona responsabile per un prodotto e/o un cliente

account for (v) essere responsabile per

account number il numero di conto

account period la periodicità del conto

accountability la responsabilità

accountant il contabile

accountant, chief il capo contabile

accounting, cost la contabilità dei costi, la contabilità industriale

accounting department la contabilità, il reparto contabilità

accounting, management la contabilità amministrativa

accounting method il sistema contabile, il sistema di contabilità

accounting period il periodo contabile, il periodo di contabilità

accounting ratio il rapporto di contabilità

accounts, group i conti di gruppo, il raggruppamento dei conti

accounts payable i conti debitori

accounts receivable i conti creditori

accounts, secured i conti garantiti, i crediti garantiti

accretion l'accrescimento

accrual la maturazione

accrual method il sistema di competenza

accrue (v) derivare, maturare
accrued assets gli attivi maturati
accrued depreciation l'ammortamento maturato
accrued expenses le spese maturate
accrued interest l'interesse maturato
accrued revenue il reddito maturato
accrued taxes le tasse maturate
accumulated depreciation il fondo ammortamento
acid-test ratio il rapporto di liquidità
acknowledge (v) ammettere, riconoscere
acknowledge receipt of (v) accusiamo ricezione di
acoustic coupler l'innesto acustico
acquire (v) ottenere, acquistare
acquired rights i diritti acquisiti
acquisition l'acquisto, la compra
acquisition profile il profilo di acquisizione, il profilo d'acquisto
acreage allotment l'allocazione del terreno
acronym l'acronimo, la sigla
across-the-board settlement la risoluzione generale
across-the-board tariff negotiation il negoziato tariffaro generale
act of God la forza maggiore
action plan il piano d'azione
action research la ricerca di azione
active account il conto operativo
active assets gli utili attivi
active debt il debito attivo
active trust il fondo d'investimento
activity chart il diagramma delle attività
activity on arrow il piano di immediata esecuzione
actual attuale, effettivo
actual cash value il valore effettivo a pronti
actual costs i costi effettivi, i costi reali
actual income il reddito effettivo
actual liability la passitività effettiva, il responsabilità effettiva
actual market volume il volume effettivo di mercato
actual total loss la perdita totale effettiva

actuary l'attuario
add-on sales le vendite aggiunte
addendum l'addendo, l'aggiunta, l'appendice
address commission la commissione di raccomandazione
adjudge (v) aggiudicare
adjudication l'aggiudicazione
adjust (v) aggiustare
adjustable peg il sistema di parità variabile
adjusted CIF price il prezzo CIF rettificato
adjusted earned income l'introito rettificato
adjusted rate il tasso rettificato
adjusting entry la scrittura contabile correttiva
adjustment process la procedura di regolamento
adjustment trigger l'evento determinante lo scatto del processo di aggiustamento
administration l'amministrazione
administrative amministrativo
administrative expense la spesa amministrativa
administrator l'amministratore
administratrix l'amministratrice
advance (v) avanzare, anticipare
advance freight il nolo anticipato
advance notice il preavviso
advance payments i pagamenti anticipati
advance refunding il rimborso anticipato
advantage, competitive il vantaggio competitivo
adverse balance il bilancio negativo
advertisement (request) for bid la richiesta d'appalto, il bando d'appalto
advertising la pubblicità
advertising agency l'agenzia pubblicitaria
advertising budget il preventivo pubblicitario
advertising campaign la campagna pubblicitaria
advertising drive la spinta pubblicitaria
advertising expenses le spese pubblicitarie
advertising manager il direttore della pubblicità, il direttore pubblicitario
advertising media i mezzi di pubblicità

advertising research lo studio pubblicitario
advice note la nota d'avviso
advise (v) avvisare
advisory council l'organo consultivo
advisory funds la previsione di spese di consulenza
advisory service il servizio consultivo
affidavit la dichiarazione scritta e giurata
affiliate la filiale
affirmative action l'azione contro la discriminazione
affreightment il noleggio
afloat a galla
after-hours trading il commercio fuori orario
after-sales service la manutenzione e servizio successivi alla vendita
after-tax real rate of return il rendimento reale al netto di tasse
afterdate (v) postdatare
against all risks contro qualsiasi rischio
agency l'agenzia
agency bank la banca d'agenzia
agency fee la commissione, la parcella dell'agenzia
agenda l'agenda
agent l'agente
agent bank la banca agente
aggregate demand la domanda aggregata
aggregate risk il rischio cumulativo
aggregate supply l'offerta aggregata
agreement l'accordo, la convenzione
agricultural paper la cambiale agraria
agricultural products i prodotti agrari
agriculture l'agricoltura
air express l'espresso aereo
air freight il trasporto via aerea
air shipment la spedizione aerea
algorithm l'algoritmo
algorithmic language il linguaggio algoritmico
alien corporation l'azienda straniera, la ditta straniera
all in cost il costo complessivo

all or none tutto o niente

allocation of costs l'allocazione dei costi

allocation of responsibilities l'allocazione di responsabilità

allocation, resources l'allocazione delle risorse

allonge (of a draft) la coda (di cambiale)

allot (v) spartire

allotment la ripartizione

allotment letter la lettera di ripartizione

allow (v) permettere

allowance l'abbuono

allowance, depreciation il fondo di ammortamento

alongside accanto

alteration l'alterazione

alternative order l'ordine alternativo

amalgamation la fusione

amend (v) emendare, revisionare

amendment l'emendamento

amortization l'ammortamento

amount la somma

amount due la somma dovuta

analog computer l'elaboratore a sistema analog

analysis l'analisi

analysis, break-even l'analisi di equilibrio tra i costi e i ricavi, il punto di pareggio

analysis, competitor l'analisi del concorrente

analysis, cost l'analisi dei costi

analysis, cost-benefit l'analisi del rapporto tra i costi ed i benefici

analysis, critical path l'analisi del percorso critico

analysis, financial l'analisi finanziaria

analysis, functional l'analisi funzionale

analysis, input-output l'analisi entrata/uscita, l'analisi dei fattori produttivi

analysis, investment l'analisi d'investimento

analysis, job l'analisi del progetto, l'analisi dell'occupazione, l'analisi del lavoro

analysis, needs l'analisi delle esigenze

analysis, product l'analisi del prodotto

analysis, profitability l'analisi del rapporto tra costo e profitto, l'analisi dei profitti, lo studio sulla profittabilità

analysis, risk l'analisi del rischio

analysis, sales l'analisi delle vendite

analysis, systems l'analisi del sistema

analyst l'analista

anchorage (dues) gli oneri d'ancoraggio

ancillary operations le operazioni ausiliari

angle of incidence l'angolo d'incidenza

annual annuale

annual accounts i conti annuali

annual audit la revisione annuale dei conti

annual report il rapporto annuale

annuitant il pensionante, il vitalizio

annuity la rendita

anti-dumping duty la tariffa protettiva, la tariffa "anti-dumping"

antique authenticity certificate il certificato antiquariale d'autenticità

antitrust laws le leggi anti-monopolistiche

apparel l'abbigliamento

application form il modulo di richiesta

applied proceeds swap il baratto, la permuta degli introiti

appointment l'appuntamento

appraisal la stima, la valutazione

appraisal, capital expenditure la stima delle spese capitali

appraisal, financial la valutazione finanziaria

appraisal, investment la valutazione degli investimenti

appraisal, market la valutazione di mercato

appreciation l'apprezzamento

apprentice l'apprendista

appropriation lo stanziamento

approval l'approvazione

approve (v) approvare

approved delivery facility lo stabilimento di consegna approvato

approved securities i titoli mobiliari approvati
arbitrage l'arbitraggio
arbitration l'arbitrato
arbitration agreement l'accordo d'arbitrato
arbitrator l'arbitro
area manager il direttore d'area
arithmetic mean la media aritmetica
arm's length a distanza
armaments gli armamenti
around (exchange term) circa
arrears gli arretrati
as, if and when come se e quando
as is goods i beni nello stato attuale, i beni senza ricorso
as per advice come per nota informativa
as soon as possible appena possibile
asking price il prezzo richiesto
assay l'analisi
assemble (v) (people) riunire
assemble (v) (things) montare
assembly il montaggio, l'assemblea
assembly line la catena di montaggio, la linea di montaggio
assess (v) valutare
assessed valuation la valutazione imponibile
assessment la valutazione
asset l'attivo, l'attività
asset turnover il giro d'attività, il movimento d'attività
asset value il valore delle attività
assets, accrued gli attivi maturati
assets, current gli attivi correnti
assets, deferred gli attivi differiti
assets, fixed gli attivi fissi, gli immobilizzi tecnici
assets, intangible gli attivi intangibili
assets, liquid gli attivi mobili, l'attivo circolante
assets, net gli attivi netti
assets, tangible i beni reali
assign (v) assegnare

assignee l'assegnatario
assignor il cedente
assistant l'assistente
assistant general manager il vice direttore generale
assistant manager il vice direttore
associate company la società in accomandita, la ditta associata
assumed liability la responsabilità presunta
at and from a e da
at best al meglio
at call a richiesta, a domanda
at or better a o meglio
at par alla pari
at sight a vista
at the close alla chiusura
at the market al mercato
at the opening all'apertura
attach (v) allegare
attaché case la borsa documenti
attended time il tempo presenziato
attestation l'attestato
attorney l'avvocato
attorney, power of la procura
attrition l'attrito
audit (v) controllare, rivedere, verificare
audit trail il bilancio di revisione
audit, internal la revisione interna
auditing balance sheet il foglio di revisione del bilancio contabile
auditor il revisore
autarky l'autarchia
authenticity (gold) l'autenticità
authority, to have (v) avere l'autorità
authorize (v) autorizzare
authorized dealer il rivenditore autorizzato
authorized shares le azioni autorizzate
authorized signature la firma autorizzata
automatic automatico
automation l'automazione

autonomous autonomo

availability, subject to in base alla disponibilità

average la media

average cost il costo medio

average life la vita media, la durata media

average price il prezzo medio

average unit cost il costo medio unitario

averaging raggiungere una media, prendere la media

avoidable costs le spese evitabili

B

back date (v) postdatare

back haul il ritorno di una parte della merce sullo stesso percorso utilizzato per il trasporto originale

back order l'ordine arretrato

back selling la rivendita del prodotto al fornitore originale

back taxes le imposte arretrate

back-to-back credit il credito documentario aperto sulla base di un altro credito originario, il credito disposto dal beneficiario di un credito

back-to-back loans i prestiti erogati sulla base di una garanzia ricevuta

backed note l'obbligazione garantita

backing and filling l'appoggio ed esecuzione

backing support il sostegno d'appoggio

backlog gli ordini inevasi

backup bonds i titoli obbligazionari dati in garanzia

backwardation il deporto

backwash effect l'effetto di risucchio

bad debt il debito insolvibile

balance, bank il bilancio bancario

balance, credit il credito disponible, il saldo e credito

balance of payments la bilancia dei pagamenti

balance of trade la bilancia commerciale

balance ratios gli indici di bilancio

balance sheet il bilancio d'esercizio

bale capacity la capacità in balle

bale cargo la merce imballata

ballast bonus il premio sulla zavorra

balloon (payment) l'ultimo pagamento rateale per un importo notevolmente più alto dei precedenti

balloon note l'obbligazione a rate con pagamento maggiorato alla maturità

bank la banca

bank acceptance l'accettazione bancaria

bank account il conto bancario

bank balance il bilancio bancario

bank carnet il carnet bancario

bank charges i costi bancari

bank check l'assegno bancario

bank deposit il deposito bancario

bank draft la tratta bancaria

bank examiner il revisore bancario

bank exchange il cambio bancario

bank holiday la festività legale

bank letter of credit la lettera di credito bancaria

bank loan il prestito bancario

bank money order il vaglia bancario

bank note la banconota

bank rate il tasso bancario

bank release il benestare bancario

bank statement il rendiconto bancario

bankruptcy il fallimento

bar chart il grafico a barra, il diagramma utilizzando barre

bareboat charter il noleggio a scafo nudo

bargain l'affare

bargaining, collective la contrattazione collettiva

bargaining power il potere di negoziazione

barratry l'incitazione alla discordia

barter (v) barattare

base currency la valuta di base

base price il prezzo di base

base rate il tasso di base

base year l'anno di base

basis point (1/100%) il punto di base (centesimo di un percento)

batch processing l'elaborazione per gruppi
batch production la produzione in lotti
batten fitted attrezzato con infissi per ancorare la merce
baud il baud
bear market la borsa in fase negativa
bearer il portatore
bearer bond l'obbligazione al portatore
bearer security il titolo al portatore
bell-shaped curve la curva a campana
below par sotto la pari
below the line capitalizzati
beneficiary il beneficiario
bequest il lascito
berth terms i termini di ormeggio
bid and asked offerto e richiesto
bill la fattura
bill broker l'intermediario di obbligazioni
bill of exchange la cambiale
bill of lading la polizza di carico
bill of sale l'atto di vendita
bill of sight il certificato d'ispezione
billboard il cartellone
binary notation la numerazione binaria, la notazione binaria
binder la caparra
bit il bit
black market il mercato nero
blanket bond l'obbligazione generale
blanket order l'ordine generale
blockage of funds il blocco dei fondi
blocked currency la valuta bloccata
blue chip stock le azioni pregiate
blue-collar worker l'operaio
blueprint la cianografia, il programma
board, executive il consiglio dirigenziale
board meeting la riunione del consiglio
board of directors il consiglio di amministrazione

board of supervisors il consiglio di sovrintendenza

boardroom la sala del consiglio

boilerplate il testo scritto senza particolare interesse

bond l'obbligazione

bond areas le aree delle obbligazioni

bond issue l'emissione di buoni, le obbligazioni

bond power il potere del buono, il potere di emettere obbligazioni

bond rating la valutazione dell'obbligazione

bonded carrier il portatore di obbligazioni

bonded goods le merci vincolate

bonded warehouse il magazzino doganale

bonus (premium) il premio

book inventory il inventario registrato, il inventario contabile

book value il valore registrato, il valore contabile

book value per share il valore registrato per azione

bookkeeping la contabilità

boom l'espansione, il "boom"

border il confine

border tax adjustment la correzione della tassa di confine

borrow (v) prendere in prestito

boycott (v) boicottare

brainstorming la conferenza-confronto idee, il dibattito costruttivo d'opinioni

branch office la filiale

brand la marca

brand acceptance l'accettazione della marca

brand image l'immagine della marca

brand loyalty la fedeltà alla marca

brand manager il dirigente responsabile per la gestione della marca

brand recognition il riconoscimento della marca

break even (v) arrivare al punto di parità

break-even analysis l'analisi di equilibrio tra i costi e i ricavi, il punto di pareggio

break-even point il punto della parità, il punto di pareggio, il volume di vendite al quale c'è equilibrio tra ricavi e costi

briefcase la borsa documenti

broken lot la partita divisa

broken stowage il carico frazionato

broker l'intermediario

broker, software il mediatore di software

budget il preventivo

budget, advertising il preventivo pubblicitario

budget appropriation lo stanziamento del preventivo

budget, cash il preventivo di cassa, il preventivo in contanti

budget forecast la previsione del preventivo

budget, investment il preventivo d'investimento

budget, marketing il preventivo per il marketing

budget, sales il preventivo per le spese di vendita

bug (defect in computer program) il difetto nel programma dell'elaboratore elettronico, il bug

bull market la borsa in fase di andamento positivo

burden rate il tasso dell'onere

bureaucrat il burocrate

business activity l'attività commerciale

business card il biglietto da visita

business cycle il ciclo commerciale

business management l'amministrazione commerciale, la gestione commerciale

business plan il piano commerciale

business policy la politica commerciale

business strategy la strategia commerciale

buy at best (v) comprare al miglior prezzo

buy back (v) riacquistare

buy on close (v) comprare alla chiusura

buy on opening (v) comprare all'apertura

buyer l'acquirente, il compratore

buyer, chief il compratore capo, il responsabile acquisti

buyer, credit l'acquirente su credito

buyer, potential il acquirente potenziale, il compratore potenziale

buyer's market il mercato favorevole all'acquirente, il mercato propenso per gli acquirenti

buyer's option all'opzione del compratore

buyer's premium il premio del compratore

buyer's responsibility la responsabilità dell'acquirente

buyout la rilevazione delle quote del soci liquidati

by-product il prodotto derivato, il prodotto secondario

bylaws le normative, i regolamenti

byte il byte

C

cable il cavo

cable transfer la rimessa telegrafica

calculator la calcolatrice

call (v) chiamare

call feature l'opzione di acquisto di valori mobiliari in qualsiasi momento a un certo prezzo

call loan il prestito rimborsabile a domanda

call money il denaro investito a brevissima scadenza

call option l'opzione di acquistare delle azioni ad un dato prezzo entro un determinato periodo di tempo

call price il prezzo al quale è redimibile un buono a richiesta

call protection la protezione dalla richiesta di un rimborso immediato (obbligazioni)

call rate il tasso di interesse per rimborsabile a brevissima scadenza

call rule le norme per la richiesta di rimborso anticipato

callback il richiamo (in genere per articoli difettosi)

campaign, advertising la campagna pubblicitaria

campaign, productivity la campagna di produttività

cancel (v) cancellare

cancelled check l'assegno versato

capacity la capacità

capacity, manufacturing la capacità di produzione, la capacità produttiva

capacity, plant la capacità produttiva della fabbrica, il potenziale di capacità produttiva di un impianto

capacity, utilization il livello d'utilizzo della capacità produttiva

capital il capitale

capital account il conto capitale

capital allowance la riserva capitale

capital asset gli attivi immobili

capital budget il preventivo capitale, il preventivo spese impianti e macchinari

capital expenditure l'investimento capitale

capital expenditure appraisal la stima delle spese capitali

capital exports (currency) l'esportazione dei capitali

capital exports (goods) l'esportazione di beni capitali

capital gain/loss gli utili di capitale/la perdita di capitale

capital goods i beni capitali, i beni d'investimento

capital increase l'aumento dei capitali

capital-intensive richiedente un notevole investimento di capitale

capital market il mercato dei capitali

capital-output ratio il rapporto tra capitale e produzione

capital, raising raccolta dei capitali

capital, return on la resa sui capitali, i proventi sul capitale

capital, risk il capitale per finanziare nuove iniziative

capital spending la spesa dei capitali

capital stock il capitale azionario

capital structure la struttura finanziaria

capital surplus l'eccedenza dei capitali

capital, working il capitale circolante, il capitale liquido

capitalism il capitalismo

capitalization la capitalizzazione

cargo la merce imbarcata

carload il carico di vettura

carnet il carnet

carrier il portatore

carrier's risk a rischio del portatore

carry forward (v) portare a nuovo

carryback la perdita detraibile dalle imposte

carrying charges le spese d'immobilizzo

carrying value il valore d'immobilizzo

carryover riportare

cartel il consorzio di industriali

cash i contanti

cash-and-carry il pagamento in contanti

cash balance il saldo liquido

cash basis in contanti

cash before delivery il pagamento prima della consegna

cash book il libro cassa

cash budget il preventivo di cassa, il preventivo in contanti

cash delivery il pagamento alla consegna, la consegna in contanti

cash discount lo sconto per contanti

cash dividend il dividendo pagato in contanti

cash entry il annotazione di movimento di contanti, la registrazione del movimento di cassa

cash flow il movimento di cassa

cash flow statement la relazione del movimento di cassa

cash in advance il pagamento anticipato

cash management l'amministrazione della cassa

cash on delivery il pagamento alla consegna

cash surrender value il valore in contanti alla resa

cashier's check l'assegno bancario

cassette la cassetta

casualty insurance l'assicurazione contro danni

catalog il catalogo

ceiling il soffitto

central bank la banca centrale

central processing unit (computers) l'unità centrale per l'elaborazione dei dati

central rate il tasso centrale

centralization l'accentramento

certificate il certificato

certificate of deposit il certificato di deposito

certificate of incorporation l'atto di costituzione

certificate of origin il certificato d'origine

certified check l'assegno garantito

certified public accountant il ragioniere diplomato dallo stato

chain of command l'organigramma dirigenziale

chain (of stores) la catena di negozi

chain store group il gruppo di grandi magazzini

chairman of the board il presidente del consiglio

chamber of commerce la camera di commercio

channel of distribution il canale di distribuzione

charge account il conto aperto

chargeoff (v) sgravare dalle tasse

charges gli oneri

chart, activity il diagramma delle attività

chart, bar il grafico a barra, il diagramma utilizzando barre

chart, flow il diagramma delle correnti

chart, management il quadro amministrativo, l'organigramma

charter il documento costitutivo

chartered accountant il ragioniere professionista

charterparty agent il mediatore per noleggio

chattel il bene mobile

chattel mortgage l'ipoteca su beni mobili

cheap a buon mercato

check l'assegno

check, counter l'assegno bancario

checking account il conto corrente

checklist la lista di controllo

chemical chimico

chief accountant il capo contabile

chief buyer il compratore capo, il responsabile degli acquisti

chief executive il direttore generale

chip il chip

civil action l'azione di parte civile

civil engineering l'ingegneria civile

claim il reclamo

classified ad la piccola pubblicità

clean document il documento pulito, il documento in ordine

clearinghouse la stanza di compensazione

closed account il conto chiuso

closely held corporation la ditta privata

closing entry la scrittura di chiusura

closing price il prezzo alla chiusura

co-ownership la comproprietà

coal il carbone

codicil il comma

coffee break l'intervallo (per caffè)

coinsurance la co-assicurazione

cold call la visita di vendita senza preavviso

collateral il collaterale

colleague il collega

collect on delivery il pagamento alla consegna

collection period il periodo di riscossione

collective agreement il patto collettivo

collective bargaining la contrattazione collettiva

collector of customs l'esattore doganale, il doganiere

colloquium il colloquio

combination la combinazione

combination duty il dazio combinato, la tariffa combinata

commerce il commercio

commercial (advertisement) l'avviso, l'avvertimento, l'annuncio

commercial bank la banca commerciale

commercial grade il livello commerciale, la qualità commerciale

commercial invoice la fattura commerciale

commission (agency) la parcella

commission (fee) la provvigione

commitment l'impegno

commodity l'oggetto di prima necessità, il bene

commodity exchange la borsa (mercato) di beni di prima necessità

common carrier il vettore

common market il mercato comune

common stock le azione ordinaria

company l'azienda

company goal l'obiettivo aziendale

company, holding la società finanziaria, la società madre

company, parent la ditta madre, l'azienda madre

company policy la politica aziendale

compensating balance lasciare una certa somma di fondi nel conto corrente presso la istituzione

compensation il compenso

compensation trade il commercio compensativo

competition la concorrenza, la competizione

competitive advantage il vantaggio competitivo

competitive edge il punto di vantaggio

competitive price il prezzo concorrenziale

competitive strategy la strategia concorrenziale

competitor il concorrente

competitor analysis l'analisi del concorrente

complimentary copy la copia in omaggio

component il componente

composite index l'indice composto

compound interest l'interesse composto

comptroller il controllore

computer il cervello elettronico, il computer

computer, analog l'elaboratore a sistema analog

computer bank il computer bank

computer center il centro per elaborati elettronici

computer, digital l'elaboratore a sistema digitale, l'elaboratore digitale

computer input l'entrata dei dati nell'elaboratore elettronico (input)

computer language il linguaggio per elaboratori elettronici

computer memory la memoria dell'elaboratore

computer output la produzione del computer (computer output)

computer program il programma dell'elaboratore, il programma del computer

computer storage l'immagazzinaggio dei dati per il computer

computer terminal il terminale dell'elaboratore, il terminale del computer

conditional acceptance l'accettazione condizionale

conditional sales contract il contratto di vendita condizionata

conference room la sala conferenze

confidential confidenziale, riservato

confirmation of order la conferma dell'ordine

conflict of interest il conflitto d'interesse

conglomerate il conglomerato

consideration (bus. law) il compenso, la considerazione

consignee il destinatario

consignment la spedizione, la consegna

consignment note la nota di spedizione

consolidated financial statement il bilancio consolidato

consolidation il consolidamento

consortium il consorzio

consular invoice la fattura consolare

consultant il consulente

consultant, management il consulente amministrativo

consumer il consumatore

consumer acceptance l'accettazione da parte del consumatore

consumer credit il credito al consumatore

consumer goods i beni di consumo

consumer price index l'indice dei prezzi al consumo

consumer research la ricerca sul consumatore

consumer satisfaction la soddisfazione del consumatore

container il contenitore, il "container"

contingencies le contingenze

contingent fund il fondo di contingenza, il fondo di previdenza

contingent liability la responsabilità contingente, la sopravvenienza passiva

contract il contratto

contract carrier il vettore contrattuale

contract month il mese contrattuale

control, cost il controllo dei costi

control, financial il controllo finanziario

control, inventory il controllo dell'inventario

control, manufacturing il controllo della produzione

control, production il controllo della produzione

control, quality il controllo di qualità

control, stock il controllo dei valori, il controllo delle azioni

controllable costs i costi controllabili

controller il controllore

controlling interest l'interesse maggioritario

convertible debentures le obbligazioni convertibili

convertible preferred stock le azioni privilegiate convertibili

cooperation agreement la convenzione di cooperazione

cooperative la cooperativa

cooperative advertising la pubblicità cooperativa (in compartecipazione)

copy (text) il testo

copy testing l'esame di un testo pubblicitario

copyright i diritti d'autore

corporate growth la crescita aziendale

corporate image l'immagine aziendale

corporate income tax l'imposta sul reddito delle persone giuridiche (IRPEG)

corporate planning la pianificazione aziendale, la programmazione aziendale

corporate structure la struttura aziendale

corporation la società per azioni, l'azienda, la ditta, la società

corporation tax l'imposta aziendale

corpus il corpo

correspondence la corrispondenza

correspondent bank la banca corrispondente

cost il costo

cost (v) costare

cost accounting la contabilità dei costi

cost analysis l'analisi dei costi

cost and freight il costo e trasporto

cost, average il costo medio

cost-benefit analysis l'analisi del rapporto tra i costi ed i benefici

cost control il controllo dei costi

cost, direct il costo diretto

cost effectiveness l'efficienza dei costi

cost factor il fattore dei costi

cost, indirect il costo indiretto

cost of capital il costo del capitale

cost of goods sold il costo dei beni venduti

cost of living il costo della vita, il carovita

cost-plus contract il contratto che garantisce un profitto in base al costo del prodotto

cost-price squeeze la riduzione della differenza tra costi e prezzi, che riduce il profitto

cost reduction la riduzione dei costi

cost, replacement il costo di ricambio

costs, allocation of l'allocazione dei costi

costs, fixed i costi fissi

costs, managed i costi amministrati, i costi controllabili

costs, production i costi di produzione

costs, set-up i costi iniziali

costs, standard i costi normali, i costi standard

costs, variable i costi variabili

cotton il cotone

counter check l'assegno bancario

counterfeit il contraffatto

countervailing duty la tariffa controvalente

country of origin il paese d'origine

country of risk il paese a rischio

coupon (bond interest) la cedola di interesse su buoni, la cedola di interesse su obbligazioni

courier service il servizio di corriere

covenant l'impegno, la promessa

cover charge il coperto

cover letter la lettera di accompagnamento

cover ratio il rapporto di copertura

coverage (insurance) la copertura
crawling peg la parità mobile
credit il credito
credit (v) accreditare
credit balance il credito disponibile, il saldo a credito
credit bank la banca di credito
credit bureau l'ufficio di credito
credit buyer l'acquirente su credito
credit card la carta di credito
credit control il controllo del credito
credit insurance l'assicurazione dei crediti
credit line la linea di credito
credit management l'amministrazione del credito
credit note la nota di accredito
credit rating la valutazione del credito
credit reference la referenza bancaria, la referenza per ottenere credito
credit terms i termini del credito
credit union l'unione creditizia
creditor il creditore
critical path analysis l'analisi del percorso critico
cross-licensing le licenze accavallate
cultural export permit il permesso d'esportazione di beni culturali
cultural property il bene culturale
cum dividend con dividendo
cumulative cumulativo
cumulative preferred stock le azioni preferenziali cumulative
currency la valuta
currency band il serpente valutario (CEE)
currency clause il comma valutaria
currency conversion la conversione di valuta
currency exchange il cambio valuta
current account il conto corrente
current assets gli attivi correnti
current liabilities gli impegni attuali, la responsabilità corrente
current ratio il rapporto corrente

current yield il rendimento corrente
customer il cliente
customer service il servizio reso al cliente
customs la dogana
customs broker lo spedizioniere doganale
customs duty la tariffa doganale, il dazio
customs entry la dichiarazione doganale
customs union l'unione doganale
cutback la riduzione
cycle billing la fatturazione a ciclo
cycle, business il ciclo commerciale

D

daily il giornaliero
dairy products i prodotti lattiero-caseari
damage il danno
data i dati
data acquisition l'acquisizione di dati
data bank la banca dati
data base il "data base," la base dei dati per elaboratori elettronici
date of delivery la data di consegna
day loan il prestito giornaliero
day order l'ordine in giornata
dead freight il nolo "vuoto per pieno"
dead rent l'affitto morto
deadline la scadenza
deadlock la situazione irresolubile, l'arresto, il punto morto
deal l'affare
deal, package la trattativa complessiva
dealer il commerciante
dealership il licenziatario
debentures le obbligazioni
debit l'addebito
debit entry la nota di debito, la registrazione a debito
debit note la nota di addebito
debt il debito

debug (v) riparare il sistema nell'elaboratore

deductible il detraibile

deduction la detrazione

deed l'atto

deed of sale l'atto di vendita

deed of transfer l'atto di passagio, l'atto di trasferimento

deed of trust l'atto fiduciario

default (v) venire meno agli obblighi

defective difettoso

deferred annuities le rendite differite

deferred assets gli attivi differiti

deferred charges gli oneri differiti

deferred delivery le consegne differite

deferred income il reddito differito

deferred liabilities le responsabilità differite, le passività differite

deferred tax le tasse differite

deficit il deficit, il disavanzo, l'ammanco

deficit financing il ricorso al prestito per finanziare un'attività

deficit spending la spesa fatta mentre la ditta è in passivo

deflation la deflazione

delay il ritardo

delinquent account il conto moroso

delivered price il prezzo alla consegna

delivery la consegna

delivery date la data di consegna

delivery notice la notifica di consegna

delivery points i punti di consegna

delivery price il prezzo di consegna

demand la richiesta

demand (v) richiedere

demand deposit il deposito a richiesta, il deposito in conto corrente

demand line of credit la linea di credito a richiesta

demographic il demografico

demotion la demozione

demurrage il ritardo

demurrage (maritime) la controstallia

department il reparto

department store il grande magazzino

depletion accounting la contabilità di riduzione

depletion control il controllo della riduzione

deposit il deposito

deposit account il conto di deposito

deposit, bank il deposito bancario

depository il deposito

depreciation il deprezzamento, l'ammortamento

depreciation, accelerated l'ammortamento accelerato

depreciation, accrued l'ammortamento maturato

depreciation allowance il fondo di ammortamento

depreciation of currency il deprezzamento della valuta

depression la depressione

deputy chairman il vice presidente

deputy manager il vice amministratore, il vice dirigente

design engineering la progettazione d'impianti, la progettazione industriale

devaluation la svalutazione

differential, price la differenziale dei prezzi

differential, tariff la tariffa differenziale

differential, wage la differenza salariale, il differenziale di stipendo

digital digitale

digital computer l'elaboratore a sistema digitale, l'elaboratore digitale

dilution of equity la diluizione del capitale azionario, la diluizione del capitale netto

dilution of labor la diluizione della manodopera, l'assorbimento del personale non specializzato

direct access storage l'immagazzinaggio con accesso diretto

direct cost il costo diretto

direct expenses le spese dirette

direct investment le investimento diretto

direct labor la manodopera diretta
direct mail la pubblicità diretta
direct papers le obbligazioni dirette
direct quotation la citazione diretta
direct selling la vendita diretta
director il direttore
disbursement il pagamento
discharge (v) scaricare
discount lo sconto
discount (v) scontare
discount rate tasso di sconto
discount securities i titoli scontati
discounted cash flow il reddito futuro scontato al valore attuale
discretionary account il fondo discrezionario
discretionary order l'ordine discrezionale
disincentive il disincentivo
disk il dischetto
dispatch l'invio, la spedizione
disposable income il reddito disponibile
dispute la disputa
dispute (v) disputare
dispute, labor la disputa di lavoro, la disputa sindacale
distribution, channel of il canale di distribuzione
distribution costs i costi di distribuzione
distribution network la rete di distribuzione
distribution policy la politica di distribuzione
distributor il distributore
diversification la diversificazione
divestment la spogliazione, la vendita
dividend il dividendo
dividend yield il rendimento del dividendo
division of labor la divisione del lavoro
dock (ship's receipt) la ricevuta del custode del molo
dock handling charges le spese di ormeggio
document il documento
dollar cost averaging la media del costo in dollari

domestic bill la fattura nazionale

domestic corporation la ditta nazionale

door-to-door (sales) porta-a-porta (vendite)

double dealing l'inganno

double-entry bookkeeping la contabilità a partita doppia

double pricing fissare due prezzi

double taxation la doppia tassazione

double time il lavoro straordinario pagato il doppio, la doppia paga per gli straordinari

down payment l'acconto, il deposito, la caparra

down period il periodo di tempo inutilizzabile, la fase negativa

down the line in ogni caso

downswing il ribasso

downtime il periodo di tempo durante il quale l'elaboratore rimane inutilizzabile

downturn il ribasso

draft la tratta

draw down (v) ridurre l'inventario

drawback il ristorno, lo svantaggio

drawee il trattario

drawer il traente

drayage il trasporto

drop shipment la spedizione fatta direttamente al dettagliante

dry cargo il carico secco

dry goods i beni solidi

dumping (goods in foreign market) il "dumping"

dun (v) sollecitare pagamento

dunnage il fondo della stiva

duopoly il duopolio

durable goods i beni durevoli

duress la pressione

duty il dazio

duty ad valorem il dazio ad valorem

duty, anti-dumping la tariffa protettiva, la tariffa "anti-dumping"

duty, combination il dazio combinato, la tariffa combinata

duty, countervailing la tariffa controvalente
duty, export la tariffa d'esportazione
duty, remission la remissione dell'imposta
duty, specific il dazio specifico, l'imposta specifica
dutyfree esente da dazio
dynamics, group la dinamica del gruppo
dynamics, market la dinamica del mercato
dynamics, product la dinamica del prodotto

E

earmark (v) contrassegnare, specificare
earnings i guadagni
earnings on assets gli utili sugli attivi
earnings per share gli utili per azione
earnings performance il rendimento sui guadagni
earnings report la relazione sugli utili
earnings, retained i profitti ritenuti, i guadagni ritenuti, gli utili ritenuti
earnings yield la rendita sui guadagni
econometrics l'econometria
economic economico
economic indicators gli indicatori economici
economic life la vita economica
economic order quantity la quantità per un ordine economico
economics l'economia
economy of scale l'economia di scala
effective yield il rendimento effettivo
efficiency l'efficienza
elasticity (of supply or demand) l'elasticità (dell'offerta e della domanda)
electrical engineering l'ingegneria elettrica
electronic whiteboard la tavola elettronica per comandi
embargo l'embargo
embezzlement l'appropriazione indebita
employee l'impiegato
employee counseling l'assistenza al personale
employee relations le relazioni con il personale

employment agency l'agenzia per la ricerca del personale

encumbrances (liens, liabilities) il gravame

end of period la fine del periodo

end product il prodotto finale

end-use certificate il certificato attestante l'uso definitivo del prodotto

endorsee il giratario

endorsement la girata

endorser il girante

endowment la dotazione

engineering l'ingegneria

engineering and design department il reparto progettazione e stilismo

engineering, design la progettazione d'impianti, la progettazione industriale

engineering, industrial l'ingegneria industriale, la progettazione industriale

engineering, systems la progettazione dei sistemi di elaborazione

engineering, value la progettazione utilizzando costi più bassi tra costi alternativi per espletare una certa attività

enlarge (v) ingrandire

enterprise l'impresa

entrepreneur l'imprenditore

entry, cash l'annotazione di movimento di contanti, la registrazione del movimento di cassa

entry, debit la nota di debito, la registrazione a debito

entry, ledger l'entrata nel libro mastro, l'entrata sul registro

entry permit il permesso d'entrata, la dichiarazione d'entrata

equal pay for equal work la stessa paga per lo stesso lavoro

equipment gli attrezzi, le attrezzatura, gli impianti e macchinari

equipment leasing l'affitto degli attrezzi

equity l'equità, la giustizia, il capitale azionario

equity, dilution of la diluizione del capitale azionario, la diluizione del capitale netto

equity investments gli investimenti azionari
equity, return on il reddito sul capitale netto
equity share la parte dovuta per il capitale netto
ergonomics l'ergonometrica
error l'errore
escalator clause il comma della scala mobile
escape clause la clausola d'uscita
escheat la proprietà incamerata
escrow il deposito presso terzi
escrow account il conto depositato presso terzi
estate il patrimonio
estate agent l'agente patrimoniale
estate tax l'imposta patrimoniale
estimate la stima
estimate (v) stimare
estimate, sales la stima delle vendite
estimated price il prezzo previsto
estimated time of arrival l'ora d'arrivo prevista
estimated time of departure l'ora di partenza prevista
Eurobond l'euro-obbligazione
Eurocurrency l'eurovaluta
Eurodollar l'eurodollaro
evaluation la valutazione
evaluation, job la valutazione del lavoro
ex dividend senza dividendo
ex dock franco porto, ex molo
ex factory franco fabbrica
ex mill franco mulino
ex mine franco miniera
ex rights ex diritti
ex ship franco nave
ex warehouse franco magazzino
ex works franco officina
exchange (stock, commodity) la borsa
exchange (v) scambiare
exchange control il controllo valutario
exchange discount lo sconto sul cambio
exchange loss la perdita sul cambio

exchange rate il tasso di cambio
exchange risk il rischio sul cambio
exchange value il controvalore
excise duty l'imposta sui consumi
excise license il permesso amministrativo per vendere beni di consumo
excise tax l'imposta sui consumi, la tassa sul consumo
executive il dirigente
executive board il consiglio dirigenziale
executive, chief il direttore generale
executive committee il comitato esecutivo
executive compensation il compenso dirigenziale
executive director il dirigente superiore
executive, line il dirigente di linea
executive search la ricerca di personale dirigenziale
executive secretary la segretaria superiore
executor l'esecutore, il testamentario
exemption l'esenzione
expected results i risultati previsti
expenditure la spesa
expense account il listino di spese rimborsabili
expenses le spese
expenses, direct le spese dirette
expenses, indirect le spese indirette
expenses, running le spese correnti, le spese operative
expenses, shipping le spese di spedizione, le spese di trasporto
expiry date la data di scadenza
export (v) esportare
export agent l'esportatore su commissione
export credit il credito all'esportazione
export duty la tariffa d'esportazione
export entry la dichiarazione d'esportazione
export, for per esportazione
export house la ditta che tratta esportazioni
export-import bank la banca import-export
export manager il responsabile delle esportazioni
export middleman l'intermediario per l'esportazione

export permit il permesso d'esportazione
export quota la quota d'esportazione
export regulations le normative per l'esportazione
export sales contract il contratto di vendita per l'esportazione
export tax l'imposta d'esportazione
expropriation l'esproprio
extra dividend il dividendo supplementare

F

face value il valore dichiarato, il valore riportato
facilities i servizi, i facilitazione, gl'impianti
fact sheet il foglio di dati
factor il fattore, il "factor"
factor analysis l'analisi dei fattori
factor, cost il fattore dei costi
factor, load il fattore del ricarico
factor, profit il fattore degli utili, il fattore dei profitti
factor rating la stima da parte del factor
factory la fabbrica
factory overhead i costi fissi d'azienda
fail (v) fallire
failure il fallimento
fair market value il valore di mercato
fair return il rendimento competitivo agli investimenti alternativi
fair trade il commercio equo, la fiera commerciale
farm out (v) dare l'incarico a terzi
feed ratio il rapporto d'alimentazione
feedback la retroazione
fidelity bond l'obbligazione fiduciaria
fiduciary il fiduciario
fiduciary issue l'emissione fiduciaria
fiduciary loan il prestito fiduciario
field warehousing la cessione di garanzie per merci depositate in un magazzino
file la cartella
finalize (v) finalizzare
finance (v) finanziare

finance company la società di finanziamento

financial analysis l'analisi finanziaria

financial appraisal la valutazione finanziaria

financial control il controllo finanziario

financial director il direttore finanziario

financial highlights i punti di maggior interesse nel rapporto finanziario

financial incentive l'incentivo finanziario

financial management l'amministrazione finanziaria

financial period il periodo finanziario

financial planning la pianificazione finanziaria

financial services i servizi finanziaria

financial statement il bilancio, la dichiarazione finanziaria

financial year l'anno fiscale

fine (penalty) la multa (l'ammenda)

finished goods inventory l'inventario dei beni finiti

fire (v) licenziare

firm la ditta, l'azienda

first in-first out la prima partita ad entrare-la prima partita ad uscire

first preferred stock la prima azione privilegiata

fiscal agent l'agente fiscale

fiscal drag il ritardo fiscale

fiscal year l'anno fiscale

fishy-back service (container) il trasporto di containers su navi

fix the price (v) fissare il prezzo

fixed assets gli attivi fissi, gli immobilizi tecnici

fixed capital i capitali fissi

fixed charges gli oneri fissi

fixed costs i costi fissi

fixed expenses le spese fisse, le spese costanti

fixed income security il titolo di mobiliare a reddito fisso

fixed investment l'investimento costante

fixed liability la responsabilità fissa

fixed rate of exchange il tasso di scambio fisso

fixed term il termine fisso

fixtures (on balance sheet) gl'impianti fissi
flat bond il buono fisso, l'obbligazione
flat rate l'importo fisso
flat yield il rendimento piatto
flatcar il carro merci senza sponde
fleet policy la polizza per un gruppo di automobili
flexible tariff l'imposta variabile
float (outstanding checks, stock) il periodo di tempo durante il quale la banca usufruisce degli assegni depositati e non incassati
float (v) (issue stock) lanciare (una nuova impresa)
floating asset l'attivo variabile
floating charge l'onere variabile
floating debt il debito fluttuante
floating exchange rate il tasso di cambio variabile
floating rate il tasso fluttuante, il tasso variabile
floor (of exchange) la sala delle contrattazioni
floppy disk il dischetto floppy, il "floppy disk"
flow chart il diagramma delle correnti
follow-up order l'ordine successivo
followup (v) far seguito
foodstuffs gli alimentari
footing (accounting) l'addizione
for export per esportazione
forecast la previsione
forecast (v) prevedere
forecast, budget la previsione del preventivo
forecast, market la previsione del mercato
forecast, sales la previsione di vendite
foreign bill of exchange la cambiale emessa all'estero
foreign corporation la ditta estera
foreign currency la valuta estera
foreign debt il debito estero
foreign exchange il cambio estero
foreign securities i titoli mobiliari esteri
foreign tax credit il credito sulle imposte estere
foreign trade il commercio estero
foreman il capo servizio

forgery la contraffazione
form letter la lettera tipo, la lettera "standard"
format il formato
forward contract il contratto a termine
forward cover la copertura a termine
forward forward il termine futuro
forward margin il margine a termine
forward market il mercato a termine
forward purchase l'acquisto a termine
forward shipment la spedizione a termine
forwarding agent lo spedizioniere
foul bill of lading la polizza di carico con riserve o eccezioni
franchise la concessione di appalto
fraud la frode
free alongside ship franco porto, F.A.S.
free and clear senza impegni
free enterprise il liberismo economico
free list (commodities without duty) le merci esentasse
free market il mercato libero
free market industry l'industria di mercato libero
free of particular average libero da medie particolari
free on board (FOB) franco bordo, F.O.B.
free on rail franco stazione ferroviaria
free port il porto franco
free time il tempo libero
free trade il commercio libero
free trade zone la zona franca
freelancer il libero professionista
freight le merci, il carico
freight all kinds le merci di tutti i tipi
freight allowed il carico permesso
freight collect i costi di spedizione a carico del destinatario
freight forwarder lo spedizioniere
freight included compreso trasporto
freight prepaid il trasporto prepagato
frequency curve la curva di frequenza

fringe benefits gli addizionali

fringe market il mercato marginale

front-end fee l'onere anticipato, la commissione anticipata

front-end financing il finanziamento anticipato

front-end loading caricare i fondi all'inizio del contratto

frozen assets gli attivi bloccati

full settlement il saldo completo

functional analysis l'analisi funzionale

fund il fondo

fund, contingent il fondo di contingenza, il fondo di previdenza

fund, sinking il fondo d'ammortamento per il ritiro di obbligazioni

fund, trust il fondo d'investimento fiduciario

funded debt il debito consolidato

funds, public i fondi pubblici

funds, working il capitale liquido, i fondi attivi

fungible goods i beni fungibili

futures il contratto a futura consegna, il contratto a termine

futures option l'opzione di acquisto o di vendita di un contratto a termine

G

garnishment il precetto

gearing l'ingranaggio

gearless senza cambio

general acceptance l'accettazione generale

general average loss la perdita media in genere

general manager l'amministratore generale

general meeting la riunione generale

general partnership la società in accomandita semplice (s.a.s.)

general strike lo sciopero generale

gentleman's agreement l'accordo sulla parola

gilt (Brit. govt. security) i titoli governativi, i buoni e obbligazioni del tesoro (Britannici)

glut la sovvrabbondanza

go around (v) fare il giro

go-go fund il fondo d'investimento molto aggressivo

go public (v) diventare una ditta per azioni

godown il magazzino commerciale nell'estremo oriente

going-concern value il valore effettivo della ditta

going rate (or price) il prezzo corrente

gold clause la clausola d'oro

gold price il prezzo dell'oro

gold reserves le riserve d'oro

good delivery (securities) la buona consegna

goods i beni

goods, capital i beni capitali, i beni d'investimento

goods, consumer i beni di consumo

goods, durable i beni durevoli

goods, industrial i beni industriali

goodwill la benevolenza

government il governo

government agency l'ente governativo

government bank la banca governativa

government bonds i buoni governativi (del tesoro)

grace period il periodo di grazia

grade, commercial il livello commerciale, la qualità commerciale

graft la baratteria

grain il grano

grant an overdraft (v) concedere uno scoperto a fido

graph il diagramma, il grafico

gratuity la gratifica

gray market il mercato grigio

grievance procedure la procedura per stabilire una lamentela

gross domestic product il prodotto interno lordo

gross income il reddito lordo

gross investment l'investimento lordo

gross loss la perdita lorda

gross margin il margine lordo

gross national product (GNP) il prodotto nazionale lordo (Pnl)

gross price il prezzo lordo

gross profit il profitto lordo, l'utile lordo

gross sales le vendite lorde

gross spread la differenza tra il prezzo di vendita e i costi di produzione

gross weight il peso lordo

gross yield il rendimento lordo

group accounts i conti di gruppo, il raggrupamento dei conti

group dynamics la dinamica del gruppo

group insurance la polizza d'assicurazione di gruppo

group, product il gruppo di prodotti

group training l'istruzione in gruppo

growth la crescita

growth, corporate la crescita aziendale

growth index l'indice di crescita

growth industry l'industria in fase di crescita

growth potential il potenziale di crescita

growth rate il tasso di crescita

growth stock l'azione d'incremento

guarantee la garanzia

guaranty bond il buono garantito, l'obbligazione garantita

guaranty company la ditta di garanzia

guesstimate la stima approssimativa

guidelines i parametri

H

half-life (bonds) la mezza scadenza (per buoni)

handicap lo svantaggio

harbor dues i diritti portuali

hard copy la copia scritta

hard currency la valuta pregiata

hard sell la vendita aggressiva

hardware la ferramenta

hardware (computer) il hardware

head office la sede centrale

headhunter l'agente ricercatore di dirigenti

headload il carico di testa

headquarters la sede

heavy industry l'industria pesante

heavy lift charges gli oneri di sollevamento di carichi pesanti

hedge (v) essere elusivo, evitare di compromettersi, bilanciare

hidden assets gli attivi nascosti

high technology l'alta tecnologia

highest bidder il miglior offrente

hire (v) assumere

hoard (v) ammassare

holder (negotiable instruments) il detentore

holder in due course il possessore in buona fede

holding company la società finanziaria, la società madre, il "holding"

holding period il periodo di detenzione

home market il mercato interno

hot money il denaro caldo

hourly earnings i guadagni orari

housing authority l'ente pubblico responsabile per gli alloggi

human resources le risorse del personale

hybrid computer l'elaboratore ibrido

hyphenate (v) dividere una parola usando trattini, creare una parola composta di due nomi utilizzando un trattino

hypothecate l'ipotecare

I

idle capacity la capacità produttiva inattiva

illegal illegale

illegal shipments le spedizioni illegali

imitation l'imitazione

impact, have an...on (v) influenzare

impact, profit l'impatto dei profitti, l'impatto sugli utili

impending changes le modifiche incombenti

implication l'implicazione

implied agreement il patto implicito, la convenzione implicita

import quota la quota d'importazione
import l'importazione
import (v) importare
import declaration la dichiarazione doganale
import deposits i depositi d'importazione
import duty il dazio
import entry l'entrata d'importazione
import license la licenza di importazione
import regulations le normative per l'importazione
import tariff la tariffa d'importazione
import tax l'imposta d'importazione
importer of record l'importatore registrato
impound (v) sequestrare
improve upon (v) migliorare
improvements i miglioramenti
impulse buying gli acquisti impulsivi
imputed l'imputato
in the red in passivo
in transit in transito
inadequate inadeguato
incentive l'incentivo
inchoate interest gl'interessi incipienti
incidental expenses le spese incidentali
income il reddito, il introito
income account il conto redditizio
income bonds i buoni redditizi
income bracket il livello di reddito
income, gross il reddito lordo
income, net il reddito netto
income statement la dichiarazione del reddito
income tax, corporate l'imposta sul reddito delle persone giuridiche (IRPEG)
income tax, personal l'imposta sul reddito delle persone fisiche (IRPEF)
income yield il rendimento
incorporate (v) incorporare
increase l'aumento, l'incremento
increase (v) aumentare, incrementare

increased costs i costi incrementati

incremental cash flow il movimento di cassa incrementale

incremental costs i costi incrementali

indebtedness l'indebitamento

indemnity l'indennità

indentured legato con un contratto

index (indicator) l'indice

index (v) indicizzare

index, growth l'indice di crescita

index linked guaranteed minimum wage la paga base minima indicizzata

indexing l'indicizzazione

indirect claim il reclamo indiretto

indirect cost il costo indiretto

indirect expenses le spese indirette

indirect labor il lavoro indiretto

indirect tax l'imposta indiretta

industrial accident l'incidente industriale

industrial arbitration l'arbitrato industriale

industrial engineering l'ingegneria industriale, la progettazione industriale

industrial goods i beni industriali

industrial insurance l'assicurazione industriale

industrial planning la pianificazione industriale

industrial relations le relazioni industriali

industrial union il sindacato industriale

industry l'industria

industrywide a livello industriale

inefficient inefficiente

inelastic demand or supply la domanda od offerta rigida o inelastica

infant industry l'industria nascente

inflation l'inflazione

inflationary inflazionistico

infrastructure l'infrastruttura

inheritance tax l'imposta di successione

injunction l'ingiunzione

inland bill of lading la polizza di carico nazionale

innovation l'innovazione, la novità
input l'entrata, l'"input"
input-output analysis l'analisi entrata/uscita, l'analisi fattori produttivi
insolvent insolvente
inspection l'ispezione
inspector l'ispettore
instability l'instabilità
installment credit il credito a rate
installment plan il sistema di vendita rateale
institutional advertising la pubblicità istituzionale
institutional investor l'investitore istituzionale
instruct (v) istruire
instrument lo strumento
instrumental capital il capitale industriale
insurance l'assicurazione
insurance broker l'agente di assicurazione
insurance company l'agenzia d'assicurazione
insurance fund il fondo di assicurazione
insurance policy la polizza d'assicurazione
insurance premium il premio d'assicurazione
insurance underwriter il sottoscrittore dell'assicurazione
intangible assets gli attivi intangibili
integrated management system il sistema di gestione integrato
interact (v) iniziare un'azione reciproca
interbank interbanca
interest l'interesse
interest arbitrage l'arbitraggio d'interesse
interest, compound l'interesse composto
interest expenses le spese d'interesse
interest income il reddito sugli interessi
interest parity la parità d'interesse
interest period il periodo d'interesse
interest rate il tasso d'interesse
interface l'"interface"
interim provvisorio

interim budget il preventivo provvisorio
interim statement la dichiarazione provvisoria
interlocking directorate le direzioni congiunte
intermediary l'intermediario
intermediary goods i beni intermediari
internal interno
internal audit la revisione interna
internal funding i fondi interni
internal rate of return il rendimento interno
internal revenue tax le imposte indirette
International Date Line la Linea Internazionale di Demarcazione (dove il giorno cambia)
interstate commerce il commercio interstatale
intervene (v) intervenire
interview l'intervista
intestate senza testamento
intrinsic value il valore intrinseco
invalidate (v) invalidare
inventory l'inventario
inventory control il controllo dell'inventario
inventory, perpetual l'inventario perpetuo
inventory, physical l'inventario fisico
inventory turnover il giro dell'inventario
inverted market il mercato invertito, il mercato capovolto
invest (v) investire
invested capital il capitale investito
investment l'investimento
investment adviser il consulente sugli investimenti
investment analysis l'analisi d'investimento
investment appraisal la valutazione dell'investimento
investment bank la banca d'investimento
investment budget il preventivo d'investimento
investment company la compagnia d'investimento
investment credit il credito per investimento
investment criteria i criteri d'investimento
investment grade il livello di qualità per investimenti
investment letter la lettera d'investimento

investment policy la politica d'investimento
investment program il programma d'investimento
investment, return on il ritorno sull'investimento, il profitto sull'investimento
investment strategy la strategia d'investimento
investment trust il fondo comune d'investimento
investor relations la relazioni con gli investitori
invisibles gli intangibili
invitation to bid la richiesta d'appalto, il bando d'appalto
invoice la fattura
invoice, commercial la fattura commerciale
invoice, consular la fattura consolare
invoice cost il costo fatturato
invoice, pro forma la fattura pro forma
issue (stock) l'emissione, il valore mobiliare
issue (v) emettere
issue price il prezzo d'emissione
issued shares le azioni emesse
item la voce
itemize (v) dettagliare
itemized account il conto dettagliato

J

Jason clause la clausola di negligenza
jawbone (v) chiacchierare
jet lag il fuso orario
jig (production) il crivello
job il lavoro, la mansione
job analysis l'analisi dell'occupazione, l'analisi del lavoro, l'analisi del progetto
job description la descrizione del lavoro
job evaluation la valutazione del lavoro
job hopper colui che cambia spesso il posto di lavoro
job lot alla rinfusa
job performance la valutazione dell'adempimento del lavoro
job security la garanzia del posto di lavoro
jobber il lavoratore a cottimo, il grossista

joint account il conto congiunto
joint estate il patrimonio congiunto
joint liability la responsabilità congiunta
joint owner il comproprietario
joint stock company la ditta a capitale sociale
joint venture il joint venture
journal il giornale
journeyman l'operaio a giornate
joystick il comando, il "joystick"
junior partner il socio secondario
junior security il titolo a garanzia secondaria
jurisdiction la giurisdizione

K

keep posted (v) tenere al corrente
key exports le esportazioni chiave
key man insurance l'assicurazione per il personale indispensabile
Keynesian economics l'economia keynesiana
keypuncher il perforatore
kickback la tangente
kiting (banking) emettere un assegno scoperto e poi depositare la somma necessaria per renderlo valido
knot (nautical) il nodo
know-how l'abilità, il "know-how"

L

labor il lavoro
labor code il codice del lavoro
labor dispute la disputa di lavoro, la disputa sindacale
labor force la forza lavoro
labor-intensive industry l'industria che dipende molto dal fattore della manodopera
labor law la normativa sul lavoro
labor leader il capo sindacale
labor market il mercato del lavoro
labor relations i rapporti sindacali

labor-saving gli accorgimenti che tendono a risparmiare sulla manodopera

labor turnover i ricambio della manodopera

labor union il sindacato

laborer il lavoratore

lagging indicator l'indicatore in ritardo

laissez-faire laissez-faire

land la terra

land grant la donazione di terra

land reform la riforma fondiaria

land tax l'imposta fondiaria

landed cost il costo alla destinazione

landing certificate il certificato per lo sbarco

landing charges gli oneri di sbarco

landing costs i costi di sbarco

landowner il proprietario

large-scale grande scala

last in-first out l'ultima partita consegnata-prima partita ad uscire

law la legge

law of diminishing returns la legge dei rendimenti decrescenti

lawsuit la causa

lawyer l'avvocato

lay-off il licenziamento

lay time il tempo di giacenza

lay up (v) disarmare

laydays le stallie

layout lo schema

lead time l'intervallo tra progettazione e produzione, il periodo di preparazione

leader il capo

leading firm la ditta primaria, la ditta "leader"

leading indicator l'indicatore principale

leads and lags gli anticipi e ritardi

leakage la dispersione, lo sconto

learning curve la curva d'insegnamento

lease il contratto d'affitto, il contratto di locazione

lease (v) affittare

leased department il reparto affittato

leave of absence l'aspettativa, la licenza

ledger il libro mastro

ledger account il conto sul libro mastro

ledger entry l'entrata nel libro mastro, l'entrata sul registro

legacy l'eredità

legal capital il capitale sociale legale

legal entity l'entità legale

legal holiday la festività legale

legal list (fiduciary investments) l'elenco legale

legal monopoly il monopolio legale, il monopolio di stato

legal tender la valuta legale

lending margin il margine di prestito

less-than-carload il carico inferiore alla capacità di una vettura

less-than-truckload il carico inferiore alla capacità di un camion

lessee il locatario

lessor il locatore

letter la lettera

letter of credit la lettera di credito

letter of guaranty la lettera di garanzia

letter of indemnity la lettera d'indennità

letter of introduction la lettera di presentazione

level out (v) livellare

leverage, financial l'ammontare di passività nella struttura finanziara dell'impresa

levy taxes (v) imporre tasse

liability la responsabilità

liability, actual la responsabilità effettiva, la passività effettiva

liability, assumed la responsabilità presunta

liability, contingent la responsabilità contingente, la sopravvenienza passiva

liability, current gli impegni attuali, la responsabilità corrente

liability, fixed la responsabilità fissa

liability insurance l'assicurazione sulla responsabilità civile

liability, unsecured l'impegno senza garanzie, la passività senza garanzia

liable for tax il responsabile per l'imposta

liable to soggetto a

liaison il legame

libel la diffamazione

license la licenza

license fees i costi di licenza

licensed warehouse il deposito

lien il pegno

life cycle of a product la durata di un prodotto

life insurance policy la polizza d'assicurazione sulla vita

life member il socio a vita

life of a patent la durata di un brevetto

lighterage lo scarico con chiatte

limit order (stock market) l'ordine a termine

limited liability la responsabilità limitata

limited partnership la società a responsabilità limitata (s.r.l.)

line executive il dirigente di linea

line management l'amministrazione dirigenziale

line of business l'attività commerciale

line, product la gamma di prodotti, la linea di prodotti

linear lineare

linear estimation la valutazione lineare

linear programming la programmazione lineare

linear terms i termini lineari

liquid assets gli attivi mobili, l'attivo circolante

liquidation la liquidazione

liquidation value il valore liquidato

liquidity la liquidità

liquidity preference (economics) la preferenza per la liquidità

liquidity ratio il rapporto di liquidità

list (v) elencare

list price il prezzo di listino

listed securities le azioni registrate presso la borsa

litigation la lite

living trust il fidecommisso vivente

load (sales charge) il carico, la commissione

load factor il fattore del ricarico

loan il prestito

loan stock i titoli mobiliari prestati a un broker

lobbying i tentativi di influenzare atti governativi con pressioni varie

local customs le usanze locali

local taxes le imposte locali

lock in (v) (rate of interest) bloccare, assicurare

lock out la serrata

logistics la logistica

logo il marchio

long hedge l'investimento di protezione a lunga scadenza

long interest l'interesse lungo

long-range planning la pianificazione a lunga scadenza

long-term capital account il conto capitale a lungo termine

long-term debt il debito a lunga termine

long ton la tonnellata metrica

loss le perdita

loss, gross la perdita lorda

loss leader l'articolo posto in vendita pubblicitaria al di sotto del prezzo necessario per guadagnare un profitto

loss-loss ratio il rapporto perdita contro perdita

loss, net la perdita netta

lot la partita, il lotto

low income il basso reddito

low-interest loans i prestiti con tasso d'interesse basso (favorevole)

low-yield bonds i buoni a basso rendimento

lump sum la somma globale

luxury goods i beni voluttuari

luxury tax l'imposta sui beni di lusso

M

machinery i macchinari

macroeconomics la macroeconomia

magnetic memory la memoria magnetica

magnetic tape il nastro magnetico

mail order l'ordine per corrispondenza

mailing list l'elenco di indirizzi per invio di materiali pubblicitari

mainframe computer l'elaboratore centrale

maintenance la manutenzione

maintenance contract il contratto di manutenzione

maintenance margin il margine di manutenzione

maize il mais, il granoturco

majority interest l'interesse maggioritario

make available (v) rendere disponibile

make-or-buy decision la decisione di fabbricare invece di comprare

maker (of a check, draft, etc.) il fattore

makeshift di fortuna, di ripiego

man (gal) Friday il factotum

man hours le ore lavorative

man-made fibers le fibre artificiali, le fibre sintetiche

manage (v) amministrare

managed costs i costi amministrati, i costi controllabili

managed economy l'economia controllata

managed float la variabilità amministrata o controllata

management l'amministrazione

management accounting la contabilità amministrativa

management, business l'amministrazione commerciale, la gestione commerciale

management by objectives la gestione per obiettivi

management chart il quadro amministrativo, l'organigramma

management consultant il consulente amministrativo

management, credit l'amministrazione del credito

management fee l'onorario amministrativo

management, financial l'amministrazione finanziaria

management group il gruppo amministrativo

management, line l'amministrazione dirigenziale

management, market l'amministrazione del mercato, la gestione del mercato

management, middle l'amministrazione intermediaria

management, office l'amministrazione dell'ufficio, la gestione dell'ufficio

management, personnel la gestione del personale

management, product la gestione del prodotto

management, sales l'amministrazione delle vendite, la gestione delle vendite

management team l'equipe amministrativa

management, top il massimo livello amministrativo, la dirigenza

manager l'amministratore, il direttore

mandate il mandato

mandatory redemption l'estinzione obbligatoria

manifest il manifesto

manpower la manodopera

manual workers gli operai

manufacturer il fabbricante, il produttore

manufacturer's agent l'agente del produttore

manufacturer's representative il rappresentante del produttore

manufacturing capacity la capacità di produzione, la capacità produttiva

manufacturing control il controllo della produzione

margin call richiedere il saldo del deposito per coprire perdite sulla borsa

margin, gross il margine lordo

margin, net il margine netto

margin of safety il margine di sicurezza

margin, profit il margine di profitto

margin requirements le esigenze di margine

marginal account il conto marginale

marginal cost il costo marginale

marginal pricing la determinazione del prezzo marginale

marginal productivity la produttività marginale

marginal revenue i ricavi marginali

marine cargo insurance l'assicurazione marittima

marine underwriter l'assicuratore marino

maritime contract il contratto marittimo

mark down (v) scontare

market il mercato

market (v) vendere, mettere sul mercato, market

market access l'accesso al mercato

market appraisal la valutazione di mercato

market, buyer's il mercato favorevole all'acquirente, il mercato propenso per gli acquirenti

market concentration la concentrazione di mercato

market dynamics la dinamica del mercato

market forces le forze di mercato

market forecast la previsione del mercato

market, fringe il mercato marginale

market index l'indice di mercato

market-maker (securities) il compratore e venditore di titoli mobiliari, colui che crea un mercato

market management l'amministrazione del mercato, la gestione del mercato

market penetration la penetrazione commerciale

market plan il piano di mercato, il programma di mercato

market position la posizione di mercato

market potential il potenziale di mercato

market price il prezzo di mercato

market rating la valutazione del mercato

market report il rapporto sul mercato

market research la ricerca di mercato

market saturation la saturazione del mercato

market share la quota di mercato

market survey l'indagine di mercato

market trends le tendenze del mercato

market value il valore di mercato

marketable securities i titoli di sicura affidabilità che possono essere posti sul mercato, i titoli mobiliari
marketing il marketing
marketing budget il preventivo per il marketing
marketing concept il concetto di marketing
marketing plan la strategia di marketing
marketplace il mercato
markup il ricarico
mass communications le comunicazioni di massa
mass marketing il marketing per il mercato di massa
mass media i mezzi di communicazione, i "mass media"
mass production la produzione di serie
matched samples i campioni uniformi
materials i materiali
maternity leave il congedo di maternità
mathematical model il modello matematico
matrix management l'amministrazione a matrice
maturity la maturità
maturity date la data di maturazione
maximize (v) ottimizzare
mean (average) la media
measure (v) misurare
mechanical engineering l'ingegneria meccanica
mechanics' lien il pegno per il mercato
median il valore mediano
mediation la mediazione
medium of exchange il mezzo di scambio
medium term il medio termine
meet the price (v) venire incontro al prezzo
meeting la riunione
meeting, board la riunione del consiglio
member firm la ditta associata
member of firm il socio
memorandum il memorandum, l'appunto
mercantile mercantile
mercantile agency l'agenzia mercantile
mercantile law la legge mercantile

merchandise i prodotti
merchandising la mercanzia
merchant il mercante
merchant bank la merchant bank
merchant guild l'associazione mercantile
merger la fusione
metals i metalli
method il metodo
metrification la metrificazione
microchip il microchip
microcomputer il micro computer
microfiche la microfiche
microfilm il microfilm
microprocessor il micro elaboratore
middle management l'amministrazione intermediaria
middleman l'intermediario
milling la macinatura, la fresatura
minicomputer il mini computer, il mini elaboratore elettronico
minimum reserves le riserve minime
minimum wage la paga minima, la paga base
minority interest l'interesse minoritario
mint la zecca
miscalculation il calcolo errato
miscellaneous varie
misleading ingannevole
misunderstanding malinteso
mixed cost il costo misto
mixed sampling la campionatura mista
mobility of labor la mobilità della manodopera
mock-up il modello
mode la maniera
model il modello
modem il modulatore per la trasmissione di dati via cavo
modular production la produzione modulare
monetary base la base monetaria
monetary credits i crediti monetari

monetary policy la politica monetaria
money il denaro
money broker il cambio valute, l'intermediario valutario
money manager l'amministratore finanziario
money market il mercato monetario
money order il vaglia postale
money shop il negozio di denaro
money supply la disponsibilità dei capitali
monitor il monitor
monopoly il monopolio
monopsony il monopsonio
Monte Carlo technique la tecnica di Monte Carlo
moonlighting il lavoro nero
morale il morale
moratorium il moratorio
mortgage l'ipoteca
mortgage bank la banca ipotecaria
mortgage bond l'obbligazione garantita da ipoteca
mortgage certificate il certificato ipotecario
mortgage debenture l'obbligazione ipotecaria
most-favored nation il paese con trattamento preferenziale
motion la mozione
motivation study lo studio motivazionale
movement of goods lo spostamento dei beni
moving average la media variabile
moving expenses le spese di trasloco
moving parity la parità variabile
multicurrency i multivalutario
multilateral agreement la convenzione multilaterale
multilateral trade il commercio multilaterale
multinational corporation la società multinazionale
multiple exchange rate il tasso di cambio multiplo
multiple taxation la tassazione multipla
multiples i multipli
multiplier il moltiplicatore
multiprogramming multiprogrammato

municipal bond l'obbligazione municipale

mutual fund il fondo d'investimento

mutual savings bank la cassa cooperativa di risparmio

mutually exclusive classes le classi mutualmente esclusive

N

named inland point in country of origin il punto interno denominato nel paese d'importazione

named point of destination la destinazione indicata

named point of exportation il punto d'esportazione indicato

named point of origin il punto d'origine indicato

named port of importation il porto d'importazione denominato

named port of shipment il porto di spedizione denominato

national bank la banca nazionale

national debt il debito nazionale

nationalism il nazionalismo

nationalization la nazionalizzazione

native produce il prodotto locale

natural resources le risorse naturali

near money l'attività finanziaria a brevissimo termine

needs analysis l'analisi delle esigenze

negative cash flow il flusso di cassa negativo

negative pledge il pegno negativo

negligent negligente

negotiable negoziabile

negotiable securities i titoli mobiliari negoziabili

negotiate (v) negoziare, trattare

negotiated sale la vendita negoziata

negotiation il negoziato

net netto

net asset value il valore netto degli attivi

net asset worth il valore netto degli attivi

net assets gli attivi netti

net borrowed reserves le riserve di capitali presi a prestito

net cash flow il flusso netto di cassa

net change il cambio netto, il cambiamento netto

net equity assets gli attivi netti sulle azioni ordinarie

net income il reddito netto

net investment l'investimento netto

net loss la perdita netta

net margin il margine netto

net position (of a trader) la posizione netta

net present value il valore attuale netto

net profit il profitto netto

net sales le vendite nette

net working capital il capitale circolante al netto

net worth il capitale azionario, il valore netto

network (v) stabilire contatti capillari

new issue la nuova emissione

new money l'infusione di fondi da nuove fonti

new product development lo sviluppo di nuovi prodotti

night depository la cassa notturna

no-load fund il fondo d'investimento senza commissioni

no par value senza valore alla pari

no problem nessun problema

nominal price il prezzo nominale

nominal yield il reddito nominale

noncumulative preferred stock le azioni privilegiate non cumulative

noncurrent assets l'attività non a breve termine

nondurable goods i beni non durevoli

nonfeasance le trasgressione

nonmember il non associato, il non socio

nonprofit senza fini di lucro

nonresident il non residente, lo straniero

nonvoting stock le azioni senza diritto di voto

norm la norma

not otherwise indexed by name non oltre indicato per nome

notary il notaio
note, credit la nota di accredito
note, debit la nota di addebito
note, promissory la cambiale, il pagherò cambiario
notes receivable le cambiali esigibili
novation la novazione
null and void nullo a tutti gli effetti
nullify (v) annullare
numerical control il controllo numerico

O

obligation l'obbligazione
obsolescence l'obsolescenza
occupation l'occupazione
occupational hazard il pericolo professionale
odd lot le rimanenze, la partita frazionata
odd lot broker il mediatore di partite sparse
off board (stock market) non ufficiale
off-line inattivo, "off-line"
off-the-books non registrato
offer (v) offrire
offer for sale (v) porre in vendita
offered price il prezzo offerto
offered rate il tasso offerto
office l'ufficio
office, branch la filiale
office, head la sede generale
office management l'amministrazione dell'ufficio, la gestione dell'ufficio
offset printing la fotolitografia
offshore company la ditta offshore
oligopoly l'oligopolio
oligopsony l'oligopsonio
omit (v) omettere
on account in conto
on consignment su rimessa
on cost su costo
on demand su richiesta

on line (computer) pronto per l'utilizzo, "on line"
on the back sul retro
on-the-job training l'istruzione sul posto di lavoro
open account il conto aperto
open cover la copertura in abbonamento
open door policy la politica di apertura
open market il mercato aperto
open market operations le operazioni di mercato aperto
open order l'ordine continuo
open shop la fabbrica aperta anche ai non iscritti al sindacato
opening balance il bilancio d'apertura
opening price il prezzo iniziale, il prezzo di apertura del mercato
operating budget il preventivo operativo
operating expenses le spese operative
operating income il reddito operativo
operating profit gli utili diretti
operating statement la dichiarazione operativa
operations audit il controllo operativo
operations headquarters la sede amministrativa
operations management la gestione delle operazioni
operator l'operatore
opportunity costs il costo dell'opportunità
option l'opzione
option index l'indice delle opzioni
option, stock l'opzione sulle azioni
optional opzionale, facoltativo
oral bid l'offerta a voce
order l'ordine
order (v) ordinare
order form il modulo
order number il numero dell'ordine
order of the day l'ordine del giorno
order, to place an (v) piazzare un ordine
ordinary capital il capitale ordinario
organization l'organizzazione
organization chart l'organigramma

original cost il costo originale
original entry l'entrata originale
original maturity la data originale di maturazione
other assets (and liabilities) le altre attività (e passività)
out-of-pocket expenses le spese di tasca propria
outbid (v) offrire di più
outlay lo sborsamento
outlet lo sbocco
outlook la prospettiva
output la produzione
outsized articles gli articoli fuori misura
outstanding contract il contratto insoluto
outstanding debt i debiti insoluti
outstanding stock le azioni in circolazione
outturn la produzione
over-the-counter quotation le quotazione fuori borsa
overage l'eccesso
overbuy (v) acquistare in quantità eccesiva
overcapitalized capitalizzato in eccesso
overcharge il sovrapprezzo
overdraft la somma in eccesso ai fondi disponibili
overdue scaduto
overhang la sporgenza
overhead le spese fisse generali
overlap la sovrapposizione
overnight nel giro di una notte
overpaid sovrappagato
overseas common point il punto comune oltremare
oversell (v) vendere più di quanto si abbia
overstock il sovraccarico
oversubscribed sottoscritto oltre il necessario
oversupply le forniture oltre il necessario
overtime il lavoro straordinario
overvalued sopravvalutato
owner il proprietario
owner's equity l'interesse del proprietario
ownership la proprietà
ownership, absentee il proprietario assente

P

p/e ratio il rapporto tra i prezzi ed i guadagni di un azione

package deal la trattativa complessiva

packaging l'imballaggio

packing case la cassa d'imballo

packing list il listino d'imballaggio

paid holiday il giorno festivo pagato

paid in full completamente pagato

paid-in surplus l'eccedenza versata

paid up capital il capitale versato

paid up shares le azioni liberate

pallet il pallet

palletized freight la merce pallettizzata

paper la carta

paper profit il profitto su carta, gli utili su carta

paper tape il nastro di carta

par pari

par, above sopra la pari

par, below sotto la pari

par value il valore al pari

parcel post il pacco postale

parent company la ditta madre, l'azienda madre

parity la parità

parity income ratio il rapporto tra il reddito e la parità

parity price il prezzo di parità

part cargo la parte della merce

partial payment il pagamento parziale

participating preferred stock le azioni preferenziali di partecipazione sugli utili

participation fee la tariffa di partecipazione

participation loan il prestito partecipato

particular average loss la perdita media particolare

partner il socio

partnership la società di persone

parts le parti

passbook il libretto di deposito bancario

passed dividend il dividendo eliminato

past due scaduto
patent il brevetto
patent application il modulo di richiesta per brevetto
patent law la legge sui brevetti
patent pending il brevetto richiesto
patent royalty i diritti di brevetto
patented process la procedura brevettata
pattern il modello, il disegno
pay (v) pagare
pay as you go pagare in contanti
pay up (v) saldare
payable on demand pagabile su richiesta
payable to bearer pagabile al portatore
payable to order pagabile all'ordine
payback period il periodo di ripagamento
payee il creditore
payer il pagante
payload il carico effettivo
paymaster il preparatore delle paghe
payment il pagamento
payment in full il pagamento completo
payment in kind il pagamento in natura
payment refused il pagamento rifiutato
payoff la liquidazione dei conti
payout period il periodo di pagamento
payroll il libro paga
payroll tax l'imposta sui salari
peak load il carico massimo
peg (v) fissare
pegged price il prezzo fissato
penalty clause la clausola di penalità
penalty-fraud action l'azione di penalità per azioni di frode
penny stock le azioni con un valore inferiore ad un dollaro
pension fund il fondo pensionistico
per capita pro capite
per diem la diaria

per share per azione
percentage earnings la percentuale di guadagni
percentage of profits la percentuale di profitti
performance bond l'assicurazione d'adempimento
periodic inventory l'inventario periodico
peripherals le aggiunte
perks i benefici
permit il permesso
perpetual inventory l'inventario perpetuo
personal deduction la detrazione personale
personal exemption l'esenzione personale
personal income tax l'imposta sul reddito delle persone fisiche (IRPEF)
personal liability la responsabilità personale
personal property la proprietà personale
personality test l'esame della personalità
personnel administration l'amministrazione del personale
personnel department il reparto personale
personnel management la gestione del personale
petrochemical la petrochimica
petrodollars i petrodollari
phase in (v) introdurre
phase out (v) eliminare
physical inventory l'inventario fisico
phytosanitary regulations le normative fitosanitarie
picket line la linea di picchettaggio
pickup and delivery il ritiro e la consegna
pie chart il grafico a fette
piecework il lavoro a cottimo
piggyback service il trasporto di containers con camion
pilferage il piccolo furto
pilotage il pilotaggio
pipage le tubazioni
place an order (v) piazzare un ordine, ordinare
place of business il posto di lavoro
placement (personnel) il collocamento
plan il piano

plan (v) progettare

plan, action il piano d'azione

plan, market il piano di mercato, il programma di mercato

planned obsolescence l'obsolescenza programmata

plant capacity la capacità produttiva della fabbrica, la potenziale di capacità produttiva di un impianto

plant location la localizzazione degli impianti

plant manager l'amministratore della fabbrica

pledge l'impegno, la promessa

plenary meeting la riunione plenaria

plow back (v) (earnings) reinvestire

plus accrued interest compreso interessi accumulati

point (percentage, mortgage term) i centesimi di percentuale per ipoteche

point, break-even il punto di pareggio, il punto della parità, il volume di vendite al quale c'è equilibrio tra ricavi e costi

point of order la questione di procedura

point of sale il punto di vendita

policy la polizza

policyholder l'assicurato

pool (of funds) il fondo monetario comune

pool (v) mettere in fondo comune

pooling of interests gli interessi in comune

portfolio la cartella, il portafoglio

portfolio management l'amministrazione della cartella degli investimenti

portfolio, stock la cartella d'azioni

portfolio theory la teoria d'azione relativa agli investimenti

position limit il limite di perdita

positive cash flow il movimento positivo dei fondi

post (v) (bookkeeping) registrare

postdated postdatato

postpone (v) posticipare

potential buyer l'acquirente potenziale, il compratore potenziale

potential sales le vendite potenziali

power of attorney la procura

practical pratico
preemptive right il diritto di prelazione
prefabrication il prefabbricazione
preferential debts i debiti preferenziali
preferred stock l'azione preferenziale
preferred tariff la tariffa preferenziale
preliminary prospectus il prospetto preliminare
premises (location) l'edificio
premium, acceleration il premio d'accelerazione
premium, insurance il premio d'assicurazione
premium offer l'offerta premio
premium payment il pagamento del premio
premium price il prezzo di premio
prepaid expenses (balance sheet) le spese prepagate
prepay (v) prepagare
president il presidente
preventive maintenance la manutenzione preventiva
price il prezzo
price (v) stabilire il prezzo
price, competitive il prezzo concorrenziale
price cutting i tagli dei prezzi, la riduzione dei prezzi
price differential il differenziale dei prezzi
price/earnings ratio il rapporto tra i prezzi ed i guadagni di un azione
price elasticity l'elasticità del prezzo
price, fix the (v) fissare il prezzo
price index l'indice dei prezzi
price limit il prezzo limite
price list il listino prezzi
price, market il prezzo di mercato
price range la gamma dei prezzi
price support il sostegno del prezzo
price tick lo sbalzo di prezzo
price war la guerra sui prezzi
primary market il mercato primario
primary reserves le riserve primarie
prime cost il costo primo
prime time le ore migliori per la pubblicità televisiva

principal il principale
printed matter le stampe
printout lo stampato
priority la priorità
private fleet la flotta privata
private label (or brand) la produzione per conto terzi
private placement (finance) la collocazione privata
pro forma invoice la fattura pro forma
pro forma statement la dichiarazione pro forma
probate l'omologazione
problem il problema
problem analysis l'analisi del problema
problem solving la risoluzione di problemi
proceeds i proventi
process (v) trasformare, lavorare
process, production il procedimento di produzione, il processo produttivo
processing error l'errore di elaborazione
procurement l'acquisto
product il prodotto
product analysis l'analisi del prodotto
product design il disegno del prodotto
product development lo sviluppo del prodotto
product dynamics la dinamica del prodotto
product group il gruppo di prodotti
product life la durata del prodotto
product line la gamma di prodotti, la linea di prodotti
product management la gestione del prodotto
product profitability l'utile del prodotto
production la produzione
production control il controllo della produzione
production costs i costi di produzione
production line la linea di produzione
production process il procedimento di produzione, il processo produttivo
production schedule il programma di produzione
productivity la produttività
productivity campaign la campagna di produttività

profession la professione

profit il profitto, gli utile

profit and loss statement la dichiarazione degli utili e delle perdite, il conto profitti e perdite

profit factor il fattore degli utili, il fattore dei profitti

profit, gross il profitto lordo, l'utile lordo

profit impact l'impatto dei profitti, l'impatto sugli utili

profit margin il margine di profitto

profit, net il profitto netto

profit projection la proiezione degli utili

profit sharing la spartizione degli utili

profit taking la vendita per la realizzazione di profitti

profitability la redditività

profitability analysis l'analisi dei profitti, l'analisi del rapporto tra costo e profitto, lo studio sulla profittabilità

program il programma

program (v) programmare

prohibited goods i beni proibiti

project il progetto

project (v) proiettare, progettare

project planning la pianificazione del progetto

promissory note la cambiale, il pagherò cambiario

promotion la promozione

promotion, sales la promozione delle vendite

prompt pronto, sollecito

proof of loss la verifica della perdita

property la proprietà

proprietary il diritto di proprietario

proprietor il proprietario

prospectus il prospetto

protectionism il protezionismo

protest (banking; law) (v) protestare

proxy la procura

proxy statement la dichiarazione per procura

prudent man rule la norma dell'uomo giudizioso

public auction l'asta pubblica

public company l'azienda pubblica

public domain il dominio pubblico

public funds i fondi pubblici

public offering l'offerta al pubblico

public opinion poll il sondaggio della opinione pubblica

public property la proprietà pubblica

public relations le pubbliche relazioni

public sale la vendita pubblica

public sector il settore pubblico

public utilities i servizi pubblici

public works i lavori pubblici

publicity la pubblicità

pump priming l'investimento di fondi per iniziare l'attività

punch card la scheda perforata

purchase (v) acquistare, comprare

purchase money mortgage l'ipoteca

purchase order l'ordine d'acquisto

purchase price il prezzo d'acquisto

purchasing agent l'agente d'acquisto

purchasing manager l'amministratore degli acquisti

purchasing power il potere d'acquisto

pure risk il rischio puro

put and call la compravendita di azioni sopra o sotto il prezzo attuale

put in a bid (v) mettere in appalto

put option l'opzione di vendita (di un'azione a un prezzo superiore a quello attuale)

pyramid selling la vendita piramidale

Q

qualifications le qualifiche

qualified acceptance endorsement la girata d'accettazione qualificata

quality control il controllo di qualità

quality goods i beni di qualità

quantity la quantità

quantity discount lo sconto per quantità

quasi-public company l'azienda quasi pubblica

quick assets le attività prontamente realizzabili
quitclaim deed la rinuncia ad un atto di proprietà
quorum il quorum
quota la quota
quota, export la quota d'esportazione
quota, sales la quota di vendita
quota system il sistema di contingentamento
quotation la quotazione, la citazione

R

rack jobber la lavorazione su commessa
rail shipment il trasporto ferroviario
rain check l'abbuono per ricevere merce esaurita in un'altra data
raising capital l'innalzamento dei capitali, il raccoglimento dei capitali
rally il rafforzamento delle azioni
random access memory la memoria d'accesso casuale
random sample il campione casuale
rate il tasso
rate, base il tasso di base
rate of growth il tasso di crescita
rate of increase il tasso d'incremento
rate of interest il tasso d'interesse
rate of return il tasso di rimunerazione, il tasso di rendimento
rating, credit la valutazione dei crediti
rating, market la valutazione del mercato
ratio la proporzione
ration (v) razionare
raw materials la materia prima
re-export (v) riesportare
ready cash il denaro disponibile
real assets gli attivi reali
real estate gli immobili
real income il reddito reale
real investment l'investimento reale
real price il prezzo reale
real time il tempo reale

real wages il salario reale
reasonable care la cura ragionevole
rebate l'abbuono, lo sconto
recapitalization la ricapitalizzazione
receipt la ricevuta
recession la recessione
reciprocal training l'istruzione reciproca
record date la data di registrazione
recourse il ricorso
recovery il ricovero
recovery of expenses il rimborso delle spese
red tape la prassi burocratica
redeemable bonds le obbligazioni redimibili
redemption allowance la deduzione convertibile
redemption fund il fondo di investimento redimibile
redemption premium il premio di redimibilità
rediscount rate il tasso di risconto
reference, credit la referenza bancaria, la referenza per ottenere credito
reference number il numero di riferimento
refinancing il rifinanziamento
reflation la riflazione
refund il rimborso
refuse acceptance (v) rifiutare accettazione
refuse payment (v) rifiutare pagamento
regard (with regard to) riguardo (al riguardo)
registered check l'assegno nominativo
registered mail la raccomandata
registered representative il rappresentante nominato
registered security il titolo nominativo
registered trademark il marchio registrato
regression analysis l'analisi di regressione
regressive tax l'imposta regressiva
regular warehouse il magazzino regolare
regulation la normativa
reimburse (v) rimborsare
reinsurer il riassicuratore
reliable source la fonte attendibile

remainder (v) liquidare
remedy (law) il rimedio
remission duty la remissione dell'imposta
remission of a tax la remissione di una tassa
remuneration la rimunerazione
renegotiate (v) rinegoziare
renew (v) rinnovare
rent l'affitto
reorder (v) riordinare
reorganize (v) riorganizzare
repay (v) ripagare
repeat order l'ordine ripetuto
replacement cost il costo di ricambio
replacement parts le parti di ricambio
reply; in reply to il riscontro; a riscontro di
reply (v) rispondere
report la relazione
repossession il rientro in possesso
representative il rappresentante
reproduction costs i costi d' riproduzione
request for bid il bando di appalto
requirements le esigenze, le requisiti
resale la rivendita
research la ricerca
research and development la ricerca e lo sviluppo
reserve la riserva
resident buyer il compratore in loco
resolution (legal document) la risoluzione
resources allocation l'allocazione delle risorse
restrictions on export le restrizioni all'esportazione
restrictive labor practices le procedure restrittive di lavoro
restructure (v) ristrutturare
résumé il curriculum vitae
retail al dettaglio
retail bank la banca al dettaglio, la banca per il consumatore
retail merchandise i beni al dettaglio

retail outlet il negozio al dettaglio

retail price il prezzo al dettaglio

retail sales tax l'imposta sulla vendita al dettaglio

retail trade il commercio al dettaglio

retained earnings i profitti ritenuti, i guadagni ritenuti, gli utili ritenuti

retirement il congedo, il pensionamento

retroactive arretrato

return on assets managed il rendimento sulle attività amministrate

return on capital i proventi sul capitale, il rendimento sul capitale

return on equity il reddito sul capitale netto

return on investment il profitto sull'investimento, il ritorno sull'investimento

return on sales la resa sulle vendite

return, rate of il tasso di rimunerazione, il tasso di rendimento

revaluation la rivalutazione

revenue l'introito, il ricavo

revenue bond l'obbligazione garantita dai ricavi dell'emittente

reverse stock split la riduzione nel numero delle azioni

revocable trust il fondo d'investimento fiduciario revocabile

revolving credit il credito rotativo

revolving fund il fondo d'investimento rotativo

revolving letter of credit la lettera di credito rotativa

reward il premio

rider (contracts) la postilla

right of recourse il diritto al ricorso

right of way la precedenza

risk il rischio

risk analysis l'analisi del rischio

risk assessment la valutazione del rischio

risk capital il capitale per finanziare nuove iniziative

rollback la riduzione

rolling stock il materiale rotante

rollover il rinvestimento degli utili di un investimento

rough draft la bozza

rough estimate la stima

round lot la partita arrotondata, la partita intera

routine la routine

royalty (payment) i diritti d'autore

running expenses le spese correnti, le spese operative

rush order l'ordine urgente

S

safe deposit box la cassetta di sicurezza

safeguard il salvaguardia

salary il salario

sale and leaseback la vendita e il riaffitto

sales le vendite

sales analysis l'analisi delle vendite

sales budget il preventivo per le spese di vendita

sales estimate la stima delle vendite, le vendite previste

sales force il personale di vendita

sales forecast le previsioni di vendita

sales management l'amministrazione delle vendite, la gestione delle vendite

sales promotion la promozione delle vendite

sales quota la quota di vendita

sales tax l'imposta sulle vendite

sales territory il territorio di vendita

sales turnover il giro delle vendite

sales volume il volume delle vendite

salvage (v) recuperare

salvage charges le spese di recupero

salvage value il valore di recupero

sample (v) campionare

sample line la linea campionaria

sample size la misura del campione

savings i risparmi

savings account il conto di risparmio

savings bank la cassa di risparmio

savings bond il buono di risparmio
scalper il bagarino
schedule l'orario
screen (v) selezionare
script il copione
sealed bid l'appalto sigillato
seasonal stagionale
second mortgage l'ipoteca secondaria
second position la posizione secondaria
secondary market (securities) il mercato secondario per titoli mobiliari
secondary offering (securities) l'offerta secondaria di titoli di sicura affidabilità
secretary la/il segretaria/o
secured accounts i conti garantiti, i crediti garantiti
secured liability l'impegno garantito, la passività garantita
securities i titoli di sicura affidabilità, i titoli mobiliari, le azioni, le obbligazioni
security la sicurezza, la garanzia
self-appraisal l'auto-critica
self-employed, be (v) lavorare per conto proprio
self-management l'autogestione
self-service il self-service
sell (v) vendere
sell direct (v) vendere diretta
sell, hard la vendita aggressiva
sell, soft la vendita non aggressiva
semi-variable costs i costi semi-variabili
senior issue l'emissione primaria
seniority l'anzianità
separation la separazione
serial bonds le obbligazioni a scadenza periodica
serial storage l'immagazzinaggio
service (v) mantenere
service, advisory il servizio consultivo
service contract il contratto di manutenzione
service, customer il servizio reso al cliente
set-up costs i costi iniziali

settlement la definizione
settlement, full il saldo completo
severance pay la bonuscita
shareholder l'azionista
shareholder's equity il capitale netto dell'azionista
shareholders' meeting la riunione degli azionisti
shares le azioni
shift (labor) il turno
shipment la spedizione, la consegna
shipper lo spedizioniere
shipping agent l'agente spedizioniere
shipping charges i costi di trasporto
shipping expenses le spese di spedizione, le spese di trasporto
shipping instructions le istruzioni per il trasporto
shopping center il centro acquisti fuori dall'area urbana
short delivery la consegna incompleta
short of, to be (v) mancare
short position la posizione scoperta
short sale la vendita allo scoperto
short shipment la spedizione incompleta
short supply le forniture carenti
short-term capital account il conto capitale a breve termine
short-term debt il debito a breve termine
short-term financing il finanziamento a breve termine
shortage la carenza, la mancanza
shrink-wrapping l'imballaggio utilizzando pellicole di plastica ristretta
sick leave il congedo per malattia
sight draft la tratta a vista
signature la firma
silent partner il socio accomandante
simulate (v) simulare
sinking fund il fondo d'ammortamento per il ritiro di obbligazioni
skilled labor la manodopera specializzata

sliding parity la parità variabile
sliding scale la scala variabile
slump la fase negativa
small business la piccola industria
soft currency la valuta debole
soft goods i beni non durevoli
soft loan il prestito con minor garanzia
soft sell la vendita non aggressiva
software il software
software broker il mediatore di software
sole agent l'agente esclusivo
sole proprietor il proprietario unico
sole rights i diritti esclusivi
solvency la liquidità
specialist (stock exchange) lo specialistà
specialty goods i beni specializzati
specific duty il dazio specifico, l'imposta specifica
speculator lo speculatore
speed up (v) accelerare
spin off (v) lanciare un nuovo prodotto sulla base di un altro prodotto
spoilage lo scarto
sponsor (of fund, partnership) lo "sponsor"
spot delivery la consegna immediata
spot market il mercato a contanti
spread la variazione
spreadsheet il modulo multiplo, lo "spreadsheet"
staff il personale
staff and line il personale e i dirigenti
staff assistant l'assistente di servizio
staff organization l'organigramma di servizio
stagflation la stagflazione
stale check l'assegno vecchio
stand-alone word processor l'elaboratore del testo autonomo
stand-alone workstation il posto di lavoro autonomo
stand in line (v) fare la coda
standard costs i costi normali, i costi standard

standard deviation lo scarto quadratico medio

standard of living il tenore di vita

standard practice le pratiche d'uso

standard time l'ora solare

standardization la standardizzazione

standing charges la tariffa fissa

standing costs i costi fissi

standing order l'ordine fisso

start-up cost i costi iniziali

statement la dichiarazione

statement, financial il bilancio, la dichiarazione finanziaria

statement of account la dichiarazione di conto

statement, pro forma la dichiarazione pro forma

statement, profit and loss la dichiarazione degli utili e delle perdite

statistics le statistiche

statute lo statuto

statute of limitations la scadenza oltre la quale non sono permesse azioni legali

stock il valore, il titolo, l'azione

stock certificate il certificato azionario

stock control il controllo dei valori, il controllo delle azioni

stock exchange la borsa

stock index l'indice della borsa

stock market la borsa

stock option l'opzione sulle azioni

stock portfolio il portafoglio azionario

stock power il potere delle azioni, l'autorizzazione a collateralizzare azioni

stock profit l'utile dalle azioni

stock purchase l'acquisto valori mobiliari

stock split il frazionamento delle azioni

stock takeover l'insediamento tramite acquisto del controllo azionario

stock turnover il giro delle azioni, il ricambio delle azioni

stockbroker il mediatore delle azioni

stockholder l'azionista

stockholders' equity il capitale degli azionisti, il capitale azionario

stop-loss order l'ordine di fermo perdita

storage l'immagazzinaggio

store (v) accumulare

stowage lo stivaggio

stowage charges i costi di stivaggio

straddle l'opzione col privilegio di acquistare o vendere un'azione allo stesso prezzo

strapping l'azione che deriva dalla richiesta di esercitare due opzioni di acquisto ed una di vendita

strategic articles gli articoli strategici

streamline (v) affusolare, scorrere in modo regolare

stress management l'amministrazione della tensione

strike (v) scioperare

strike, wildcat lo sciopero selvaggio

strikebreaker (scab) il crumiro

stuffing l'imbottitura

subcontract (v) subappaltare

subcontractor il subappaltatore

sublet il subaffitto

subscription price il prezzo di sottoscrizione

subsidiary la filiale

subsidy il sussidio

substandard deficiente, sotto norma

sum of the year's digits la somma dei numeri dell'anno precedente, il metodo di ammortamento accellerato

supersede (v) sostituire

supervisor il supervisore

supplier il fornitore

supply and demand l'offerta e la domanda

support activities le funzioni di sostegno

surcharge il sovraccarico, il soprapprezzo

surety company la ditta garante

surplus capital il capitale eccedente

surplus goods i beni eccedenti

surtax la soprattassa

suspend payment (v) sospendere il pagamento
switching charges le spese di scambio
sworn statement la dichiarazione sotto giuramento
syndicate (v) costituire un sindacato
systems analysis l'analisi dei sistemi
systems design la progettazione dei sistemi di elaborazione
systems engineering la progettazione dei sistemi di elaborazione
systems management l'amministrazione dei sistemi di elaborazione

T

table of contents l'indice
take down (v) smontare, ritirare
take off (v) decollare
take-home pay lo stipendio netto
take out (v) eliminare, togliere
takeover l'insediamento
takeover bid l'offerta d'insediamento
tangible assets i beni reali
tanker la petroliera
target price il prezzo indicativo
tariff la tariffa
tariff barriers le barriere doganali, le barriere tariffarie
tariff charges i costi tariffari
tariff classification la classificazione doganale
tariff commodity la voce tariffaria
tariff differential il differenziale tariffario
tariff war la guerra tariffaria
task force il gruppo di esperti
tax la tassa, l'imposta
tax allowance lo sgravio fiscale
tax base la base delle tasse imponibili
tax burden l'onere fiscale
tax collector l'esattore delle tasse
tax deduction la detrazione dalle imposte
tax evasion l'evasione fiscale

tax, excise l'imposta sui consumi, la tassa sul consumo

tax, export l'imposta d'esportazione

tax-free income il reddito esentasse

tax haven il rifugio fiscale, il paradiso fiscale

tax, import l'imposta d'importazione

tax relief lo sgravio fiscale

tax, sales l'imposta sulle vendite

tax shelter la riduzione delle tasse tramite facilitazioni permesse dal governo

taxation la tassazione

team, management l'equipe amministrativa

telecommunications le telecomunicazioni

telemarketing il marketing telefonico

teleprocessing la tele-elaborazione

teller il cassiere

tender l'offerta

tender, legal la valuta legale

tender offer dare in appalto, offerta d'acquisto

term bond il buono a termine

term insurance l'assicurazione a scadenza

term loan il prestito a termine

terminal il terminale

terminate (v) terminare

terms of sale le condizioni di vendita

terms of trade le condizioni di commercio

territorial waters le acque territoriali

territory il territorio

thin market il mercato debole, i pochi ordini di acquisto a un dato prezzo

third-party exporter l'esportatore per conto terzi

third window la terza finestra, il terzo sbocco

through bill of lading la tramite polizza di carico

throughput la quantità di materiale messa in produzione durante un determinato periodo

tick, price lo sbalzo di prezzo

ticker tape il nastro della telescrivente

tied aid l'assistenza vincolata

tied loan il prestito vincolato

tight market il mercato ristretto

time and motion study lo studio del rapporto tra tempo e movimento

time bill (of exchange) la cambiale a termine

time deposit il deposito a tempo

time, lead l'intervallo tra progettazione e produzione, il periodo di preparazione

time order l'ordine a scadenza

time sharing la multiproprietà

time zone il fuso orario

timetable l'orario, la tabella

tip (inside information) l'informazione riservata

title il titolo

title insurance l'assicurazione del diritto di possesso

to the bearer al portatore

tombstone il avviso al pubblico di sottoscrizione di azione o obbligazione su giornali finanziari

tonnage la stazza

tools gli attrezzi, gli utensili

top management i dirigenti, il massimo livello amministrativo

top price il prezzo massimo

top quality la migliore qualità

top up (v) riempire

tort il torto

trade il commercio

trade (v) commerciare

trade acceptance l'accetazione commerciale

trade agreement il patto commerciale, la convenzione commerciale

trade association l'associazione settoriale, l'associazione commerciale

trade barrier la barriera commerciale

trade commission l'ufficio commerciale

trade credit il credito commerciale

trade date il giorno di vendita per azioni

trade discount lo sconto agli operatori settoriali

trade, fair il commercio equo, la fiera commerciale

trade house la ditta che tratta scambi commerciali

trade-off lo scambio

trade union il sindacato

trademark il marchio registrato

trader il commerciante

trading company la ditta import/export, il "trading company"

trading floor (stock exchange) la sala delle negoziazioni

trading limit il limite generalmente giornaliero dell'aumento o decremento dei valori

trainee l'impiegato in fase d'addestramento

tranche la tranche, la fetta

transaction la transazione

transfer la trasferta, il trasferimento

transfer agent l'agente che effettua i trasferimenti dei titoli

transit, in in transito

translator il traduttore

transportation il trasporto

traveler's check l'assegno per il viaggiatore, il "traveler's check"

treasurer il tesoriere

treasury bills i buoni del tesoro a breve termine

treasury bonds le obbligazioni del tesoro

treasury notes le banconota

treasury stock le azioni riacquistate

treaty il trattato

trend la tendenza

trial balance il bilancio provvisorio

troubleshoot (v) scoprire e localizzare i guasti

truckload il carico di un camion

trust il fondo d'investimento

trust company la società per la gestione degli investimenti

trust fund il fondo d'investimento fiduciario

trust receipt la ricevuta fiduciaria

trustee l'amministratore fiduciario

turnkey le chiavi in mano

turnover, asset il giro d'attività, il movimento d'attività

turnover, inventory il giro dell'inventario
turnover, sales il giro delle vendite
turnover, stock il giro delle azioni, il ricambio delle azioni
two-name paper il credito intestato a due
two-tiered market il mercato a due livelli

U

ultra vires acts gli atti arbitrari
unaccompanied goods i beni non accompagnati
uncollectible accounts i conti inesigibili
undercapitalized sotto-capitalizzato
undercut (v) vendere sotto il prezzo del concorrente
underdeveloped nations i paesi in via di sviluppo
underestimate (v) sottovalutare
underpaid sottopagato
undersigned il sottoscritto
understanding (agreement) l'accordo
undertake (v) intraprendere
undervalue (v) sottovalutare
underwriter l'assicuratore, il sottoscrittore
undeveloped non sviluppato
unearned increment il plusvalore
unearned revenue il reddito non da lavoro
unemployment la disoccupazione
unemployment compensation la cassa integrazione
unfair non equo
unfavorable sfavorevole
unfeasible inattuabile
union contract il contratto sindacale
union label l'etichetta sindacale
union, labor il sindacato
unit cost il costo unitario
unit load discount lo sconto applicato sulle unità di carico
unit price il prezzo unitario
unlisted non elencato
unload (v) scaricare

unsecured liability l' impegno senza garanzie, la passività senza garanzia

unsecured loan il prestito senza garanzia

unskilled labor il lavoro manuale, il lavoro non specializzato

up to our expectations alle nostre aspettative

upmarket il mercato privilegiato

upturn la svolta positiva

urban renewal la ristrutturazione urbana

urban sprawl la crescita incontrollata della zona urbana

use tax l'imposta sul consumo

useful life la durata utile

user-friendly user friendly

usury l'usuria

utility l'utilità

V

valid valido

validate (v) validare

valuation la valutazione

value il valore

value-added tax l'imposta sul valore aggiunto (IVA)

value, asset il valore delle attività

value, book il valore contabile

value engineering la progettazione utilizzando costi più bassi tra costi alternativi per espletare una certa attività

value, face il valore dichiarato, il valore riportato

value for duty il valore daziabile

value, market il valore di mercato

variable annuity il reddito annuale variabile

variable costs i costi variabili

variable import levy l'imposta variabile di importazione

variable margin il margine variabile

variable rate il tasso variabile

variable rate mortgage l'ipoteca con tasso d'interesse variabile

variance la variazione

velocity of money la velocità della circolazione monetaria

vendor il venditore

vendor's lien il privilegio del venditore

venture capital il capitale d'investimento in nuove iniziative

vertical integration l'integrazione verticale

vested interests gli interessi acquisiti

vested rights i diritti acquisiti

veto il veto

vice-president il vice-presidente

visible balance of trade il bilancio commerciale visibile

voice-activated attivato a voce

voiced check l'ispezione a voce

void invalido, nullo

volatile market il mercato instabile, il mercato volatile

volume il volume, la mole

volume discount lo sconto di volume

volume, sales il volume delle vendite

voting right il diritto al voto

voucher la ricevuta

W

wage lo stipendio, la paga

wage differential la differenza salariale, il differenziale di stipendio

wage dispute la disputa salariale

wage drift lo slittamento salariale

wage earner il salariato

wage freeze il blocco degli stipendi

wage level il livello salariale

wage-price spiral la spirale dei salari e dei prezzi

wage scale la scala salariale

wage structure la struttura salariale

wages la paga, lo stipendio, il salario

waiver clause la clausola di rinuncia

walkout lo sciopero

want ad la piccola pubblicità
warehouse il magazzino
warehouseman il magazziniere
warrant (v) garantire
warranty la garanzia
wasted asset l'attivo sprecato, l'attività deperibile
waybill la lettera di vettura
wealth la ricchezza
wear and tear l'usura
weekly return la rendita settimanale
weight il peso
weighted average la media ponderata
wharfage charges gli oneri per l'uso del molo
when issued quando emesso, a seguito dell'emmissione
white-collar worker l'impiegato
wholesale market il mercato all'ingrosso
wholesale price il prezzo all'ingrosso
wholesale trade il commercio all'ingrosso
wholesaler il grossista
wildcat strike lo sciopero selvaggio
will il testamento
windfall profits i profitti inattesi
window dressing (increase appeal) (v) dare un miglior aspetto al prodotto
wire transfer il trasferimento via cavo
with average con una media
withholding tax l'imposta ritenuta alla fonte
witness il testimone
word processor il word processor
work (v) lavorare
work committee il comitato di lavoro
work council il consiglio di lavoro
work cycle il ciclo lavorativo
work day il giorno lavorativo
work in progress il lavoro in corso
work load la mole di lavoro, la quantità di lavoro
work on contract il lavoro per contratto

work order la commessa

work station il posto di lavoro, il "work station"

workforce la forza di lavoro

working assets le attività non di capitale, le attività liquide

working balance il bilancio d'esercizio

working capital il capitale circolante, il capitale liquido

working class la classe lavorativa

working contract il contratto di lavoro

working funds il capitale liquido, i fondi attivi

working hours le ore di lavoro

working papers il permesso di lavoro

working tools gli attrezzi per il lavoro

workplace il posto di lavoro

workshop il laboratorio

World Bank la banca mondiale

worth, net il capitale azionario, il valore netto

worthless senza valore

writ il mandato

write down (v) svalutare

write off (v) cancellare un'obbligazione dovuta

written agreement la convenzione scritta

written bid (stock exchange) l'offerta scritta

Y

yardstick il metro

year l'anno

year-end il fine anno

year, fiscal l'anno fiscale

yield il reddito, il rendimento

yield to maturity il reddito alla maturità, il rendimento

Z

zero coupon l'obbligazione senza cedole per ricevere interessi

zip code il codice d'avviamento postale, C.A.P.

zone la zona

zoning law la normativa per la costruzione in varie città

ITALIAN TO ENGLISH

A

a buon mercato cheap
a distanza arm's length
a domanda at call
a e da at and from
a galla afloat
a livello industriale industrywide
a o meglio at or better
a richiesta at call
a risconto di in reply to
a rischio del portatore carrier's risk
a seguito dell'emmissione when issued
a vista at sight
abbandonare abandon (v)
abbandono (m) abandonment
abbigliamento (m) apparel
abbuono (m) allowance, rebate
abbuono per ricevere merce esaurita in un'altra data rain check
abilità (f) know-how
accanto alongside
accelerare speed up (v)
accentramento (m) centralization
accesso (m) al mercato market access
accettante (f) acceptor
accettare accept (v)
accettazione (f) acceptance
accettazione bancaria bank acceptance
accettazione cambiaria acceptance bill
accettazione commerciale trade acceptance
accettazione condizionale conditional acceptance
accettazione da parte del consumatore consumer acceptance
accettazione della marca brand acceptance
accettazione generale general acceptance
acconto (m) down payment

accordo (m) agreement, understanding
accordo d'accettazione acceptance agreement
accordo d'arbitrato arbitration agreement
accordo e la soddisfazione accord and satisfaction
accordo sulla parola gentleman's agreement
accorgimenti (m) che tendono a risparmiare sulla manodopera labor-saving
accreditare credit (v)
accrescimento (m) accretion
accumulare store (v)
accusiamo ricezione di acknowledge receipt of (v)
acque (f) territoriali territorial waters
acquirente (m/f) buyer
acquirente potenziale potential buyer
acquirente su credito credit buyer
acquisizione (f) di dati data acquisition
acquistare acquire (v), purchase (v)
acquistare in quantità eccesiva overbuy (v)
acquisti (m) impulsivi impulse buying
acquisto (m) acquisition, procurement
acquisto a termine forward purchase
acquisto valori mobiliari stock purchase
acronimo (m) acronym
addebito (m) debit
addendo (m) addendum
addizionali (m) fringe benefits
addizione (f) footing (accounting)
affare (m) bargain, deal
affittare lease (v)
affitto (m) rent
affitto degli attrezzi equipment leasing
affitto morto dead rent
affusolare streamline (v)
agenda (f) agenda
agente (m/f) agent
agente che effettua i trasferimenti dei titoli transfer agent
agente d'acquisto purchasing agent

agente del produttore manufacturer's agent
agente di assicurazione insurance broker
agente esclusivo sole agent
agente fiscale fiscal agent
agente patrimoniale estate agent
agente ricercatore di dirigenti headhunter
agente spedizioniere shipping agent
agenzia (f) agency
agenzia d'assicurazione insurance company
agenzia mercantile mercantile agency
agenzia per la ricerca del personale employment agency
agenzia pubblicitaria advertising agency
aggiudicare adjudge (v)
aggiudicazione (f) adjudication
aggiunta (f) addendum, (pl) peripherals
aggiustare adjust (v)
agricoltura (f) agriculture
al dettaglio retail
al meglio at best
al mercato at the market
al portatore to the bearer
algoritmo (m) algorithm
alimentari (m) foodstuffs
all'apertura at the opening
all'opzione del compratore buyer's option
alla chiusura at the close
alla pari at par
alla rinfusa job lot
alle nostre aspettative up to our expectations
allegare attach (v)
allocazione (f) dei costi allocation of costs
allocazione del terreno acreage allotment
allocazione delle risorse resources allocation
allocazione di responsabilità allocation of responsibilities
alta tecnologia (f) high technology

alterazione (f) alteration

altre attività (f) (e passività) other assets (and liabilities)

ammanco (m) deficit

ammassare hoard (v)

ammettere acknowledge (v)

amministrare manage (v)

amministrativo administrative

amministratore (m) administrator, manager

amministratore degli acquisti purchasing manager

amministratore della fabbrica plant manager

amministratore fiduciario trustee

amministratore finanziario money manager

amministratore generale general manager

amministratrice (f) administratrix

amministrazione (f) administration, management

amministrazione a matrice matrix management

amministrazione commerciale business management

amministrazione dei sistemi di elaborazione systems management

amministrazione del credito credit management

amministrazione del mercato market management

amministrazione del personale personnel administration

amministrazione dell'ufficio office management

amministrazione della cartella degli investimenti portfolio management

amministrazione della cassa cash management

amministrazione della tensione stress management

amministrazione delle vendite sales management

amministrazione dirigenziale line management

amministrazione finanziaria financial management

amministrazione intermediaria middle management

ammontare (m) di passività nella struttura finanziara dell'impresa leverage (financial)

ammortamento (m) amortization, depreciation

ammortamento accelerato accelerated depreciation

ammortamento maturato accrued depreciation
analisi (f) analysis, assay
analisi d'investimento investment analysis
analisi dei costi cost analysis
analisi dei fattori factor analysis
analisi dei fattori produttivi input-output analysis
analisi dei profitti profitability analysis
analisi dei sistemi systems analysis
analisi del concorrente competitor analysis
analisi del lavoro job analysis
analisi del percorso critico critical path analysis
analisi del problema problem analysis
analisi del prodotto product analysis
analisi del progetto job analysis
analisi del rapporto tra costo e profitto profitability analysis
analisi del rapporto tra i costi ed i benefici cost-benefit analysis
analisi del rischio risk analysis
analisi dell'occupazione job analysis
analisi delle esigenze needs analysis
analisi delle vendite sales analysis
analisi di equilibrio tra i costi e i ricavi break-even analysis
analisi di regressione regression analysis
analisi entrata/uscita input-output analysis
analisi finanziaria financial analysis
analisi funzionale functional analysis
analista (m/f) analyst
angolo (m) d'incidenza angle of incidence
anno (m) year
anno di base base year
anno finanziario financial year
anno fiscale fiscal year
annotazione (f) di movimento di contanti cash entry
annuale annual
annullare nullify (v)
annuncio (m) commercial (advertisement)
anticipare advance (v)

anticipi (m) e ritardi leads and lags
anzianità (f) seniority
appalto (m) sigillato sealed bid
appena possibile as soon as possible
appendice (f) addendum
appoggio (m) ed esecuzione backing and filling
apprendista (m/f) apprentice
apprezzamento (m) appreciation
appropriazione (m) indebita embezzlement
approvare approve (v)
approvazione (f) approval
appuntamento (m) appointment
appunto (m) memorandum
arbitraggio (m) arbitrage
arbitraggio d'interesse interest arbitrage
arbitrato (m) arbitration
arbitrato industriale industrial arbitration
arbitro (m) arbitrator
aree (f) delle obbligazioni bond areas
armamenti (m) armaments
arresto (m) deadlock
arretrati (m) arrears
arretrato retroactive
arrivare al punto di parità break even (v)
articoli (m) fuori misura outsized articles
articoli strategici strategic articles
articolo (m) posto in vendita pubblicitaria al di sotto del prezzo necessario per guadagnare un profitto loss leader
aspettativa (f) leave of absence
assegnare assign (v)
assegnatario/a (m/f) assignee
assegno (m) check
assegno bancario bank check, cashier's check, counter check
assegno garantito certified check
assegno nominativo registered check
assegno per il viaggiatore traveler's check
assegno vecchio stale check

assegno versato cancelled check
assemblea (f) assembly
assenteismo (m) absenteeism
assicurare lock in (v) (rate of interest)
assicurato/a (m/f) policyholder
assicuratore/trice (m/f) underwriter
assicuratore marino marine underwriter
assicurazione (f) insurance
assicurazione a scadenza term insurance
assicurazione contro danni casualty insurance
assicurazione d'adempimento performance bond
assicurazione dei crediti credit insurance
assicurazione del diritto di possesso title insurance
assicurazione industriale industrial insurance
assicurazione marittima marine cargo insurance
assicurazione per il personale indispensabile key man insurance
assicurazione sulla responsabilità civile liability insurance
assistente (m/f) assistant
assistente di servizio staff assistant
assistenza (f) al personale employee counseling
assistenza vincolata tied aid
associazione (f) commerciale trade association
associazione mercantile merchant guild
associazione settoriale trade association
assorbimento (m) del personale non specializzato dilution of labor
assorbire absorb (v)
assorbire la perdita absorb the loss (v)
assumere hire (v)
asta (f) pubblica public auction
attestato (m) attestation
atti (m) arbitrari ultra vires acts
attivato a voce voice-activated
attivi (m) bloccati frozen assets
attivi correnti current assets
attivi differiti deferred assets
attivi fissi fixed assets

attivi immobili capital asset
attivi intangibili intangible assets
attivi maturati accrued assets
attivi mobili liquid assets
attivi nascosti hidden assets
attivi netti net assets
attivi netti sulle azioni ordinarie net equity assets
attivi reali real assets
attività (f) asset
attività commerciale business activity, line of business
attività deperibile wasted asset
attività finanziaria a brevissimo termine near money
attività liquide working assets
attività non a breve termine noncurrent assets
attività non di capitale working assets
attività prontamente realizzabili quick assets
attivo (m) asset
attivo circolante liquid assets
attivo sprecato wasted asset
attivo variabile floating asset
atto (m) deed
atto di costituzione certificate of incorporation
atto di passagio deed of transfer
atto di trasferimento deed of transfer
atto di vendita bill of sale, deed of sale
atto fiduciario deed of trust
attrezzato con infissi per ancorare la merce batten fitted
attrezzatura (f) equipment
attrezzi (m) equipment, tools
attrezzi per il lavoro working tools
attrito (m) attrition
attuale actual
attuario (m) actuary
aumentare increase (v)
aumento (m) increase
aumento dei capitali capital increase

autarchia (f) autarky
autenticità (f) authenticity (gold)
auto-critica (f) self-appraisal
autogestione (f) self-management
automatico automatic
automazione (f) automation
autonomo autonomous
autorizzare authorize (v)
autorizzazione (f) a collateralizzare azioni stock power
avanzare advance (v)
avere l'autorità authority, to have (v)
avvertimento (m) commercial (advertisement)
avvisare advise (v)
avviso (m) commercial (advertisement)
avviso al pubblico di sottoscrizione di azione o obbligazione su giornali finanziari tombstone
avvocato (m) attorney, lawyer
azienda (f) company, corporation, firm
azienda madre parent company
azienda pubblica public company
azienda quasi pubblica quasi-public company
azienda straniera alien corporation
azione (f) action, stock
azione che deriva dalla richiesta di esercitare due opzioni di acquisto ed una di vendita strapping
azione contro la discriminazione affirmative action
azione d'incremento growth stock
azione di parte civile civil action
azione di penalità per azioni di frode penalty-fraud action
azione ordinaria common stock
azione preferenziale preferred stock
azioni (f) securities, shares
azioni autorizzate authorized shares
azioni con un valore inferiore ad un dollaro penny stock
azioni emesse issued shares
azioni in circolazione outstanding stock

KEY TO PRONUNCIATION

VOWELS

ITALIAN LETTER(S)	SOUND IN ENGLISH	EXAMPLE
a	ah (yacht)	casa (kAH-sah), house
è	eh (net)	lèggere (lEH-jeh-reh), to read
e	ay (hay)	mela (mAY-lah), apple
i	ee (feet)	libri (lEE-bree), books
o	oh (rope)	boccone (boh-kOH-neh), mouthful
u	oo (cool)	tutto (tOOt-toh), everything

CONSONANTS

ci	chee (cheese)	cinema (chEE-nay-mah), movies
ce	chay (chair)	piacere (pee-ah-chAY-reh), pleasure
ca	kah (cot)	casa (kAH-sah), house
co	koh (cold)	cotto (kOHt-toh), cooked
che	kay (kent)	perchè (pehr-kAY), because
chi	key (key)	pochi (pOH-key), few
gi	jee (jeep)	giro (jEE-roh), turn
ge	jay (general)	generale (jay-nay-rAH-leh), general
gh	gh (spaghetti)	spaghetti (spah-ghAY-tee)
gli	ll (million)	egli (AY-ly-ee), he bottiglia (boht-tEE-ly-ee-ah), bottle
gn	ny (canyon)	magnifico (mah-ny-EE-fee-koh), magnificent
qu	koo (quiet)	àquila (AH-koo-ee-lah), eagle
sce sci	sh (fish)	pesce (pAY-sheh), fish sciòpero (shee-OH-peh-roh), strike
z or zz	ts (eats)	pizza (pEE-tsah), pizza zero (tsEH-roh), zero

The remaining Italian sounds and letters correspond, more or less, to English ones. For example:

Bologna (boh-lOH-nyah)
Firenze (fee-rEHn-tseh)
Napoli (nAH-poh-lee)
Pisa (pEE-sah)
Roma (rOH-mah)
Torino (toh-rEE-noh)

Barron's Bilingual Business Guides
Talking Business in Italian
© Copyright 1987 by Barron's Educational Series, Inc.

PHRASES FOR THE SUCCESSFUL BUSINESS DAY

The First Meeting		
Hello. Good Morning.	Buon giorno.	(boo-OHn jee-OHr-noh)
How are you?	Come sta?	(KOH-meh stah)
Very well, thank you.	Bene, grazie.	(beh-neh grAH-tse-eh)
And you?	E lei?	(ay-lEH-ee)
My name is...	Mi chiamo...	(mEE key-AH-mo)
Do you speak English?	Parla ingelese?	(pAHr-lah een-glAY-seh)
I speak a little Italian.	Parlo poco l'italiano.	(pAHr-loh pOH-koh lee-tah-lee-AH-noh)
What did you say?	Che cosa ha detto?	(keh kOH-sah ah dEH-toh)
Please speak more slowly.	Parli più piano, per favore.	(pAHr-lee peeOO pee-AH-noh per fah-vOH-reh)
Please repeat that.	Ripeta quello, per favore.	(ree-pEH-tah koo-AYl-loh per fah-vOH-reh)
What does this mean?	Che significa questo?	(keh see-ny-EE-fee-kah koo-AYs-toh)
I don't understand	Non capisco.	(nohn kah-pEEs-koh)
Where are the rest rooms?	Dove soni i gabinetti?	(dOH-veh sOH-noh ee gah-bee-nAY-tee)
Goodbye.	Arrivederci.	(ahr-ree-veh-dAYr-chee)
At the Restaurant		
This is a good restaurant.	Questo è un buon ristorante.	(koo-AYs-toh eh oon boo-OHn ree-stoh-rAHn-teh)
The menu, please.	Il menù, per piacere.	(eel may-noo pehr pee-ah-chAY-reh)
Waiter, I would like...	Cameriere, vorrie...	(kah-meh-ree-EH-reh vohr-rEH-ee)
Please bring me a glass of red wine.	Mi porti un bicchiere di vino rosso, per favore.	(mee pOHr-tee oon bee-key-EH-reh dee vEE-noh rOH-soh pehr fah-vOH-reh)
Bring us some white wine.	Ci porti del vino bianco.	(chee pOHr-tee dayl vEE-noh bee-AHn-koh)
The check, please.	Il conto, per favore.	(eel kOHn-toh pehr fah-vOH-reh)
Thank you very much.	Mille grazie.	(mEEl-leh grAH-tsee-eh)
What time is it?	Che ora è?	(kay OH-rah EH)
At the Hotel		
I need...	Ho bisogno di...	(oh bee-sOH-ny-oh dee)
Where can I buy an English-language newspaper?	Dove posso comprare un giornale in lingua inglese?	(dOH-veh pOHs-soh kohm-prAH-reh oon jee-ohr-nAH-leh een lEEn-goo-ah een-glAY-seh)
Good evening.	Buona sera	(boo-OH-nah sAY-rah)
Looking for Help		
I am lost.	Non so dove mi trovo.	(nohn sOH dOH-vee me trOH-voh)
Where is the bus stop?	Dov'è la fermata dell auto bus?	(doh-vEH lah fehr-mAH-tah dayl AH-oo-toh-boos)
Where is the post office?	Dov'è l'ufficio postale?	(doh-vEH loof-fEE-chee-oh poh-stAH-leh)
Where is a mail box?	Dov'è una cassetta postale?	(doh-vEH OO-nah kas-sAYt-tah poh-stah-leh)
I would like to make a telephone call.	Vorrei fare una telefonata.	(vohr-rEH-ee fAH-reh OO-nah teh-leh-foh-nAH-tah)

azioni liberate paid up shares

azioni preferenziali cumulative cumulative preferred stock

azioni preferenziali di partecipazione sugli utili participating preferred stock

azioni pregiate blue chip stock

azioni privilegiate convertibili convertible preferred stock

azioni privilegiate non cumulative noncumulative preferred stock

azioni registrate presso la borsa listed securities

azioni riacquistate treasury stock

azioni senza diritto di voto nonvoting stock

azionista (m/f) shareholder, stockholder

B

bagarino (m) scalper

banca (f) bank

banca agente agent bank

banca al dettaglio retail bank

banca centrale central bank

banca commerciale commercial bank

banca corrispondente correspondent bank

banca d'agenzia agency bank

banca d'investimento investment bank

banca dati data bank

banca di credito credit bank

banca governativa government bank

banca import-export export-import bank

banca ipotecaria mortgage bank

banca mondiale World Bank

banca nazionale national bank

banca per il consumatore retail bank

banconota (f) bank note, treasury note

bando (m) d'appalto advertisement for bid (request), invitation to bid

barattare barter (v)

baratteria (f) graft

baratto (m) applied proceeds swap

barriera (f) commerciale trade barrier
barriere doganali tariff barriers
barriere tariffarie tariff barriers
base (f) dei dati per elaboratori elettronici data base
base delle tasse imponibili tax base
base monetaria monetary base
basso (m) reddito low income
baud (m) baud
bene (m) commodity
bene culturale cultural property
bene mobile chattel
benefici (m) perks
beneficiario (m) beneficiary
benestare (m) bancario bank release
benevolenza (f) goodwill
beni (m) goods
beni accompagnati accompanied goods
beni al dettaglio retail merchandise
beni capitali capital goods
beni d'investimento capital goods
beni di consumo consumer goods
beni di qualità quality goods
beni durevoli durable goods
beni eccedenti surplus goods
beni fungibili fungible goods
beni industriali industrial goods
beni intermediari intermediary goods
beni nello stato attuale as is goods
beni non accompagnati unaccompanied goods
beni non durevoli nondurable goods, soft goods
beni proibiti prohibited goods
beni reali tangible assets
beni senza ricorso as is goods
beni solidi dry goods
beni specializzati specialty goods
beni voluttuari luxury goods
biglietto (m) da visita business card
bilancia (f) commerciale balance of trade

bilancia dei pagamenti balance of payments

bilanciare hedge (v)

bilancio (m) financial statement

bilancio bancario bank balance

bilancio commerciale visibile visible balance of trade

bilancio consolidato consolidated financial statement

bilancio d'apertura opening balance

bilancio d'esercizio balance sheet, working balance

bilancio di revisione audit trail

bilancio negativo adverse balance

bilancio provvisorio trial balance

bit (m) bit

bloccare lock in (v) (rate of interest)

blocco (m) degli stipendi wage freeze

blocco dei fondi blockage of funds

boicottare boycott (v)

bonuscita (f) severance pay

borsa stock exchange, stock market

borsa (mercato) di beni di prima necessità commodity exchange

borsa documenti attache case, briefcase

borsa in fase di andamento positivo bull market

borsa in fase negativa bear market

bozza (f) rough draft

brevetto (m) patent

brevetto richiesto patent pending

bug (m) bug (defect in computer program)

buona consegna (f) good delivery (securities)

buoni (m) a basso rendimento low-yield bonds

buoni del tesoro a breve termine treasury bills

buoni e obbligazioni del tesoro (Britannici) gilt (Brit. govt. security)

buoni governativi (del tesoro) government bonds

buoni redditizi income bonds

buono (m) a termine term bond

buono di risparmio savings bond

buono fisso flat bond

buono garantito guaranty bond
burocrate (m) bureaucrat
byte (m) byte

C

calcolatrice (f) calculator
calcolo (m) errato miscalculation
cambio (m) valute money broker
cambiale (f) bill of exchange, promissory note
cambiale a termine time bill (of exchange)
cambiale agraria agricultural paper
cambiale di comodo accommodation bill, accommodation paper
cambiale emessa all'estero foreign bill of exchange
cambiali (f) esigibili notes receivable
cambio (m) bancario bank exchange
cambio estero foreign exchange
cambio netto, il cambiamento netto net change
cambio valuta currency exchange
camera (f) di commercio chamber of commerce
campagna (f) di produttività productivity campaign
campagna pubblicitaria advertising campaign
campionare sample (v)
campionatura (f) mista mixed sampling
campionatura per accettazione acceptance sampling
campione (m) casuale random sample
campioni uniformi matched samples
canale (m) di distribuzione channel of distribution
cancellare cancel (v)
cancellare un'obbligazione dovuta write off (v)
capacità (f) capacity
capacità di produzione, capacità produttiva manufacturing capacity
capacità in balle bale capacity
capacità produttiva della fabbrica plant capacity
capacità produttiva inattiva idle capacity
caparra (f) binder, down payment
capitale (m) capital

capitale azionario capital stock, equity, net worth

capitale circolante al netto net working capital

capitale d'investimento in nuove iniziative venture capital

capitale degli azionisti stockholders' equity

capitale eccedente surplus capital

capitale industriale instrumental capital

capitale investito invested capital

capitale liquido working capital, working funds

capitale ordinario ordinary capital

capitale per finanziare nuove iniziative risk capital

capitale sociale legale legal capital

capitale versato paid up capital

capitali fissi fixed capital

capitalismo (m) capitalism

capitalizzati below the line

capitalizzato in eccesso overcapitalized

capitalizzazione (f) capitalization

capitalizzazione dei costi fissi nel costo dell'inventario absorption costing

capo (m) leader

capo contabile chief accountant

capo servizio foreman

capo sindacale labor leader

carbone (m) coal

carenza (f) shortage

caricare i fondi all'inizio del contratto front-end loading

carico (m) freight, load (sales charge)

carico di testa headload

carico di un camion truckload

carico di un camion inferiore alla capacità less-than-truckload

carico di una vettura inferiore alla capacità less-than-carload

carico di vettura carload

carico effettivo payload

carico frazionato broken stowage

carico massimo peak load

carico permesso freight allowed
carico secco dry cargo
carnet (m) carnet
carnet bancario bank carnet
carovita (m) cost of living
carro (m) merci senza sponde flatcar
carta (f) paper
carta di credito credit card
cartella (f) file, portfolio
cartella d'azioni portfolio, stock
cartellone (m) billboard
casa (f) di accettazione acceptance house
cassa cooperativa di risparmio mutual savings bank
cassa d'imballo packing case
cassa di risparmio savings bank
cassa integrazione unemployment compensation
cassa notturna night depository
cassetta (f) cassette
cassetta di sicurezza safe deposit box
cassiere (m) teller
catalogo (m) catalog
catena (f) di montaggio assembly line
catena di negozi chain (of stores)
causa (f) lawsuit
cavo (m) cable
cedente (m) assignor
cedola (f) di interesse su obbligazioni coupon (bond interest)
cedola di interesse su buoni coupon (bond interest)
centesimi (m) di percentuale per ipoteche point (percentage, mortgage term)
centro (m) acquisti fuori dall'area urbana shopping center
centro per elaborati elettronici computer center
certificato (m) certificate
certificato antiquariale d'autenticità antique authenticity certificate
certificato attestante l'uso definitivo del prodotto end-use certificate

certificato azionario stock certificate
certificato d'ispezione bill of sight
certificato d'origine certificate of origin
certificato di deposito certificate of deposit
certificato ipotecario mortgage certificate
certificato per lo sbarco landing certificate
cervello (m) elettronico computer
cessione (f) di garanzie per merci depositate in un magazzino field warehousing
chiacchierare jawbone (v)
chiamare call (v)
chiavi (f) in mano turnkey
chimico chemical
chip (m) chip
cianografia (f) blueprint
ciclo (m) commerciale business cycle
ciclo lavorativo work cycle
circa around (exchange term)
citazione (f) quotation
citazione diretta direct quotation
classe (f) lavorativa working class
classi mutualmente esclusive mutually exclusive classes
classificazione (f) doganale tariff classification
clausola (f) d'accelerazione acceleration clause
clausola d'oro gold clause
clausola d'uscita escape clause
clausola di negligenza Jason clause
clausola di penalità penalty clause
clausola di rinuncia waiver clause
cliente (m) customer
co-assicurazione (f) coinsurance
coda (di cambiale) (f) allonge (of a draft)
codice (m) d'avviamento postale, C.A.P. zip code
codice del lavoro labor code
collaterale (m) collateral
collega (m) colleague
collocamento (m) placement (personnel)

collocazione (f) privata private placement (finance)
colloquio (m) colloquium
colui che cambia spesso il posto di lavoro job hopper
colui che crea un mercato market-maker (securities)
comando (m), "joystick" (m) joystick
combinazione (f) combination
come per nota informativa as per advice
come se e quando as, if and when
comitato (m) di lavoro work committee
comitato esecutivo executive committee
comma (m) codicil
comma della scala mobile escalator clause
comma valutaria currency clause
commerciante (m) dealer, trader
commerciare trade (v)
commercio (m) commerce, trade
commercio al dettaglio retail trade
commercio all'ingrosso wholesale trade
commercio compensativo compensation trade
commercio equo fair trade
commercio estero foreign trade
commercio fuori orario after-hours trading
commercio interstatale interstate commerce
commercio libero free trade
commercio multilaterale multilateral trade
commessa (f) work order
commissione (f) agency fee, load (sales charge)
commissione anticipata front-end fee
commissione di raccomandazione address commission
compagnia (f) d'investimento investment company
compendio (m) del documento probatorio della titolarità di diritti abstract of title
compenso (m) compensation, consideration (bus. law)
compenso dirigenziale executive compensation
compra (f) acquisition

competizione (f) competition
completamente pagato paid in full
componente (m) component
comprare purchase (v)
comprare al miglior prezzo buy at best (v)
comprare alla chiusura buy on close (v)
comprare all'apertura buy on opening (v)
compratore (m) buyer
compratore capo chief buyer
compratore e venditore di titoli mobiliari market-maker (securities)
compratore in loco resident buyer
compratore potenziale potential buyer
compravendita (f) di azioni sopra o sotto il prezzo attuale put and call
compreso interessi accumulati plus accrued interest
compreso trasporto freight included
comproprietà (f) co-ownership
comproprietario (m) joint owner
computer (m) computer
comunicazioni (f) di massa mass communications
con dividendo cum dividend
con una media with average
concedere uno scoperto a fido grant an overdraft (v)
concentrazione (f) di mercato market concentration
concessione (f) di appalto franchise
concetto (m) di marketing marketing concept
concetto di solvibilità ability-to-pay concept
concorrente (m) competitor
concorrenza (f) competition
condizioni (f) di commercio terms of trade
condizioni di vendita terms of sale
conferenza-confronto (f) idee brainstorming
conferma (f) dell'ordine confirmation of order
confidenziale confidential
confine (m) border
conflitto (m) d'interesse conflict of interest

congedo (m) retirement
congedo di maternità maternity leave
congedo per malattia sick leave
conglomerato (m) conglomerate
consegna (f) consignment, delivery, shipment
consegna immediata spot delivery
consegna in contanti cash delivery
consegna incompleta short delivery
consegne differite deferred delivery
considerazione (f) consideration (bus. law)
consiglio (m) di amministrazione board of directors
consiglio di lavoro work council
consiglio di sovrintendenza board of supervisors
consiglio dirigenziale executive board
consolidamento (m) consolidation
consorzio (m) consortium
consorzio di industriali cartel
consulente (m) consultant
consulente amministrativo management consultant
consulente sugli investimenti investment adviser
consumatore (m) consumer
contabile (m) accountant
contabilità (f) accounting department, bookkeeping
contabilità a partita doppia double-entry bookkeeping
contabilità amministrativa management accounting
contabilità dei costi, contabilità industriale cost accounting
contabilità di riduzione depletion accounting
contanti (m) cash
contenitore (m) container
conti (m) annuali annual accounts
conti creditori accounts receivable
conti debitori accounts payable
conti di gruppo group accounts
conti garantiti secured accounts
conti inesigibili uncollectible accounts
contingenze (f) contingencies

conto (m) account

conto aperto charge account, open account

conto bancario bank account

conto capitale capital account

conto capitale a breve termine short-term capital account

conto capitale a lungo termine long-term capital account

conto chiuso closed account

conto congiunto joint account, joint cost

conto corrente checking account, current account

conto depositato presso terzi escrow account

conto dettagliato itemized account

conto di deposito deposit account

conto di risparmio savings account

conto marginale marginal account

conto moroso delinquent account

conto operativo active account

conto profitti e perdite profit and loss statement

conto redditizio income account

conto sul libro mastro ledger account

contraffatto (m) counterfeit

contraffazione (f) forgery

contrassegnare earmark (v)

contrattazione (f) collettiva collective bargaining

contratto (m) contract

contratto a futura consegna futures

contratto a termine forward contract, futures

contratto che garantisce un profitto in base al costo del prodotto cost-plus contract

contratto d'affitto lease

contratto di lavoro working contract

contratto di locazione lease

contratto di manutenzione maintenance contract, service contract

contratto di vendita condizionata conditional sales contract

contratto di vendita per l'esportazione export sales contract

contratto insoluto outstanding contract
contratto marittimo maritime contract
contratto sindacale union contract
contro qualsiasi rischio against all risks
controllare audit (v)
controllo (m) dei costi cost control
controllo dei valori stock control
controllo del credito credit control
controllo dell'inventario inventory control
controllo della produzione manufacturing control, production control
controllo della riduzione depletion control
controllo delle azioni stock control
controllo di qualità quality control
controllo finanziario financial control
controllo numerico numerical control
controllo operativo operations audit
controllo valutario exchange control
controllore (m) comptroller, controller
controstallia (f) (maritime) demurrage
controvalore (m) exchange value
convenzione (f) agreement
convenzione commerciale trade agreement
convenzione d'accettazione acceptance agreement
convenzione di cooperazione cooperation agreement
convenzione implicita implied agreement
convenzione multilaterale multilateral agreement
convenzione scritta written agreement
conversione (f) di valuta currency conversion
cooperativa (f) cooperative
coperto (m) cover charge
copertura (f) coverage (insurance)
copertura a termine forward cover
copertura in abbonamento open cover
copia (f) in omaggio complimentary copy
copia scritta hard copy
copione (m) script

corpo (m) corpus

correzione (f) della tassa di confine border tax adjustment

corrispondenza (f) correspondence

costare cost (v)

costi (m) amministrati managed costs

costi bancari bank charges

costi controllabili controllable costs, managed costs

costi di distribuzione distribution costs

costi di licenza license fees

costi di produzione production costs

costi di riproduzione reproduction costs

costi di sbarco landing costs

costi di spedizione a carico del destinatario freight collect

costi di stivaggio stowage charges

costi di trasporto shipping charges

costi effettivi actual costs

costi fissi fixed costs, standing costs

costi fissi d'azienda factory overhead

costi incrementali incremental costs, increased costs

costi iniziali set-up costs, start-up cost

costi normali standard costs

costi reali actual costs

costi semi-variabili semi-variable costs

costi standard standard costs

costi tariffari tariff charges

costi variabili variable costs

costituire un sindacato syndicate (v)

costo (m) cost

costo alla destinazione landed cost

costo complessivo all in cost

costo congiunto joint cost

costo dei beni venduti cost of goods sold

costo del capitale cost of capital

costo dell'opportunità opportunity costs

costo della vita cost of living

costo di ricambio replacement cost

costo diretto direct cost
costo e trasporto cost and freight
costo fatturato invoice cost
costo indiretto indirect cost
costo marginale marginal cost
costo medio average cost
costo medio unitario average unit cost
costo misto mixed cost
costo originale original cost
costo primo prime cost
costo unitario unit cost
cotone (m) cotton
creare una parola composta di due nomi utilizzando un trattino hyphenate (v)
crediti (m) garantiti secured accounts
crediti monetari monetary credits
credito (m) credit
credito a rate installment credit
credito al consumatore consumer credit
credito all'esportazione export credit
credito commerciale trade credit
credito d'accettazione acceptance credit
credito disponibile credit balance
credito disposto dal beneficiario di un credito back-to-back credit
credito documentario aperto sulla base di un altro credito originario back-to-back credit
credito intestato a due two-name paper
credito per investimento investment credit
credito rotativo revolving credit
credito sulle imposte estere foreign tax credit
creditore (m) creditor, payee
crescita (f) growth
crescita aziendale corporate growth
crescita incontrollata della zona urbana urban sprawl
criteri (m) d'investimento investment criteria
crivello (m) jig (production)
crumiro (m) strikebreaker (scab)
cumulativo cumulative

cura (f) ragionevole reasonable care
curriculum (m) vitae resume
curva (f) a campana bell-shaped curve
curva d'insegnamento learning curve
curva di frequenza frequency curve

D

danno (m) damage
danno accidentale accidental damage
dare in appalto tender offer
dare l'incarico a terzi farm out (v)
dare un miglior aspetto al prodotto window dressing (increase appeal) (v)
data (f) di consegna date of delivery
data di maturazione maturity date
data di registrazione record date
data di scadenza expiry date
data originale di maturazione original maturity
dati (m) data
dazio (m) duty (customs, import)
dazio ad valorem duty ad valorem
dazio combinato combination duty
dazio specifico specific duty
debiti (m) insoluti outstanding debt
debiti preferenziali preferential debts
debito (m) debt
debito a breve termine short-term debt
debito a lunga termine long-term debt
debito attivo active debt
debito consolidato debt
debito estero foreign debt
debito fluttuante floating debt
debito insolvibile bad debt
debito nazionale national debt
decisione (f) di fabbricare invece di comprare make-or-buy decision
decollare take off (v)
deduzione (f) convertibile redemption allowance
deficiente substandard

deficit (m) deficit
definizione (f) settlement
deflazione (f) deflation
demografico (m) demographic
demozione (f) demotion
denaro (m) money
denaro caldo hot money
denaro disponibile ready cash
denaro investito a brevissima scadenza call money
deporto (m) backwardation
depositi (m) d'importazione import deposits
deposito (m) deposit, depository, down payment, licensed warehouse
deposito a richiesta demand deposit
deposito a tempo time deposit
deposito bancario bank deposit
deposito in conto corrente demand deposit
deposito presso terzi escrow
depressione (f) depression
deprezzamento (m) depreciation
deprezzamento della valuta depreciation of currency
derivare accrue (v)
descrizione (f) del lavoro job description
destinatario (m) consignee
destinazione (f) indicata named point of destination
detentore (m) holder (negotiable instruments)
determinazione (f) del prezzo marginale marginal pricing
detraibile (m) deductible
detrazione (f) deduction
detrazione dalle imposte tax deduction
detrazione personale personal deduction
dettagliare itemize (v)
di fortuna makeshift
di ripiego makeshift
diagramma (m) graph
diagramma delle attività activity chart
diagramma delle correnti flow chart

diagramma utilizzando barre bar chart
diaria (f) per diem
dibattito (m) costruttivo d'opinioni brainstorming
dichiarazione (f) statement
dichiarazione d'entrata entry permit
dichiarazione d'esportazione export entry
dichiarazione degli utili e delle perdite profit and loss statement
dichiarazione del reddito income statement
dichiarazione di conto statement of account
dichiarazione doganale customs entry, import declaration
dichiarazione finanziaria financial statement
dichiarazione operativa operating statement
dichiarazione per procura proxy statement
dichiarazione pro forma pro forma statement
dichiarazione provvisoria interim statement
dichiarazione scritta e giurata affidavit
dichiarazione sotto giuramento sworn statement
difetto (m) nel programma dell'elaboratore elettronico bug (defect in computer program)
difettoso defective
diffamazione (f) libel
differenza (f) salariale wage differential
differenza tra il prezzo di vendita e i costi di produzione gross spread
differenziale (m) dei prezzi price differential
differenziale di stipendio wage differential
differenziale tariffario tariff differential
digitale digital
diluizione (f) del capitale azionario dilution of equity
diluizione del capitale netto dilution of equity
diluizione della manodopera dilution of labor
dinamica (f) del gruppo group dynamics
dinamica del mercato market dynamics
dinamica del prodotto product dynamics
direttore (m) director, manager
direttore d'area area manager

direttore della pubblicità, direttore pubblicitario advertising manager
direttore finanziario financial director
direttore generale chief executive
direzioni congiunte interlocking directorate
dirigente (m) executive
dirigente di linea line executive
dirigente responsabile per la gestione della marca brand manager
dirigente superiore executive director
dirigenti (m), dirigenza (f) top management
diritti (m) acquisiti acquired rights, vested rights
diritti d'autore copyright, royalty (payment)
diritti di brevetto patent royalty
diritti esclusivi sole rights
diritti portuali harbor dues
diritto al ricorso right of recourse
diritto al voto voting right
diritto di prelazione preemptive right
diritto di proprietario proprietary
disarmare lay up (v)
disavanzo (m) deficit
dischetto (m) disk
dischetto floppy floppy disk
disegno (m) pattern
disegno del prodotto product design
disincentivo (m) disincentive
disoccupazione (f) unemployment
dispersione (f) leakage
disponsibilità (f) dei capitali money supply
disputa (f) dispute
disputa di lavoro labor dispute
disputa salariale wage dispute
disputa sindacale labor dispute
disputare dispute (v)
distributore (m) distributor
ditta (f) corporation, firm
ditta a capitale sociale joint stock company

ditta associata associate company, member firm
ditta che tratta esportazioni export house
ditta che tratta scambi commerciali trade house
ditta di garanzia guaranty company
ditta estera foreign corporation
ditta garante surety company
ditta import/export trading company
ditta madre parent company
ditta nazionale domestic corporation
ditta offshore offshore company
ditta primaria, ditta "leader" leading firm
ditta privata closely held corporation
ditta straniera alien corporation
diventare una ditta per azioni go public (v)
diversificazione (f) diversification
dividendo (m) dividend
dividendo eliminato passed dividend
dividendo pagato in contanti cash dividend
dividendo supplementare extra dividend
dividere una parola usando trattini hyphenate (v)
divisione (f) del lavoro division of labor
documento (m) document
documento costitutivo charter
documento in ordine clean document
documento pulito clean document
dogana (f) customs
doganiere (m) collector of customs
domanda (f) aggregata aggregate demand
domanda od offerta rigida o inelastica inelastic demand or supply
dominio (m) pubblico public domain
donazione (f) di terra land grant
doppia (f) tassazione double taxation
doppia paga per gli straordinari double time
dotazione (f) endowment
dumping (m) dumping (goods in foreign market)
duopolio (m) duopoly
durata (f) del prodotto product life

durata di un brevetto life of a patent
durata di un prodotto life cycle of a product
durata media average life
durata utile useful life

E

eccedenza (f) dei capitali capital surplus
eccedenza versata paid-in surplus
eccesso (m) overage
econometria (f) econometrics
economia (f) economics
economia controllata managed economy
economia di scala economy of scale
economia keynesiana Keynesian economics
economico economic
edificio (m) premises (location)
effettivo actual
effetto (m) di risucchio backwash effect
efficienza (f) efficiency
efficienza dei costi cost effectiveness
elaboratore (m) a sistema analog analog computer
elaboratore a sistema digitale, elaboratore digitale digital computer
elaboratore centrale mainframe computer
elaboratore del testo autonomo stand-alone word processor
elaboratore ibrido hybrid computer
elaborazione (f) per gruppi batch processing
elasticità (f) (dell'offerta e della domanda) elasticity (of supply or demand)
elasticità del prezzo price elasticity
elencare list (v)
elenco (m) di indirizzi per invio di materiali pubblicitari mailing list
elenco legale legal list (fiduciary investments)
eliminare phase out (v), take out (v)
embargo (m) embargo
emendamento (m) amendment
emendare amend (v)

emettere issue (v)

emettere un assegno scoperto e poi depositare la somma necessaria per renderlo valido kiting (banking)

emissione (f) issue (stock)

emissione di buoni bond issue

emissione fiduciaria fiduciary issue

emissione primaria senior issue

ente (m) governativo government agency

ente pubblico responsabile per gli alloggi housing authority

entità (f) legale legal entity

entrata (f) input

entrata d'importazione import entry

entrata dei dati nell'elaboratore elettronico computer input

entrata nel libro mastro ledger entry

entrata originale original entry

entrata sul registro ledger entry

equipe (f) amministrativa management team

equità (m) equity

eredità (f) legacy

ergonometrica (f) ergonomics

errore (m) error

errore di elaborazione processing error

esame (m) d'accettazione acceptance test

esame della personalità personality test

esame di un testo pubblicitario copy testing

esattore (m) delle tasse tax collector

esattore doganale collector of customs

esecutore/trice (m/f) executor

esente da dazio dutyfree

esenzione (f) exemption

esenzione personale personal exemption

esigenze (f) requirements

esigenze di margine margin requirements

espansione (f) boom

esportare export (v)

esportatore/trice (m/f) per conto terzi third-party exporter

esportatore su commissione export agent

esportazione (f) dei capitali capital exports (currency)

esportazione di beni capitali capital exports (goods)

esportazioni chiave key exports

espresso (m) aereo air express

esproprio (m) expropriation

essere elusivo hedge (v)

essere responsabile per account for (v)

estinzione (f) obbligatoria mandatory redemption

etichetta (f) sindacale union label

euro-obbligazione (f) Eurobond

eurodollaro (m) Eurodollar

eurovaluta (f) Eurocurrency

evasione (f) fiscale tax evasion

evento (m) determinante lo scatto del processo di aggiustamento adjustment trigger

evitare di compromettersi hedge (v)

ex diritti ex rights

ex molo ex dock

F

fabbrica (f) factory

fabbrica aperta anche ai non iscritti al sindacato open shop

fabbricante (m) manufacturer

facilitazione (f) facilities

facilitazione d'appoggio creditizio accommodation credit

facoltativo optional

factotum (m) man/gal Friday

fallimento (m) bankruptcy, failure

fallire fail (v)

far seguito followup (v)

fare il giro go around (v)

fare la coda stand in line (v)

fase (f) negativa down period, slump
fattore (m) factor, maker (of a check, draft, etc.)
fattore degli utili profit factor
fattore dei costi cost factor
fattore dei profitti profit factor
fattore del ricarico load factor
fattura (f) bill, invoice
fattura commerciale commercial invoice
fattura consolare consular invoice
fattura nazionale domestic bill
fattura pro forma pro forma invoice
fatturazione (f) a ciclo cycle billing
fedeltà (f) alla marca brand loyalty
ferramenta (f) hardware
festività (f) legale bank holiday, legal holiday
fetta (f) tranche
fibre (f) artificiali, fibre sintetiche man-made fibers
fidecommisso (m) vivente living trust
fiduciario (m) fiduciary
fiera (f) commerciale fair trade
la filiale (f) affiliate, branch office, subsidiary
finalizzare finalize (v)
finanziamento (m) a breve termine short-term financing
finanziamento anticipato front-end financing
finanziare finance (v)
fine anno (m) year-end
fine (f) del periodo end of period
firma (f) signature
firma autorizzata authorized signature
fissare peg (v)
fissare due prezzi double pricing
fissare il prezzo fix the price (v)
flotta (f) privata private fleet
flusso (m) di cassa negativo negative cash flow
flusso netto di cassa net cash flow
foglio (m) di dati fact sheet

foglio di revisione del bilancio contabile auditing balance sheet

fondi attivi working funds

fondi interni internal funding

fondi pubblici public funds

fondo (m) fund

fondo ammortamento accumulated depreciation

fondo comune d'investimento investment trust

fondo d'ammortamento per il ritiro di obbligazioni sinking fund

fondo d'investimento active trust, mutual fund

fondo d'investimento fiduciario trust fund

fondo d'investimento fiduciario revocabile revocable trust

fondo d'investimento molto aggressivo go-go fund

fondo d'investimento rotativo revolving fund

fondo d'investimento senza commissioni no-load fund

fondo della stiva dunnage

fondo di ammortamento depreciation allowance

fondo di assicurazione insurance fund

fondo di contingenza contingent fund

fondo di investimento redimibile redemption fund

fondo di previdenza contingent fund

fondo discrezionario discretionary account

fondo monetario comune pool (of funds)

fondo pensionistico pension fund

fonte (f) attendible reliable source

formato (m) format

fornitore (m) supplier

forniture (f) carenti short supply

forniture oltre il necessario oversupply

forza (f) di lavoro workforce, labor force

forza maggiore act of God

forze di mercato market forces

fotolitografia (f) offset printing

franco fabbrica ex factory

franco magazzino ex warehouse

franco miniera ex mine

franco mulino ex mill
franco nave ex ship
franco officina ex works
franco porto ex dock, free alongside ship
franco stazione ferroviaria free on rail
frazionamento (m) delle azioni stock split
fresatura (f) milling
frode (f) fraud
funzioni (f) di sostegno support activities
fusione (f) amalgamation, merger
fuso (m) orario jet lag, time zone

G

gamma (f) dei prezzi price range
gamma di prodotti product line
garanzia (f) guarantee, security, warranty
garanzia del posto di lavoro job security
gestione (f) commerciale business management
gestione del mercato market management
gestione del personale personnel management
gestione del prodotto product management
gestione dell'ufficio office management
gestione delle operazioni operations management
gestione delle vendite sales management
gestione per obiettivi management by objectives
giornale (m) journal
giornaliero (m) daily
giorno (m) di liquidazione account day
giorno di vendita per azioni trade date
giorno festivo pagato paid holiday
giorno lavorativo work day
girafario (m) endorsee
girante (m) endorser
girata (f) endorsement
girata d'accettazione qualificata qualified acceptance endorsement
girata di comodo accommodation endorsement

giro (m) d'attività asset turnover
giro dell'inventario inventory turnover
giro delle azioni stock turnover
giro delle vendite sales turnover
giurisdizione (f) jurisdiction
giustizia (f) equity
governo (m) government
grafico (m) graph
grafico a barra bar chart
grafico a fette pie chart
grande (m) magazzino department store
grande scala large-scale
grano (m) grain
granoturco (m) maize
gratifica (f) gratuity
gravame (m) encumbrances (liens, liabilities)
grossista (m) jobber, wholesaler
gruppo (m) amministrativo management group
gruppo di esperti task force
gruppo di grandi magazzini chain store group
gruppo di prodotti product group
guadagni (m) earnings
guadagni orari hourly earnings
guadagni ritenuti retained earnings
garantire warrant (v)
guerra (m) sui prezzi price war
guerra tariffaria tariff war

H

hardware (m) hardware (computer)

I

illegale illegal
imballaggio (m) packaging
imballaggio utilizzando pellicole di plastica ristretta shrink-wrapping
imbottitura (f) stuffing

imitazione (f) imitation
immagazzinaggio (m) storage, serial storage
immagazzinaggio con accesso diretto direct access storage
immagazzinaggio dei dati per il computer computer storage
immagine (f) aziendale corporate image
immagine della marca brand image
immobili (m) real estate
immobilizi (m) tecnici fixed assets
impatto (m) dei profitti profit impact
impatto sugli utili profit impact
impegni (m) attuali current liabilities
impegno (m) commitment, covenant, pledge
impegno garantito secured liability
impegno senza garanzie unsecured liability
impianti (m) facilities
impianti e macchinari equipment
impianti fissi fixtures (on balance sheet)
impiegato (m) employee, white-collar worker
impiegato in fase d'addestramento trainee
implicazione (f) implication
imporre tasse levy taxes (v)
importare import (v)
importatore/trice (m/f) registrato importer of record
importazione (f) import
importo (m) fisso flat rate
imposta (f) tax
imposta aziendale corporation tax
imposta d'esportazione export tax
imposta d'importazione import tax
imposta di successione inheritance tax
imposta fondiaria land tax
imposta indiretta indirect tax
imposta patrimoniale estate tax
imposta regressiva regressive tax
imposta ritenuta alla fonte withholding tax
imposta specifica specific duty

imposta sui beni di lusso luxury tax
imposta sui consumi excise tax, excise duty
imposta sui salari payroll tax
imposta sul consumo use tax
imposta sul reddito delle persone fisiche (IRPEF) personal income tax
imposta sul reddito delle persone giuridiche (IRPEG) corporate income tax
imposta sul valore aggiunto (IVA) value-added tax
imposta sulla vendita al dettaglio retail sales tax
imposta sulle vendite sales tax
imposta variabile flexible tariff
imposta variabile di importazione variable import levy
imposte arretrate back taxes
imposte indirette internal revenue tax
imposte locali local taxes
imprenditore/trice (m/f) entrepreneur
impresa (f) enterprise
imputato (m) imputed
in base alla disponibilità availability, subject to
in contanti cash basis
in conto on account
in ogni caso down the line
in passivo in the red
in transito in transit
inadeguato inadequate
inattivo off-line
inattuabile unfeasible
incentivo (m) incentive
incentivo finanziario financial incentive
incidente (m) industriale industrial accident
incitazione (f) alla discordia barratry
incorporare incorporate (v)
incrementare increase (v)
incremento (m) increase
indagine (f) di mercato market survey
indebitamento (m) indebtedness
indennità (f) indemnity

indicatore (m) in ritardo lagging indicator
indicatore principale leading indicator
indicatori economici economic indicators
indice (m) index (indicator), table of contents
indice composto composite index
indice dei prezzi price index
indice dei prezzi al consumo consumer price index
indice della borsa stock index
indice delle opzioni option index
indice di crescita growth index
indice di mercato market index
indici di bilancio balance ratios
indicizzare index (v)
indicizzazione (f) indexing
industria (f) industry
industria che dipende molto dal fattore della manodopera labor-intensive industry
industria di mercato libero free market industry
industria in fase di crescita growth industry
industria nascente infant industry
industria pesante heavy industry
inefficiente inefficient
inflazione (f) inflation
inflazionistico inflationary
influenzare impact, have an...on (v)
informazione (f) riservata tip (inside information)
infrastruttura (f) infrastructure
infusione (f) di fondi da nuove fonti new money
ingannevole misleading
inganno (m) double dealing
ingegneria (f) engineering
ingegneria civile civil engineering
ingegneria elettrica electrical engineering
ingegneria industriale industrial engineering
ingegneria meccanica mechanical engineering
ingiunzione (f) injunction
ingranaggio (f) gearing
ingrandire enlarge (v)

iniziare un'azione reciproca interact (v)
innalzamento (m) dei capitali raising capital
innesto (m) acustico acoustic coupler
innovazione (f) innovation
insediamento (f) takeover
insediamento tramite acquisto del controllo azionario stock takeover
insolvente insolvent
instabilità (f) instability
intangibili (m) invisibles
integrazione (f) verticale vertical integration
interbanca interbank
interesse (m) interest
interesse composto compound interest
interesse del proprietario owner's equity
interesse lungo long interest
interesse maggioritario controlling interest, majority interest
interesse maturato accrued interest
interesse minoritario minority interest
interessi acquisiti vested interests
interessi in comune pooling of interests
interessi incipienti inchoate interest
interface (m) interface
intermediario (m) broker, intermediary, middleman
intermediario di obbligazioni bill broker
intermediario per l'esportazione export middleman
intermediario valutario money broker
interno internal
intervallo (m) (per caffè) coffee break
intervallo tra progettazione e produzione lead time
intervenire intervene (v)
intervista (f) interview
intraprendere undertake (v)
introdurre phase in (v)
introito (m) income, revenue
introito rettificato adjusted earned income
invalidare invalidate (v)

invalido void
inventario (m) inventory
inventario contabile book inventory
inventario dei beni finiti finished goods inventory
inventario fisico physical inventory
inventario periodico periodic inventory
inventario perpetuo perpetual inventory
inventario registrato book inventory
investimenti (m) azionari equity investments
investimento (m) investment
investimento capitale capital expenditure
investimento costante fixed investment
investimento di fondi per iniziare l'attività pump priming
investimento di protezione a lunga scadenza long hedge
investimento diretto direct investment
investimento lordo gross investment
investimento netto net investment
investimento reale real investment
investire invest (v)
investitore/trice (m/f) istituzionale institutional investor
invio (m) dispatch
ipoteca (f) mortgage, purchase money mortgage
ipoteca con tasso d'interesse variabile variable rate mortgage
ipoteca secondaria second mortgage
ipoteca su beni mobili chattel mortgage
ipotecare (v) hypothecate
ispettore/trice (m/f) inspector
ispezione (f) inspection
ispezione a voce voiced check
istruire instruct (v)
istruzione (f) in gruppo group training
istruzione reciproca reciprocal training
istruzione sul posto di lavoro on-the-job training
istruzioni (f) per il trasporto shipping instructions

J

joint venture (m) joint venture

L

laboratorio (m) workshop
laissez-faire laissez-faire
lanciare (una nuova impresa) float (v) (issue stock)
lanciare un nuovo prodotto sulla base di un altro prodotto spin off (v)
lasciare una certa somma di fondi nel conto corrente presso la istituzione compensating balance
lascito (m) bequest
lavorare process (v), work (v)
lavorare per conto proprio self-employed, be (v)
lavoratore (m) laborer
lavoratore a cottimo (m) jobber
lavorazione (f) su commessa rack jobber
lavori (m) pubblici public works
lavoro (m) job, labor
lavoro a cottimo piecework
lavoro in corso work in progress
lavoro indiretto indirect labor
lavoro manuale unskilled labor
lavoro nero moonlighting
lavoro non specializzato unskilled labor
lavoro per contratto work on contract
lavoro straordinario overtime
lavoro straordinario pagato il doppio double time
legame (m) liaison
legato con un contratto indentured
legge (f) law
legge dei rendimenti decrescenti law of diminishing returns
legge mercantile mercantile law
legge sui brevetti patent law
leggi anti-monopolistiche antitrust laws
lettera (f) letter
lettera d'indennità letter of indemnity

lettera d'investimento investment letter
lettera di accompagnamento cover letter
lettera di credito letter of credit
lettera di credito bancaria bank letter of credit
lettera di credito rotativa revolving letter of credit
lettera di garanzia letter of guaranty
lettera di presentazione letter of introduction
lettera di ripartizione allotment letter
lettera di vettura waybill
lettera tipo, lettera "standard" form letter
liberismo (m) economico free enterprise
libero da medie particolari free of particular average
libero professionista (m/f) freelancer
libretto (m) di deposito bancario passbook
libro (m) cassa cash book
libro mastro ledger
libro paga payroll
licenza (f) leave of absence, license
licenza di importazione import license
licenze accavallate cross-licensing
licenziamento (m) lay-off
licenziare fire (v)
licenziatario (m) dealership
limite (m) di perdita position limit
limite generalmente giornaliero dell'aumento o decremento dei valori trading limit
linea (f) campionaria sample line
linea di credito credit line
linea di credito a richiesta demand line of credit
linea di montaggio assembly line
linea di picchettaggio picket line
linea di prodotti product line
linea di produzione production line
Linea Internazionale di Demarcazione (dove il giorno cambia) International Date Line
lineare linear
linguaggio (m) algoritmico algorithmic language
linguaggio per elaboratori elettronici computer language

liquidare remainder (v)
liquidazione (f) liquidation
liquidazione dei conti payoff
liquidità (f) liquidity, solvency
lista (f) di controllo checklist
listino (m) d'imballaggio packing list
listino di spese rimborsabili expense account
listino prezzi price list
lite (f) litigation
livellare level out (v)
livello (m) commerciale commercial grade
livello d'utilizzo della capacità produttiva capacity, utilization
livello di qualità accettabile acceptable quality level
livello di qualità per investimenti investment grade
livello di reddito income bracket
livello salariale wage level
localizzazione (f) degli impianti plant location
locatario (m) lessee
locatore/trice (m/f) lessor
logistica (f) logistics
lotto (m) lot

M

macchinari (m) machinery
macinatura (f) milling
macroeconomia (f) macroeconomics
magazziniere (m) warehouseman
magazzino (m) warehouse
magazzino commerciale nell'estremo oriente godown
magazzino doganale bonded warehouse
magazzino regolare regular warehouse
mais (m) maize
malinteso misunderstanding
mancanza (f) shortage
mancare short of, to be (v)
mandato (m) mandate, writ
maniera (f) mode

manifesto (m) manifest
manodopera (f) manpower
manodopera diretta direct labor
manodopera specializzata skilled labor
mansione (f) job
mantenere service (v)
manutenzione (f) maintenance
manutenzione e servizio successivi alla vendita after-sales service
manutenzione preventiva preventive maintenance
marca (f) brand
marchio (m) logo
marchio registrato trademark, registered trademark
margine (m) a termine forward margin
margine di manutenzione maintenance margin
margine di prestito lending margin
margine di profitto profit margin
margine di sicurezza margin of safety
margine lordo gross margin
margine netto net margin
margine variabile variable margin
market market (v)
marketing (m) marketing
marketing per il mercato di massa mass marketing
marketing telefonico telemarketing
massimo (m) livello amministrativo top management
materia (f) prima raw materials
materiale (m) rotante rolling stock
materiali materials
maturare accrue (v)
maturazione (f) accrual
maturità (f) maturity
media (f) average, mean
media aritmetica arithmetic mean
media del costo in dollari dollar cost averaging
media ponderata weighted average
media variabile moving average

mediatore (m) delle azioni stockbroker
mediatore di partite sparse odd lot broker
mediatore di software software broker
mediatore per noleggio charterparty agent
mediazione (f) mediation
medio termine (m) medium term
memorandum (m) memorandum
memoria (f) d'accesso casuale random access memory
memoria dell'elaboratore computer memory
memoria magnetica magnetic memory
mercante (m) merchant
mercantile mercantile
mercanzia (f) merchandising
mercato (m) market, marketplace
mercato a contanti spot market
mercato a due livelli two-tiered market
mercato a termine forward market
mercato all'ingrosso wholesale market
mercato aperto open market
mercato capovolto inverted market
mercato comune common market
mercato debole thin market
mercato dei capitali capital market
mercato del lavoro labor market
mercato favorevole all'acquirente buyer's market
mercato grigio gray market
mercato instabile volatile market
mercato interno home market
mercato invertito inverted market
mercato libero free market
mercato marginale fringe market
mercato monetario money market
mercato nero black market
mercato primario primary market
mercato privilegiato upmarket
mercato propenso per gli acquirenti buyer's market
mercato ristretto tight market

mercato secondario per titoli mobiliari secondary market (securities)
mercato volatile volatile market
merce (f) imballata bale cargo
merce imbarcata cargo
merce pallettizzata palletized freight
merchant (f) bank merchant bank
merci (f) freight
merci di tutti i tipi freight all kinds
merci esentasse free list (commodities without duty)
merci vincolate bonded goods
mese (m) contrattuale contract month
metalli (m) metals
metodo (m) method
metodo di ammortamento accellerato sum of the year's digits
metrificazione (f) metrification
metro (m) yardstick
mettere in appalto put in a bid (v)
mettere in fondo comune pool (v)
mettere sul mercato market (v)
mezza (f) scadenza (per buoni) half-life (bonds)
mezzi di communicazione mass media
mezzi di pubblicità advertising media
mezzo di scambio medium of exchange
micro computer (m) microcomputer
micro elaboratore (m) microprocessor
microchip (m) microchip
microfiche (f) microfiche
microfilm (m) microfilm
miglior offrente (m) highest bidder
miglioramenti (m) improvements
migliorare improve upon (v)
migliore qualità (f) top quality
mini computer (m) minicomputer
mini elaboratore elettronico (m) minicomputer
misura (f) del campione sample size
misurare measure (v)

mobilità (f) della manodopera mobility of labor
modello (m) mock-up, model, pattern
modello matematico mathematical model
modifiche (f) incombenti impending changes
modulatore (m) per la trasmissione di dati via cavo modem
modulo (m) order form
modulo di richiesta application form
modulo di richiesta per brevetto patent application
modulo multiplo spreadsheet
mole (f) volume
moltiplicatore (m) multiplier
monitor (m) monitor
monopolio (m) monopoly
monopolio di stato legal monopoly
monopolio legale legal monopoly
monopsonio (m) monopsony
montaggio (m) assembly
montare assemble (v) (things)
morale (m) morale
moratorio (m) moratorium
movimento (m) d'attività asset turnover
movimento di cassa cash flow
movimento di cassa incrementale incremental cash flow
movimento positivo dei fondi positive cash flow
mozione (f) motion
multa (f) (l'ammenda) fine (penalty)
multipli (m) multiples
multiprogrammato multiprogramming
multiproprietà (f) time sharing
multivalutario (m) multicurrency

N

nastro (m) della telescrivente ticker tape
nastro di carta paper tape
nastro magnetico magnetic tape
nazionalismo (m) nationalism

nazionalizzazione (f) nationalization
negligente negligent
negoziabile negotiable
negoziare negotiate (v)
negoziato (m) negotiation
negoziato tariffaro generale across-the-board tariff negotiation
negozio (m) al dettaglio retail outlet
negozio di denaro money shop
nel giro di una notte overnight
nessun problema no problem
netto net
nodo (m) knot (nautical)
noleggio (m) affreightment
noleggio a scafo nudo bareboat charter
nolo (m) anticipato advance freight
nolo "vuoto per pieno" dead freight
non associato (m) nonmember
non elencato unlisted
non equo unfair
non oltre indicato per nome not otherwise indexed by name
non registrato off-the-books
non residente (m) nonresident
non socio (m) nonmember
non sviluppato undeveloped
non ufficiale off board (stock market)
norma (f) norm
norma dell'uomo giudizioso prudent man rule
normativa (f) regulation
normativa per la costruzione in varie città zoning law
normativa sul lavoro labor law
normative bylaws
normative fitosanitarie phytosanitary regulations
normative per l'esportazione export regulations
normative per l'importazione import regulations
norme (f) per la richiesta di rimborso anticipato call rule
nota (f) d'avviso advice note

nota di accredito credit note
nota di addebito debit note
nota di debito debit entry
nota di spedizione consignment note
notaio (m) notary
notazione (f) binaria binary notation
notifica (f) di consegna delivery notice
novazione (f) novation
novità (f) innovation
nullo void
nullo a tutti gli effetti null and void
numerazione (f) binaria binary notation
numero (m) dell'ordine order number
numero di conto account number
numero di riferimento reference number
nuova (f) emissione new issue

O

obbligazione (f) bond, flat bond, obligation
obbligazione a rate con pagamento maggiorato alla maturità balloon note
obbligazione al portatore bearer bond
obbligazione fiduciaria fidelity bond
obbligazione garantita backed note, guaranty bond
obbligazione garantita da ipoteca mortgage bond
obbligazione garantita dai ricavi dell'emittente revenue bond
obbligazione generale blanket bond
obbligazione ipotecaria mortgage debenture
obbligazione municipale municipal bond
obbligazione senza cedole per ricevere interessi zero coupon
obbligazioni bond issue, debentures, securities
obbligazioni a scadenza periodica serial bonds
obbligazioni convertibili convertible debentures
obbligazioni del tesoro treasury bonds
obbligazioni dirette direct papers
obbligazioni redimibili redeemable bonds
obiettivo (m) aziendale company goal

obsolescenza (f) obsolescence
obsolescenza programmata planned obsolescence
occupazione (f) occupation
offerta (f) tender
offerta a voce oral bid
offerta aggregata aggregate supply
offerta al pubblico public offering
offerta d'acquisto tender offer
offerta d'insediamento takeover bid
offerta e la domanda supply and demand
offerta premio premium offer
offerta scritta written bid (stock exchange)
offerta secondaria di titoli di sicura affidabilità secondary offering (securities)
offerto e richiesto bid and asked
offrire offer (v)
offrire di più outbid (v)
oggetto di prima necessità commodity
oligopolio oligopoly
oligopsonio oligopsony
oltre la linea above-the-line
omettere omit (v)
omologazione (f) probate
onere (m) anticipato front-end fee
onere fiscale tax burden
onere variabile floating charge
oneri charges
oneri d'ancoraggio anchorage (dues)
oneri di sbarco landing charges
oneri di sollevamento di carichi pesanti heavy lift charges
oneri differiti deferred charges
oneri fissi fixed charges
oneri per l'uso del molo wharfage charges
onorario (m) amministrativo management fee
operai (m) manual workers, blue-collar worker
operaio a giornate journeyman

operatore (m) operator

operazioni (f) ausiliari ancillary operations

operazioni di mercato aperto open market operations

opzionale optional

opzione (f) option

opzione col privilegio di acquistare o vendere un'azione allo stesso prezzo straddle

opzione di acquistare delle azioni ad un dato prezzo entro un determinato periodo di tempo call option

opzione di acquisto di valori mobiliari in qualsiasi momento a un certo prezzo call feature

opzione di acquisto o di vendita di un contratto a termine futures option

opzione di vendita (di un'azione a un prezzo superiore a quello attuale) put option

opzione sulle azioni stock option

ora (f) d'arrivo prevista estimated time of arrival

ora di partenza prevista estimated time of departure

ora solare standard time

orario (m) schedule, timetable

ordinare order (v), place, an order (v)

ordine (m) order

ordine a scadenza time order

ordine a termine limit order (stock market)

ordine alternativo alternative order

ordine arretrato back order

ordine continuo open order

ordine d'acquisto purchase order

ordine del giorno order of the day

ordine di fermo perdita stop-loss order

ordine discrezionale discretionary order

ordine fisso standing order

ordine generale blanket order

ordine in giornata day order

ordine per corrispondenza mail order

ordine ripetuto repeat order

ordine successivo follow-up order

ordine urgente rush order

ordini inevasi backlog

ore (f) di lavoro working hours
ore lavorative man hours
ore migliori per la pubblicità televisiva prime time
organigramma (f) management chart, organization chart
organigramma di servizio staff organization
organigramma dirigenziale chain of command
organizzazione (f) organization
organo (f) consultivo advisory council
ottenere acquire (v)
ottimizzare maximize (v)

P

pacco (m) postale parcel post
paese (m) a rischio country of risk
paese con trattamento preferenziale most-favored nation
paese d'origine country of origin
paesi in via di sviluppo underdeveloped nations
paga (f) wage, wages
paga base minimum wage
paga base minima indicizzata index linked guaranteed minimum wage
paga minima minimum wage
pagabile al portatore payable to bearer
pagabile all'ordine payable to order
pagabile su richiesta payable on demand
pagamenti (m) anticipati advance payments
pagamento (m) disbursement, payment
pagamento alla consegna cash delivery, collect on delivery
pagamento anticipato cash in advance
pagamento completo payment in full
pagamento del premio premium payment
pagamento in contanti cash-and-carry
pagamento in natura payment in kind
pagamento parziale partial payment
pagamento prima della consegna cash before delivery
pagamento rifiutato payment refused
pagante (m) payer

pagare pay (v)
pagare in contanti pay as you go
pagherò (m) cambiario promissory note
pallet (m) pallet
paradiso (m) fiscale tax haven
parametri (m) guidelines
parcella (f) (agency) commission
parcella dell'agenzia agency fee
pari par
parità (f) parity, sliding parity
parità d'interesse interest parity
parità di comodo accommodation parity
parità mobile crawling peg
parità variabile moving parity
parte della merce part cargo
parte dovuta per il capitale netto equity share
parti parts
parti di ricambio replacement parts
partita (f) lot
partita arrotondata round lot
partita divisa broken lot
partita frazionata odd lot
partita intera round lot
partita variabile sliding parity
passività differite deferred liabilities
passività garantita liability secured
passività senza garanzia unsecured liability
patrimonio (m) estate
patrimonio congiunto joint estate
patto (m) collettivo collective agreement
patto commerciale trade agreement
patto implicito implied agreement
pegno (m) lien
pegno negativo negative pledge
pegno per il mercato mechanics' lien
penetrazione (f) commerciale market penetration
pensionamento (m) retirement

pensionante (m/f) annuitant
per azione per share
per esportazione for export
percentuale di guadagni percentage earnings
percentuale (f) di profitti percentage of profits
perdita (f) loss
perdita detraibile dalle imposte carryback
perdita lorda gross loss
perdita media in genere general average loss
perdita media particolare particular average loss
perdita netta net loss
perdita sul cambio exchange loss
perdita totale effettiva actual total loss
perforatore (m) keypuncher
pericolo (m) professionale occupational hazard
periodicità (f) del conto account period
periodo (m) contabile, il periodo di contabilità accounting period
periodo d'interesse interest period
periodo di detenzione holding period
periodo di grazia grace period
periodo di pagamento payout period
periodo di preparazione lead time
periodo di ripagamento payback period
periodo di riscossione collection period
periodo di tempo durante il quale l'elaboratore rimane inutilizzabile downtime
periodo di tempo durante il quale la banca usufruisce degli assegni depositati e non incassati float (outstanding checks, stock)
periodo di tempo inutilizzabile down period
periodo finanziario financial period
permesso (m) permit
permesso amministrativo per vendere beni di consumo excise license
permesso d'entrata entry permit
permesso d'esportazione export permit
permesso d'esportazione di beni culturali cultural export permit

permesso di lavoro working papers
permettere allow (v)
permuta (f) degli introiti applied proceeds swap
persona (f) responsabile per un prodotto e/o un cliente account executive
personale (m) staff
personale di vendita sales force
personale e i dirigenti staff and line
peso (m) weight
peso lordo gross weight
petrochimica (f) petrochemical
petrodollari (m) petrodollars
petroliera (f) tanker
pianificazione (f) a lunga scadenza long-range planning
pianificazione aziendale corporate planning
pianificazione del progetto project planning
pianificazione finanziaria financial planning
pianificazione industriale industrial planning
piano (m) plan
piano commerciale business plan
piano d'azione action plan
piano di immediata esecuzione activity on arrow
piano di mercato market plan
piattaforma (f) di comodo accommodation platform
piazzare un ordine place an order (v)
piccola industria (f) small business
piccola pubblicità (f) classified ad, want ad
piccolo furto (m) pilferage
pilotaggio (m) pilotage
plusvalore (m) unearned increment
pochi (m) ordini di acquisto a un dato prezzo thin market
politica (f) aziendale company policy
politica commerciale business policy
politica d'investimento investment policy
politica di apertura open door policy
politica di distribuzione distribution policy

politica monetaria monetary policy

polizza (f) policy

polizza d'assicurazione insurance policy

polizza d'assicurazione di gruppo group insurance

polizza d'assicurazione sulla vita life insurance policy

polizza di carico bill of lading

polizza di carico con riserve o eccezioni foul bill of lading

polizza di carico nazionale inland bill of lading

polizza per un gruppo di automobili fleet policy

porre in vendita offer for sale (v)

porta-a-porta (vendite) door-to-door (sales)

portafoglio (m) portfolio

portafoglio azionario stock portfolio

portare a nuovo carry forward (v)

portatore (m) bearer, carrier

portatore di obbligazioni bonded carrier

porto (m) d'importazione denominato named port of importation

porto di spedizione denominato named port of shipment

porto franco free port

posizione (f) di mercato market position

posizione netta net position, (of a trader)

posizione scoperta short position

posizione secondaria second position

possessore in buona fede holder in due course

postdatare afterdate (v), back date (v)

postdatato postdated

posticipare postpone (v)

postilla (f) (contracts) rider

posto (m) di lavoro place of business, work station, workplace

posto di lavoro autonomo stand-alone work station

potenziale (m) di capacità produttiva di un impianto plant capacity

potenziale di crescita growth potential

potenziale di mercato market potential

potere (m) d'acquisto purchasing power
potere del buono bond power
potere delle azioni stock power
potere di emettere obbligazioni bond power
potere di negoziazione bargaining power
prassi (f) burocratica red tape
pratiche (f) d'uso standard practice
pratico practical
preavviso (m) advance notice
precedenza (f) right of way
precetto (m) garnishment
prefabbricazione (m) prefabrication
preferenza (f) per la liquidità liquidity preference, (economics)
premio (m) bonus, (premium), reward
premio d'accelerazione acceleration premium
premio d'assicurazione insurance premium
premio d'assicurazione premium, insurance
premio del compratore buyer's premium
premio di redimibilità redemption premium
premio sulla zavorra ballast bonus
prendere in prestito borrow (v)
prendere la media averaging
prepagare prepay (v)
preparatore (m) delle paghe paymaster
presidente (m) president
presidente del consiglio chairman of the board
pressione (f) duress
prestiti (m) con tasso d'interesse basso (favorevole) low-interest loans
prestiti erogati sulla base di una garanzia ricevuta back-to-back loans
prestito (m) loan
prestito a termine term loan
prestito bancario bank loan
prestito con minor garanzia soft loan
prestito fiduciario fiduciary loan
prestito giornaliero day loan
prestito partecipato participation loan

prestito rimborsabile a domanda call loan
prestito senza garanzia unsecured loan
prestito vincolato tied loan
prevedere forecast (v)
preventivo (m) capitale capital budget
preventivo d'investimento investment budget
preventivo di cassa cash budget
preventivo in contanti cash budget
preventivo operativo operating budget
preventivo per il marketing marketing budget
preventivo per le spese di vendita sales budget
preventivo provvisorio interim budget
preventivo pubblicitario advertising budget
preventivo spese impianti e macchinari capital budget
previsione (f) forecast
previsione del mercato market forecast
previsione del preventivo budget forecast
previsione di spese di consulenza advisory funds
previsioni di vendita sales forecast
prezzo (m) price
prezzo CIF rettificato adjusted CIF price
prezzo al dettaglio retail price
prezzo al quale è redimibile un buono a richiesta call price
prezzo all'ingrosso wholesale price
prezzo alla chiusura closing price
prezzo alla consegna delivered price
prezzo concorrenziale competitive price
prezzo corrente going rate, (or price)
prezzo d'acquisto purchase price
prezzo d'emissione issue price
prezzo dell'oro gold price
prezzo di apertura del mercato opening price
prezzo di base base price
prezzo di consegna delivery price
prezzo di listino list price
prezzo di mercato price, market
prezzo di parità parity price

prezzo di premio premium price
prezzo di sottoscrizione subscription price
prezzo di una opzione di acquisto call price
prezzo fissato pegged price
prezzo indicativo target price
prezzo iniziale opening price
prezzo limite price limit
prezzo lordo gross price
prezzo massimo top price
prezzo medio average price
prezzo nominale nominal price
prezzo offerto offered price
prezzo previsto estimated price
prezzo reale real price
prezzo richiesto asking price
prezzo unitario unit price
prima azione (f) privilegiata first preferred stock
prima partita ad entrare/la prima partita ad uscire first in-first out
principale (m) principal
priorità (f) priority
privilegio (m) del venditore vendor's lien
pro capite per capita
problema (m) problem
procedimento di produzione production process
procedura (f) brevettata patented process
procedura di regolamento adjustment process
procedura per stabilire una lamentela grievance procedure
procedure restrittive di lavoro restrictive labor practices
processo produttivo production process
procura (f) power of attorney, proxy
prodotti (m) merchandise
prodotti agrari agricultural products
prodotti lattiero-caseari dairy products
prodotto (m) product
prodotto locale native produce

prodotto derivato by-product

prodotto finale end product

prodotto interno lordo gross domestic product

prodotto nazionale lordo (Pnl) gross national product, (GNP)

prodotto secondario by-product

produttività (f) productivity

produttività marginale marginal productivity

produttore (m) manufacturer

produzione (f) output, outturn, production

produzione del computer computer output

produzione di serie mass production

produzione in lotti batch production

produzione modulare modular production

produzione per conto terzi private label, (or brand)

professione (f) profession

profilo (m) di acquisizione, profilo d'acquisto acquisition profile

profitti (m) inattesi windfall profits

profitti ritenuti retained earnings

profitto (m) profit

profitto lordo gross profit

profitto netto net profit

profitto su carta paper profit

profitto sull'investimento return on investment

progettare plan (v)

progettare project (v)

progettazione (f) d'impianti design engineering

progettazione (f) dei sistemi di elaborazione systems design, systems engineering

progettazione industriale design engineering

progettazione industriale industrial engineering

progettazione utilizzando costi più bassi tra costi alternativi per espletare una certa attività value engineering

progetto (m) project

programma (m) program

programma d'investimento investment program

programma del computer computer program

programma dell'elaboratore computer program
programma di mercato market plan
programma di produzione production schedule
programmare program (v)
programmazione (f) aziendale corporate planning
programmazione lineare linear programming
proiettare project (v)
proiezione (f) degli utili profit projection
promessa (f) covenant, pledge
promozione (f) promotion
promozione delle vendite sales promotion
pronto prompt
pronto per l'utilizzo (computer) on line
proporzione (f) ratio
proprietà (f) ownership, property
proprietà incamerata escheat
proprietà personale personal property
proprietà pubblica public property
proprietario (m) landowner, owner, proprietor
proprietario assente absentee ownership
proprietario unico sole proprietor
prospettiva (f) outlook
prospetto (m) prospectus
prospetto preliminare preliminary prospectus
protestare protest (banking; law) (v)
protezione (f) dalla richiesta di un rimborso immediato (obbligazioni) call protection
protezionismo (m) protectionism
proventi (m) proceeds
proventi sul capitale return on capital
provvigione (f) (fee) commission
provvisorio interim
pubbliche (f) relazioni public relations
pubblicità (f) advertising, publicity
pubblicità cooperativa (in compartecipazione) co-operative advertising
pubblicità diretta direct mail

pubblicità istituzionale institutional advertising

punti (m) di consegna delivery points

punti di maggior interesse nel rapporto finanziario financial highlights

punto (m) comune oltremare overseas common point

punto d'esportazione indicato named point of exportation

punto d'origine indicato named point of origin

punto della parità break-even point

punto (centesimo di un percento di base) basis point, (1/100%)

punto di pareggio break-even point

punto di vantaggio competitive edge

punto di vendita point of sale

punto interno denominato nel paese d'importazione named inland point in country of origin

punto morto deadlock

Q

quadro (m) amministrativo management chart

qualifiche (f) qualifications

qualità (f) commerciale commercial grade

quando emesso when issued

quantità (f) quantity

quantità di lavoro work load

quantità di materiale messa in produzione durante un determinato periodo throughput

quantità per un ordine economico economic order quantity

questione (f) di procedura point of order

quorum (m) quorum

quota (f) quota

quota d'esportazione export quota

quota d'importazione import quota

quota di mercato market share

quota di vendita sales quota

quotazione (f) quotation

quotazione fuori borsa over-the-counter quotation

R

raccoglimento (m) dei capitali raising capital
raccolta dei capitali capital, raising
raccomandata (f) registered mail
rafforzamento (m) delle azioni rally
raggiungere una media averaging
raggrupamento (m) dei conti group accounts
ragioniere (m) diplomato dallo stato certified public accountant
ragioniere professionista chartered accountant
rapporti (m) sindacali labor relations
rapporto (m) annuale annual report
rapporto corrente current ratio
rapporto d'alimentazione feed ratio
rapporto di contabilità accounting ratio
rapporto di copertura cover ratio
rapporto di liquidità acid-test ratio
rapporto di liquidità liquidity ratio
rapporto perdita contro perdita loss-loss ratio
rapporto sul mercato market report
rapporto tra capitale e produzione capital-output ratio
rapporto tra i prezzi ed i guadagni di un azione price/earnings ratio, p/e ratio
rapporto tra il reddito e la parità parity income ratio
rappresentante (m) representative
rappresentante del produttore manufacturer's representative
rappresentante nominato registered representative
razionare ration (v)
recessione (f) recession
reclamo (m) claim
reclamo indiretto indirect claim
recuperare salvage (v)
redditività (f) profitability
reddito (m) income, yield
reddito alla maturità yield to maturity

reddito annuale variabile variable annuity
reddito differito deferred income
reddito disponibile disposable income
reddito effettivo actual income
reddito esentasse tax-free income
reddito futuro scontato al valore attuale discounted cash flow
reddito lordo gross income
reddito maturato accrued revenue
reddito netto net income
reddito nominale nominal yield
reddito non da lavoro unearned revenue
reddito operativo operating income
reddito reale real income
reddito sugli interessi interest income
reddito sul capitale netto return on equity
referenza (f) bancaria credit reference
referenza per ottenere credito credit reference
registrare post (v) (bookkeeping)
registrazione (f) a debito debit entry
registrazione del movimento di cassa cash entry
regolamenti (m) bylaws
reinvestire plow back (v) (earnings)
relazione (f) report
relazione del movimento di cassa cash flow statement
relazione sugli utili earnings report
relazioni con gli investitori investor relations
relazioni con il personale employee relations
relazioni industriali industrial relations
remissione (f) dell'imposta remission duty
remissione di una tassa remission of a tax
rendere disponibile make available (v)
rendiconto (m) bancario bank statement
rendimento (m) income yield, yield, yield to maturity
rendimento competitivo agli investimenti alternativi fair return
rendimento corrente current yield
rendimento del dividendo dividend yield

rendimento effettivo effective yield
rendimento interno internal rate of return
rendimento lordo gross yield
rendimento piatto flat yield
rendimento reale al netto di tasse after-tax real rate of return
rendimento sui guadagni earnings performance
rendimento sul capitale return on capital
rendimento sulle attività amministrate return on assets managed
rendita (f) annuity
rendita settimanale weekly return
rendita sui guadagni earnings yield
rendite differite deferred annuities
reparto (m) department
reparto affittato leased department
reparto contabilità accounting department
reparto personale personnel department
reparto progettazione e stilismo engineering and design department
requisiti (f) requirements
resa (f) sui capitali return on capital
resa sulle vendite return on sales
responsabile (m) degli acquisti chief buyer
responsabile delle esportazioni export manager
responsabile per l'imposta liable for tax
responsabilità (f) accountability, liability
responsabilità congiunta joint liability
responsabilità contingente contingent liability
responsabilità corrente current liabilities
responsabilità differite deferred liabilities
responsabilità effettiva actual liability
responsabilità fissa fixed liability
responsabilità limitata limited liability
responsabilità personale personal liability
responsabilità presunta assumed liability
responsabilità dell'acquirente buyer's responsibility
responsabilità effettiva actual liability
restrizioni (f) all'esportazione restrictions on export

rete (f) di distribuzione distribution network
retroazione (f) feedback
revisionare amend (v)
revisione (f) annuale dei conti annual audit
revisione interna internal audit
revisore (m) auditor
revisore bancario bank examiner
riacquistare buy back (v)
riassicuratore (m) reinsurer
ribasso (m) downswing, downturn
ricambio (m) della manodopera labor turnover
ricambio delle azioni stock turnover
ricapitalizzazione (f) recapitalization
ricarico (m) markup
ricavi (m) marginali marginal revenue
ricavo (m) revenue
ricchezza (f) wealth
ricerca (f) research
ricerca di azione action research
ricerca di mercato market research
ricerca di personale dirigenziale executive search
ricerca e lo sviluppo research and development
ricerca sul consumatore consumer research
ricevuta (f) receipt, voucher
ricevuta del custode del molo dock, (ship's receipt)
ricevuta fiduciaria trust receipt
richiamo (m) (in genere per articoli difettosi) callback
richiedente un notevole investimento di capitale capital-intensive
richiedere demand (v)
richiedere il saldo del deposito per coprire perdite sulla borsa margin call
richiesta (f) demand
richiesta d'appalto advertisement, (request) for bid
richiesta d'appalto invitation to bid
riconoscere acknowledge (v)
riconoscimento (m) della marca brand recognition
ricorso (m) recourse

ricorso al prestito per finanziare un'attività deficit financing

ricovero (m) recovery

ridurre l'inventario draw down (v)

riduzione (f) abatement, cutback, rollback

riduzione dei costi cost reduction

riduzione dei prezzi price cutting

riduzione della differenza tra costi e prezzi che riduce il profitto cost-price squeeze

riduzione delle tasse tramite facilitazioni permesse dal governo tax shelter

riduzione nel numero delle azioni reverse stock split

riempire top up (v)

rientro (m) in possesso repossession

riesportare re-export (v)

rifinanziamento (m) refinancing

rifiutare accettazione refuse acceptance (v)

rifiutare pagamento refuse payment (v)

riflazione (f) reflation

riforma (f) fondiaria land reform

rifugio (m) fiscale tax haven

riguardo (al riguardo) regard (with regard to)

rilevazione (f) delle quote del soci liquidati buyout

rimanenze (f) odd lot

rimborsare reimburse (v)

rimborso (m) refund

rimborso anticipato advance refunding

rimborso delle spese recovery of expenses

rimedio (m) remedy, (law)

rimessa (f) telegrafica cable transfer

rimunerazione (f) remuneration

rinegoziare renegotiate (v)

rinnovare renew (v)

rinuncia (f) ad un atto di proprietà quitclaim deed

rinvestimento (m) degli utili di un investimento rollover

riordinare reorder (v)

riorganizzare reorganize (v)

ripagare repay (v)

riparare il sistema nell'elaboratore debug (v)
ripartizione (f) allotment
riportare carryover
rischio (m) risk
rischio cumulativo aggregate risk
rischio puro pure risk
rischio sul cambio exchange risk
riscontro (m) reply
riserva (f) reserve
riserva capitale capital allowance
riservato confidential
riserve (f) d'oro gold reserves
riserve di capitali presi a prestito net borrowed reserves
riserve minime minimum reserves
riserve primarie primary reserves
risoluzione (f) resolution, (legal document)
risoluzione di problemi problem solving
risoluzione generale across-the-board settlement
risorse (f) del personale human resources
risorse naturali natural resources
risparmi (m) savings
rispondere reply (v)
ristorno (m) drawback
ristrutturare restructure (v)
ristrutturazione (f) urbana urban renewal
risultati (m) previsti expected results
il ritardo (m) delay, demurrage
ritardo fiscale fiscal drag
ritirare take down (v)
ritiro (m) e la consegna pickup and delivery
ritorno (m) di una parte della merce sullo stesso percorso utilizzato per il trasporto originale back haul
ritorno sull'investimento return on investment
riunione (f) meeting
riunione degli azionisti shareholders' meeting
riunione del consiglio board meeting
riunione generale general meeting

riunione plenaria plenary meeting
riunire assemble (v) (people)
rivalutazione (f) revaluation
rivedere audit (v)
rivendita (f) resale
rivendita del prodotto al fornitore originale back selling
rivenditore (m) autorizzato
authorized dealer routine (f)
routine

S

sala (f) conferenze conference room
sala del consiglio boardroom
sala delle contrattazioni floor, (of exchange)
sala delle negoziazioni trading floor, (stock exchange)
salariato (m) wage earner
salario (m) salary, wages
salario reale real wages
saldare pay up (v)
saldo (m) a credito credit balance
saldo completo full settlement
saldo contabile account balance
saldo e credito balance, credit
saldo liquido cash balance
salvaguardia (m) safeguard
saturazione (f) del mercato market saturation
sbalzo (m) di prezzo price tick
sbocco (m) outlet
sborsamento (m) outlay
scadenza (f) deadline
scadenza oltre la quale non sono permesse azioni legali statute of limitations
scaduto overdue, past due
scala (f) salariale wage scale
scala variabile sliding scale
scambiare exchange (v)
scambio (m) trade-off

scaricare discharge (v), unload (v)
scarico (m) con chiatte lighterage
scarto (m) spoilage
scarto quadratico medio standard deviation
scheda (f) perforata punch card
schema (m) layout
scioperare strike (v)
sciopero (m) walkout
sciopero generale general strike
sciopero selvaggio wildcat strike
scontare discount (v), mark down (v)
sconto (m) abatement, discount, leakage, rebate
sconto agli operatori settoriali trade discount
sconto applicato sulle unità di carico unit load discount
sconto di volume volume discount
sconto per contanti cash discount
sconto per quantità quantity discount
sconto sul cambio exchange discount
scoprire e localizzare i guasti troubleshoot (v)
scorrere in modo regolare streamline (v)
scrittura (f) contabile correttiva adjusting entry
scrittura di chiusura closing entry
sede (f) headquarters
sede amministrativa operations headquarters
sede centrale head office
segretario (m) superiore executive secretary
selezionare screen (v)
self-service (m) self-service
senza cambio gearless
senza dividendo ex dividend
senza fini di lucro nonprofit
senza impegni free and clear
senza testamento intestate
senza valore worthless
senza valore alla pari no par value
separazione (f) separation
sequestrare impound (v)

serpente (m) valutario (CEE) currency band
serrata (f) lock out
servizi (m) facilities
servizi finanziaria financial services
servizi pubblici public utilities
servizio consultivo service advisory
servizio di corriere courier service
servizio reso al cliente customer service
settore (m) pubblico public sector
sfavorevole unfavorable
sgravare dalle tasse chargeoff (v)
sgravio (m) fiscale tax allowance, tax relief
sicurezza (f) security
sigla (f) acronym
simulare simulate (v)
sindacato (m) labor union, trade union
sindacato industriale industrial union
sistema (m) contabile, sistema di contabilità accounting method
sistema di competenza accrual method
sistema di contingentamento quota system
sistema di gestione integrato integrated management system
sistema di parità variabile adjustable peg
sistema di vendita rateale installment plan
situazione irresolubile deadlock
slittamento (m) salariale wage drift
smontare take down (v)
società (f) corporation
società a responsabilità limitata (s.r.l.) limited partnership
società di finanziamento finance company
società di persone partnership
società finanziaria holding company
società in accomandita associate company
società in accomandita semplice (s.a.s.) general partnership

società madre holding company

società multinazionale multinational corporation

società per azioni corporation

società per la gestione degli investimenti trust company

socio member of firm, partner

socio a vita life member

socio accomandante silent partner

socio secondario junior partner

soddisfazione (f) del consumatore consumer satisfaction

soffitto (m) ceiling

software (m) software

soggetto a liable to

sollecitare pagamento dun (v)

sollecito prompt

somma (f) amount

somma dei numeri dell'anno precedente sum of the year's digits

somma dovuta amount due

somma globale lump sum

somma in eccesso ai fondi disponibili overdraft

sondaggio (m) della opinione pubblica public opinion poll

sopra la pari above par

soprapprezzo (m) surcharge

soprattassa (f) surtax

sopravvalutato overvalued

sopravvenienza (f) passiva contingent liability

sospendere il pagamento suspend payment (v)

sostegno (m) d'appoggio backing support

sostegno del prezzo price support

sostituire supersede (v)

sotto la pari below par

sotto norma substandard

sotto-capitalizzato undercapitalized

sottopagato underpaid

sottoscritto (m) undersigned

sottoscritto oltre il necessario oversubscribed
sottoscrittore (m) underwriter
sottoscrittore dell'assicurazione insurance underwriter
sottovalutare underestimate (v), undervalue (v)
sovrabbondanza (f) glut
sovraccarico (m) overstock, surcharge
sovrappagato overpaid
sovrapposizione (f) overlap
sovrapprezzo (m) overcharge
spartire allot (v)
spartizione (f) degli utili profit sharing
specialistà (m) specialist, (stock exchange)
specificare earmark (v)
speculatore (m) speculator
spedizione (f) consignment
spedizione a termine forward shipment
spedizione aerea air shipment
spedizione fatta direttamente al dettagliante drop shipment
spedizione incompleta short shipment
spedizioni illegali illegal shipments
spedizioniere (f) forwarding agent, freight forwarder, shipper
spedizioniere doganale customs broker
spedizione (f) dispatch, shipment
spesa (f) expenditure
spesa amministrativa administrative expense
spesa dei capitali capital spending
spesa fatta mentre la ditta è in passivo deficit spending
spese expenses
spese (f) correnti running expenses
spese costanti fixed expenses
spese d'immobilizzo carrying charges
spese d'interesse interest expenses
spese di ormeggio dock handling charges
spese di recupero salvage charges

spese di scambio switching charges
spese di spedizione shipping expenses
spese di tasca propria out-of-pocket expenses
spese di trasloco moving expenses
spese di trasporto shipping expenses
spese dirette direct expenses
spese evitabili avoidable costs
spese fisse fixed expenses
spese fisse generali overhead
spese incidentali incidental expenses
spese indirette indirect expenses
spese maturate accrued expenses
spese operative operating expenses, running expenses
spese prepagate prepaid expenses, (balance sheet)
spese pubblicitarie advertising expenses
spinta pubblicitaria advertising drive
spirale (f) dei salari e dei prezzi wage-price spiral
spogliazione (f) divestment
sponsor (m) sponsor, (of fund, partnership)
sporgenza (f) overhang
spostamento (m) dei beni movement of goods
stabilimento (m) di consegna approvato approved delivery facility
stabilire contatti capillari network (v)
stabilire il prezzo price (v)
stagflazione (f) stagflation
stagionale seasonal
stallie (f) laydays
stampato (m) printout
stampe (f) printed matter
standardizzazione (f) standardization
stanza (f) di compensazione clearinghouse
stanziamento (m) appropriation
stanziamento (m) del preventivo budget appropriation
statistiche (f) statistics
statuto (m) statute
stazza (f) tonnage

stessa paga (f) per lo stesso lavoro equal pay for equal work
stima (f) appraisal, estimate, rough estimate
stima approssimativa guesstimate
stima da parte del factor factor rating
stima delle spese capitali capital expenditure appraisal
stima delle vendite sales estimate
stimare estimate (v)
stipendio (m) salary, wage, wages
stipendio netto take-home pay
stivaggio (m) stowage
straniero (m) nonresident
strategia (f) commerciale business strategy
strategia concorrenziale competitive strategy
strategia d'investimento investment strategy
strategia di marketing marketing plan
strumento (m) instrument
struttura aziendale corporate structure
struttura finanziaria capital structure
struttura salariale wage structure
studio (m) del rapporto tra tempo e movimento time and motion study
studio motivazionale motivation study
studio pubblicitario advertising research
studio sulla profittabilità profitability analysis
su costo on cost
su richiesta on demand
su rimessa on consignment
subaffitto (m) sublet
subappaltare subcontract (v)
subappaltatore (m) subcontractor
succitato (m) above-mentioned
sul retro on the back
summenzionato (m) above-mentioned
supervisore (m) supervisor
sussidio (m) subsidy
svalutare write down (v)
svalutazione (f) devaluation

svantaggio (m) drawback, handicap
sviluppo (m) del prodotto product development
sviluppo di nuovi prodotti new product development
svolta (f) positiva upturn

T

tabella (f) timetable
tagli (m) dei prezzi price cutting
tangente (f) kickback
tariffa (f) tariff
tariffa combinata combination duty
tariffa controvalente countervailing duty
tariffa d'esportazione export duty
tariffa d'importazione import tariff
tariffa di partecipazione participation fee
tariffa differenziale differential tariff
tariffa doganale customs duty
tariffa fissa standing charges
tariffa preferenziale preferred tariff
tariffa protettiva, tariffa "anti-dumping" anti-dumping duty
tassa (f) tax
tassa sul consumo excise tax
tassazione (f) taxation
tassazione multipla multiple taxation
tasse differite deferred tax
tasse maturate accrued taxes
tasso (m) rate
tasso bancario bank rate
tasso centrale central rate
tasso d'adesione accession rate
tasso d'incremento rate of increase
tasso d'interesse interest rate
tasso dell'onere burden rate
tasso di base base rate
tasso di cambio exchange rate

tasso di cambio multiplo multiple exchange rate
tasso di cambio variabile floating exchange rate
tasso di crescita rate of growth
tasso di interesse per rimborsabile a brevissima scadenza call rate
tasso di rendimento rate of return
tasso di rimunerazione rate of return
tasso di risconto rediscount rate
tasso di scambio fisso fixed rate of exchange
tasso di sconto discount rate
tasso fluttuante floating rate
tasso offerto offered rate
tasso rettificato adjusted rate
tasso variabile floating rate, variable rate
tavola (f) elettronica per comandi electronic whiteboard
tecnica (f) di Monte Carlo Monte Carlo technique
tele-elaborazione (f) teleprocessing
telecomunicazioni (f) telecommunications
tempo (m) di giacenza lay time
tempo libero free time
tempo presenziato attended time
tempo reale real time
tendenza (f) trend
tendenze del mercato market trends
tenere al corrente keep posted (v)
tenore (m) di vita standard of living
tentativi (m) di influenzare atti governativi con pressioni varie lobbying
teoria (f) d'azione relativa agli investimenti portfolio theory
terminale (m) terminal
terminale del computer computer terminal
terminale dell'elaboratore computer terminal
terminare terminate (v)
termine (m) fisso fixed term
termine futuro forward forward
termini del credito credit terms

termini di ormeggio berth terms
termini lineari linear terms
terra (f) land
territorio (m) territory
territorio di vendita sales territory
terza (f) finestra third window
terzo sbocco third window
tesoriere (m) treasurer
testamentario (m) executor
testamento (m) will
testimone (m) witness
testo (m) (text) copy
testo scritto senza particolare interesse boilerplate
titoli (m) di sicura affidabilità securities
titoli di sicura affidabilità che possono essere posti sul mercato marketable securities
titoli governativi gilt, (Brit. govt. security)
titoli mobiliari marketable securities, securities
titoli mobiliari approvati approved securities
titoli mobiliari esteri foreign securities
titoli mobiliari negoziabili negotiable securities
titoli mobiliari prestati a un broker loan stock
titoli obbligazionari dati in garanzia backup bonds
titoli scontati discount securities
titolo (m) stock, title
titolo a garanzia secondaria junior security
titolo al portatore bearer security
titolo di mobiliare a reddito fisso fixed income security
titolo nominativo registered security
togliere take out (v)
tonnellata (f) metrica long ton
torto (m) tort
traduttore (m) translator
traente (m) drawer
tramite (f) polizza di carico through bill of lading
tranche (f) tranche

transazione (f) transaction
trasferimento (m) transfer
trasferimento via cavo wire transfer
trasferta (f) transfer
trasformare process (v)
trasgressione (f) nonfeasance
trasporto (m) drayage, transportation
trasporto di containers con camion piggyback service
trasporto di containers su navi fishy-back service, (container)
trasporto ferroviario rail shipment
trasporto prepagato freight prepaid
trasporto via aerea air freight
tratta (f) draft
tratta a vista sight draft
tratta bancaria bank draft
trattare negotiate (v)
trattario (m) drawee
trattativa (f) complessiva package deal
trattato (m) treaty
tubazioni (f) pipage
turno (m) (labor) shift
tutto o niente all or none

U

ufficio (m) office
ufficio commerciale trade commission
ufficio di credito credit bureau
ultima partita consegnata-prima partita ad uscire last in-first out
ultimo pagamento (m) rateale per un importo notevolmente più alto dei precedenti balloon (payment)
unione (f) creditizia credit union
unione doganale customs union
unità (f) centrale per l'elaborazione dei dati central processing unit, (computers)

usanze (f) locali local customs
user friendly user-friendly
usura (f) wear and tear
usuria (f) usury
utensili (m) tools
utile (m) profit
utile dalle azioni stock profit
utile del prodotto product profitability
utile lordo gross profit
utili attivi active assets
utili di capitale/la perdita di capitale capital gain/loss
utili diretti operating profit
utili per azione earnings per share
utili ritenuti retained earnings
utili su carta paper profit
utili sugli attivi earnings on assets
utilità (f) utility

V

vaglia (m) bancario bank money order
vaglia postale money order
validare validate (v)
valido valid
valore (m) stock, value
valore al pari par value
valore attuale netto net present value
valore daziabile value for duty
valore delle attività asset value
valore di mercato fair market value, market value
valore di recupero salvage value
valore dichiarato face value
valore effettivo a pronti actual cash value
valore effettivo della ditta going-concern value
valore in contanti alla resa cash surrender value
valore intrinseco intrinsic value
valore liquidato liquidation value

valore mediano median
valore mobiliare issue (stock)
valore netto net worth
valore netto degli attivi net asset value
valore registrato book value
valore registrato per azione book value per share
valore riportato face, value
valuta (f) currency
valuta bloccata blocked currency
valuta debole soft currency
valuta di base base currency
valuta estera foreign currency
valuta legale legal tender
valuta pregiata hard currency
valutare assess (v)
valutazione (f) appraisal, assessment, evaluation
valutazione degli investimenti investment, appraisal
valutazione del credito credit rating
valutazione del lavoro job evaluation
valutazione del mercato market rating
valutazione del rischio risk assessment
valutazione dell'adempimento del lavoro job performance rating
valutazione dell'investimento investment appraisal
valutazione dell'obbligazione bond rating
valutazione di mercato market appraisal
valutazione finanziaria financial appraisal
valutazione imponibile assessed valuation
valutazione lineare linear estimation
vantaggio (m) competitivo competitive advantage
variabilità (f) amministrata o controllata managed float
variazione (f) spread, variance
varie miscellaneous
velocità (f) della circolazione monetaria velocity of money
vendere market (v), sell (v)
vendere diretta sell direct (v)

vendere più di quanto si abbia oversell (v)
vendere sotto il prezzo del concorrente undercut (v)
vendita (f) divestment, sale
vendita aggressiva hard sell
vendita allo scoperto short sale
vendita diretta direct selling
vendita e il riaffitto sale and leaseback
vendita negoziata negotiated sale
vendita non aggressiva soft sell
vendita per la realizzazione di profitti profit taking
vendita piramidale pyramid selling
vendita pubblica public sale
vendite (f) sales
vendite aggiunte add-on sales
vendite lorde gross sales
vendite nette net sales
vendite potenziali potential sales
vendite previste sales estimate
venditore (m) vendor
venire incontro al prezzo meet the price (v)
venire meno agli obblighi default (v)
verifica (f) della perdita proof of loss
verificare audit (v)
veto (m) veto
vettore (m) common carrier
vettore contrattuale contract carrier
vice amministratore/trice (m/f) deputy manager
vice direttore/trice (m/f) assistant manager
vice direttore generale assistant general manager
vice dirigente (m/f) deputy manager
vice-presidente/essa (m/f) vice-president
visita (f) di vendita senza preavviso cold call
vita (f) economica economic life
vita media average life
vitalizio (m) annuitant
voce (f) item
voce tariffaria tariff commodity
volume (m) volume

volume delle vendite sales volume

volume di vendite al quale c'è equilibrio tra ricavi e costi break-even point

volume effettivo di mercato actual market volume

W

word processor (m) word processor

Z

zecca (f) mint

zona (f) zone

zona franca free trade zone

KEY WORDS FOR KEY INDUSTRIES

The dictionary that forms the centerpiece of *Talking Business in Italian* is a compendium of some 3000 words that you are likely to use or encounter as you do business abroad. It will greatly facilitate fact-finding about the business possibilities that interest you, and will help guide you through negotiations as well as reading documents. To supplement the dictionary, we have added a special feature—groupings of key terms about ten industries. As you explore any of these industries, you'll want to have *Talking Business* at your fingertips to help make sure you don't misunderstand or overlook an aspect that could have a material effect on the outcome of your business decision. The industries covered in the vocabulary lists are the following:

- *chemicals*
- *chinaware and tableware*
- *electronics*
- *fashion*
- *iron and steel*
- *leather goods*
- *motor vehicles*
- *pharmaceuticals*
- *printing and publishing*
- *winemaking*

Chemicals—English to Italian

acetate l'acetato
acetic acid l'acido acetico
acetone l'acetone
acid l'acido
amine l'amina
ammonia l'ammoniaca
analysis l'analisi
atom l'atomo
atomic atomica
base la base
benzene il benzolo
biochemistry la biochimica
biology la biologia
carbon il carbonio
catalyst la catalisi
chemistry la chimica
chloride il cloruro
chloroform il cloroformio
composition la composizione
compound il composto
concentration la concentrazione
cracking la piroscissione
crystallization la cristalizzazione
degree il grado
density la densità
distillation la distillazione
electrolysis l'elettrolisi
electron l'elettrone
element l'elemento
engineer l'ingegnere
enzyme l'enzima
ethane l'etano
ether l'etere
evaporation l'evaporazione
experiment l'esperimento, la prova
formula la formula
gas chromatography la gascromatografia
gram il grammo
homogeneity l'omogeneità
hydrocarbon l'idrocarbonio
hydrochloric acid l'acido cloridico
hydrolysis l'idrolisi
impurity l'impurezza
inorganic chemistry la chimica inorganica
isotope l'isotopo
laboratory il laboratorio
methane il metano
molar il molare
mole il grammo molecola
molecule la molecola
natural gas il gas naturale
neutral neutro
neutralization la neutralizzazione
neutron il neutrone
nitrate il nitrato
nitric acid acido nitrico
nitrite il nitrito
oxidation l'ossidazione
oxygen l'ossigeno
petroleum il petrolio
phosphate il fosfato
polymer il polimero
product il prodotto
proton il protone
purification la purificazione
reagent il reagente, il reattivo
reduction la riduzione
refine (v) raffinare
refinery la raffineria
research la ricerca
salt il sale
saponification la saponificazione
solubility la solubilità
solute il soluto
solution la soluzione
solvent il solvente
spectrophotometry la spettrofotometria
spectrum lo spettro
sulfate il solfato
sulfuric acid l'acido solforico
titration la titolazione
viscosity la viscosità
yield la resa
yield (v) rendere

Chemicals—Italian to English

acetato (m) acetate
acetone (m) acetone
acido (m) acid
acido acetico acetic acid
acido cloridico hydrochloric acid
acido nitrico nitric acid
acido solforico sulfuric acid
amina (f) amine
ammoniaca (f) ammonia
analisi (f) analysis
atomica atomic
atomo (m) atom
base (f) base
benzolo (f) benzene
biochimica (f) biochemistry
biologia (f) biology
carbonio (m) carbon
catalisi (f) catalyst
chimica (f) chemistry
chimica inorganica inorganic chemistry
cloroformio (m) chloroform
cloruro (m) chloride
composizione (f) composition
composto (m) compound
concentrazione (f) concentration
cristalizzazione (f) crystallization
densità (f) density
distillazione (f) distillation
elemento (m) element
elettrolisi (f) electrolysis
elettrone (m) electron
enzima (m) enzyme
esperimento (m) experiment
etano (m) ethane
etere (m) ether
evaporazione (f) evaporation
formula (f) formula
fosfato (m) phosphate
gas (m) naturale natural gas
gascromatografia (f) gas chromatography
grado (m) degree
grammo (m) gram
grammo molecola mole
idrocarbonio (m) hydrocarbon
idrolisi (f) hydrolysis
impurezza (f) impurity
ingegnere (m) engineer
isotopo (m) isotope
laboratorio (m) laboratory
metano (m) methane
molare (m) molar
molecola (f) molecule
neutralizzazione (f) neutralization
neutro neutral
neutrone (m) neutron
nitrato (m) nitrate
nitrito (m) nitrite
omogeneità (f) homogeneity
ossidazione (f) oxidation
ossigeno (m) oxygen
petrolio (m) petroleum
piroscissione (f) cracking
polimero (m) polymer
prodotto (m) product
protone (m) proton
prova (f) experiment
purificazione (f) purification
raffinare refine (v)
raffineria (f) refinery
reagente (m) reagent
reattivo (m) reagent
rendere yield (v)
resa (f) yield
ricerca (f) research
riduzione (f) reduction
sale (m) salt
saponificazione (f) saponification
solfato (m) sulfate
solubilità (f) solubility
soluto (f) solute
soluzione (f) solution
solvente (m) solvent
spettro (m) spectrum
spettrofotometria (f) spectrophotometry
titolazione (f) titration
viscosità (f) viscosity

Chinaware and Tableware—English to Italian

bone china la porcellana "bone"
bowl la scodella
breadbasket il cestino per il pane
butter dish il piattino per il burro
candlestick il candeliere
carving knife il trinciante
champagne glass il flute, la coppa per lo spumante
cheese tray il vassoio per formaggi
china la porcellana fine
coffeepot la caffettiera
crystal glass il vetro di cristallo
cup la tazza
cutlery la posateria
decanter la caraffa
dessert plate il piatto per dolci
dish il piatto
earthenware la terraglia
espresso cup la tazzina da espresso
flute il flute
fork la forchetta
glass il bicchiere
gravy boat la salsiera
hand-painted dipinto a mano
hand-blown glass il bicchiere soffiato a bocca
hand-embroidered napkins i tovaglioli ricamati a mano
knife il coltello
lace il merletto
linen la biancheria da tavola
napkin il tovagliolo
napkin ring l'anello per tovagliolo
oilcloth la tela cerata
pastry server la paletta
pepper mill il macinapepe
pepper shaker il porta pepe
pitcher la caraffa, la brocca
place setting il coperto
plate il piatto
pottery le stoviglie
salad plate il piatto per l'insalata
salt shaker la saliera
saucer il piattino
silverware l'argenteria
soup dish la zuppiera
spoon il cucchiaio
stainless steel l'acciaio inossidabile
stoneware il grès
sugar bowl la zuccheriera
tablecloth la tovaglia
tablespoon il cucchiaio
teapot la teiera
teaspoon il cucchiaino da tè
thread il filo
tureen la terrina
unbleached linen il lino grezzo

Major Chinaware Regions

Toscana (Tuscany)
Umbria
Veneto

Chinaware and Tableware—Italian to English

acciaio (m) inossidabile stainless steel
anello (m) per tovagliolo napkin ring
argenteria (m) silverware
biancheria (f) da tavola linen
bicchiere (m) glass
bicchiere soffiato a bocca hand-blown glass
brocca (f) pitcher
caffettiera (f) coffeepot
candeliere (m) candlestick
caraffa (f) decanter, pitcher
cestino (m) per il pane breadbasket
coltello (m) knife
coperto (m) place setting
coppa (f) per lo spumante champagne glass
cucchiaino (m) da tè teaspoon
cucchiaio (m) spoon
dipinto a mano hand-painted
filo (m) thread
flute (m) champagne glass, flute
forchetta (f) fork
grès (m) stoneware
lino (m) grezzo unbleached linen
macinapepe (m) pepper mill
merletto (m) lace
paletta (f) pastry server
piattino (m) saucer
piattino per il burro butter dish
piatto (m) dish, plate
piatto per dolci dessert plate
piatto per insalata salad plate
porcellana (f) "bone" bone china
porcellana fine china
porta (m) pepe pepper shaker
posateria (f) cutlery
saliera (f) salt shaker
salsiera (f) gravy boat
scodella (f) bowl
stoviglie (f) pottery
tazza (f) cup
tazzina (f) da espresso espresso cup
teiera (f) teapot
tela cerata (f) oilcloth
terraglia (f) earthenware
terrina (f) tureen
tovaglia (f) tablecloth
tovaglioli (m) ricamati a mano hand-embroidered napkins
tovagliolo (m) napkin
trinciante (m) carving knife
vassoio (m) per formaggi cheese tray
vetro (m) di cristallo crystal glass
zuccheriera (f) sugar bowl
zuppiera (f) soup dish

Electronics—English to Italian

alternating current la corrente alternata
ampere l'ampere
amplifier l'amplificatore
amplitude modulation (AM) la modulazione di ampiezza
antenna l'antenna
beam il fascio
binary code il codice binario
broadcast (v) trasmettere
cable television la filodiffusione
camera la telecamera
cassette la cassetta
cathode il catodo
channel il canale
circuit il circuito
coaxial cable il cavo coassiale
computer l'elaboratore elettronico, il "computer"
condenser il condensatore
conductor il conduttore
current la corrente
detector la valvola rivelatrice
digital digitale
diode il diodo
electricity l'elettricità
electrode l'elettrodo
electron l'elettrone
electronic elettronico
electrostatic elettrostatico
fiber optic la fibra ottica
filament il filamento
filter il filtro
frequency la frequenza
frequency modulation (FM) la modulazione di frequenza
generator il generatore
germanium il germanio
high fidelity l'alta fedeltà
induction l'induzione
insulator l'isolante
integrated circuit il circuito integrato
kilowatt il kilowatt
laser il laser
microphone il microfono
microwave la microonda
mixer il miscelatore
motor il motore
negative il negativo
ohm l'ohm
optic ottico
oscillator l'oscillatore
panel il pannello
parallel circuit il circuito in parallelo
pole il polo
positive il positivo
power la potenza, il rendimento
printed circuit il circuito stampato
program il programma
radar il radar
radio la radio
receiver il ricevitore
record il disco
record (v) incidere
resistance la resistenza
resonance la risonanza
scanning la scansione, l'esplorazione
screen lo schermo
semiconductor il semiconduttore
short wave le onde corte
silicon il silicone
sound il suono
speaker l'altoparlante
stereophonic stereofonico
switch l'interruttore
tape il nastro
telecommunications le telecomunicazioni
tube il tubo
tune (v) captare
vacuum il vuoto
vector il vettore
videocassette recorder (VCR) il videoregistratore
volt il volt
voltage il voltaggio
watt il watt
wave l'onda
wire il filo

Electronics—Italian to English

alta fedeltà (f) high fidelity
altoparlante (m) speaker
ampere (m) ampere
amplificatore (m) amplifier
antenna (f) antenna
canale (m) channel
captare tune (v)
cassetta (f) cassette
catodo (m) cathode
cavo (m) coassiale coaxial cable
circuito (m) circuit
circuito in parallelo parallel circuit
circuito integrato integrated circuit
circuito stampato printed circuit
codice (m) binario binary code
condensatore (m) condenser
conduttore (m) conductor
corrente (f) current
corrente alternata alternating current
digitale digital
diodo (m) diode
disco (m) record
elaboratore (m) elettronico computer
elettricità (f) electricity
elettrodo (m) electrode
elettrone (m) electron
elettronico electronic
elettrostatico electrostatic
esplorazione (f) scanning
fascio (m) beam
fibra ottica (f) fiber optic
filamento (m) filament
filo (m) wire
filodiffusione (f) cable television
filtro (m) filter
frequenza (f) frequency
generatore (m) generator
germanio (m) germanium
incidere record (v)
induzione (f) induction
interruttore (m) switch
isolante (m) insulator
kilowatt (m) kilowatt
laser (m) laser
microfono (m) microphone
microonda (f) microwave
miscelatore (m) mixer
modulazione (f) di ampiezza amplitude modulation (AM)
modulazione di frequenza frequency modulation (FM)
motore (m) motor
nastro (m) tape
negativo (m) negative
ohm (m) ohm
onda (f) wave
onde corte short wave
oscillatore (m) oscillator
ottico optic
pannello (m) panel
polo (m) pole
positivo (m) positive
potenza (f) power
programma (m) program
radar (m) radar
radio (f) radio
rendimento (m) power
resistenza (f) resistance
ricevitore (m) receiver
risonanza (f) resonance
scansione (f) scanning
schermo (m) screen
semiconduttore (m) semiconductor
silicone (m) silicon
stereofonico stereophonic
suono (m) sound
telecamera (f) camera
telecomunicazioni (f) telecommunications
trasmettere broadcast (v)
tubo (m) tube
valvola (f) rivelatrice detector
vettore (m) vector
videoregistratore (m) videocassette recorder (VCR)
volt (m) volt
voltaggio (m) voltage
vuoto (m) vacuum
watt (m) watt

Fashion—English to Italian

angora l'angora
blazer la giacca sportiva, il "blazer"
batiste la batista
belt la cintura
blouse la camicetta
bow tie la cravatta a farfalla
button il bottone
buttonhole l'occhiello, l'asola
cape il mantello
cashmere il cachemire
coat il cappotto
collar il colletto
color il colore
cuff link il gemello da camicia
cut (v) tagliare
design (v) disegnare
designer lo stilista, il "designer"
drape (v) drappeggiare
dress il vestito
elegance l'eleganza
fabric il tessuto
fashion la moda
fashionable alla moda
flannel la flanella
gabardine la gabardina
hem l'orlo
hood il cappuccio
jewel la gioiello
length la lunghezza
lingerie l'abbigliamento intimo
lining la foderatura
long sleeves le maniche lunghe
model il modello, il capo, la modella
muslin la mussola
needle l'ago
out of style fuori moda
pattern il modello
pleat la piega
pleated pieghettato
polyester il poliestirolo
poplin il popeline
print lo stampato
raincoat l'impermeabile
rayon il raion, la seta artificiale
ready-to-wear moda confezionata
scarf la sciarpa, il foulard
sew (v) cucire
sewing machine la macchina da cucire
shirt la camicia
shoe la scarpa
short sleeves le maniche corte
silk la seta
silkworm il baco di seta
silk factory il setificio
size il numero, la taglia
skirt la gonna
sleeve la manica
slacks i pantaloni, i calzoni
socks i calzini
sportswear l'abbigliamento sportivo
stitch il punto
stockings le calze
style lo stile
stylist lo stilista
suede lo scamosciato
suit l'abito
sweater il maglione
synthetic sintetico, artificiale
taffeta il taffetà
tailor il sarto
thread il filo
tie la cravatta
trousers i calzoni, i pantaloni
tuxedo l'abito da sera, lo smoking
veil il velo
vest il gilet
waist la vite
weaver il tessitore
width la larghezza, l'ampiezza
wool la lana
yarn il filato
zipper la cerniera lampo

Fashion—Italian to English

abbigliamento (m) intimo lingerie
abbigliamento sportivo sportswear
abito (m) suit
abito da sera tuxedo
ago (m) needle
alla moda fashionable
ampiezza (f) width
artificiale synthetic
asola (f) buttonhole
baco (m) di seta silkworm
batista (f) batiste
bottone (m) button
cachemire (m) cashmere
calze (f) stockings
calzini (m) socks
calzoni (m) slacks, trousers
camicetta (f) blouse
camicia (f) shirt
capo (m) model
cappotto (m) coat
cappuccio (m) hood
cerniera (f) lampo zipper
cintura (f) belt
colletto (m) collar
colore (m) color
cravatta (f) tie
cravatta a farfalla bow tie
cucire sew (v)
disegnare design (v)
drappeggiare drape (v)
eleganza (f) elegance
filato (m) yarn
filo (m) thread
flanella (f) flannel
foderatura (f) lining
foulard (m) scarf
fuori moda out of style
gabardina (f) gabardine
gemello (m) da camicia cuff link
giacca (f) sportiva blazer
gilet (m) vest
gioiello (f) jewel
gonna (f) skirt
impermeabile (m) raincoat
lana (f) wool
lana d'angora angora
larghezza (f) width
lunghezza (f) length
macchina (f) da cucire sewing machine
maglione (m) sweater
manica (f) sleeve
maniche (f) corte short sleeves
maniche lunghe long sleeves
mantello (m) cape
moda (f) fashion
moda confezionata ready-to-wear
modello/a (m/f) model, pattern
mussola (f) muslin
numero (m) size
occhiello (m) buttonhole
orlo (m) hem
pantaloni (m) slacks, trousers
piega (f) pleat
pieghettato pleated
poliestirolo (m) polyester
popeline (m) poplin
punto (m) stitch
raion (m) rayon
sarto (m) tailor
scamosciato (m) suede
scarpa (f) shoe
sciarpa (f) scarf
seta (f) silk
seta artificiale rayon
setificio (m) silk factory
sintetico synthetic
smoking (m) tuxedo
stampato (m) print
stile (m) style
stilista (m) designer, stylist
taffetà (m) taffeta
taglia (f) size
tagliare cut (v)
tessitore (m) weaver
tessuto (m) fabric
velo (m) veil
vestito (m) dress
vite (f) waist

Iron And Steel—English to Italian

alloy steel la lega d'acciaio
aluminum l'alluminio
annealing la ricottura
bars le barre
billets le billette
blast furnace l'altoforno
carbon steel l'acciaio al carbonio
cast iron il ferro fuso, la ghisa di seconda fusione
chromium il cromo
coal il carbone
coil la serpentina, la bobina
coke il coke
cold rolling la laminatura a freddo
conveyor il trasportatore
conveyor belt il trasportatore a cinghia
copper il rame
crucible il crogiuolo
cupola la cupola
electric arc furnace l'altoforno ad arco elettrico
electrodes gli elettrodi
electrolytic process la procedura elettrolitica
ferrite la ferrite
ferroalloys le leghe di ferro
ferromanganese il ferromanganese
ferronickel il ferronichel
finished products i prodotti finiti
finishing mill il laminatoio finitore
flat products i prodotti piatti
foundry la fonderia
furnace la fornace
galvanizing la galvanizzazione, la zincatura
grinding la molatura
heat il calore
hot rolling la laminatura a caldo
induction furnace il forno ad induzione
ingot mold la lingottiera
ingots i lingotti
iron ore il minerale ferroso
limestone il calce
malleability la malleabilità, la duttilità
manganese ore il minerale manganese
molybdenum il molibdeno
nickel il nichelio
nitrogen il nitrogeno
ore il minerale
pickling il decapaggio
pig iron la ghisa, la ghisa di prima fusione
pipes and tubes le condotte e i tubi
plate la lamiera, la piastra
powder la polvere
pressure la pressione
process la procedura
refractories i refrattari
rod l'asta, il ferro tondo
rolling mill il laminatoio
scale la scaglia, l'incrostatura
scrap i rottami
sheets le lastre
slabs le sbarre
specialty steels gli acciai con lavorazione particolare
stainless steel l'acciaio inossidabile
steel mill l'acciaieria
super alloys la superleghe
temper il rinvenimento
titanium il titanio
toughness la durezza
tungsten il tungstenio
vacuum melting furnace fornace per la colatura sotto vuoto
vanadium il vanadio
wire il filo metallico

Iron and Steel—Italian to English

acciai (m) con lavorazione particolare specialty steels
acciaieria (f) steel mill
acciaio (m) al carbonio carbon steel
acciaio inossidabile stainless steel
alluminio (m) aluminum
altoforno (m) blast furnace
altoforno ad arco elettrico electric arc furnace
asta (f) rod
barre (f) bars
billette (f) billets
bobina (f) coil
calce (m) limestone
calore (m) heat
carbone (m) coal
coke (m) coke
condotte (f) e tubi (m) pipes and tubes
crogiuolo (m) crucible
cromo (m) chromium
cupola (f) cupola
decapaggio (m) pickling
durezza (f) toughness
duttilità (f) malleability
elettrodi (m) electrodes
ferrite (f) ferrite
ferro (m) fuso cast iron
ferro tondo rod
ferromanganese (m) ferromanganese
ferronichel ferronickel
filo (m) metallico wire
fonderia (f) foundry
fornace (f) furnace
fornace per la colatura sotto vuoto vacuum melting furnace
forno (m) ad induzione induction furnace
galvanizzazione (f) galvanizing
ghisa (f) pig iron
ghisa di prima fusione pig iron
ghisa di seconda fusione cast iron
incrostatura (f) scale
lamiera (f) plate
laminatoio (m) rolling mill
laminatoio finitore finishing mill
laminatura a caldo (f) hot rolling
laminatura a freddo cold rolling
lastre (f) sheets
lega d'acciaio (f) alloy steel
leghe (f) di ferro ferroalloys
lingotti (m) ingots
lingottiera (f) ingot mold
malleabilità (f) malleability
minerale (m) ore
minerale ferroso iron ore
minerale manganese manganese ore
molatura (f) grinding
molibdeno (m) molybdenum
nichelio (m) nickel
nitrogeno (m) nitrogen
piastra (f) plate
polvere (f) powder
pressione (f) pressure
procedura (f) process
procedura elettrolitica electrolytic process
prodotti (m) finiti finished products
prodotti piatti flat products
rame (m) copper
refrattari (m) refractories
ricottura (f) annealing
rinvenimento (m) temper
rottami (m) scrap
sbarre (f) slabs
scaglia (f) scale
serpentina (f) coil
superleghe (f) super alloys
titanio (m) titanium
trasportatore (m) conveyor
trasportatore a cinghia conveyor belt
tungstenio (m) tungsten
vanadio (m) vanadium
zincatura (f) galvanizing

Leather Goods—English to Italian

ankle boots gli stivaletti
astrakan l'astrakan
attaché case la cartella
beaver il castoro
belt la cintura
billfold il portafogli
blotter il tampone di carta assorbente
boot shop la stivaleria
bootmaker lo stivalaio
boots gli stivali
briefcase la borsa documenti
calfskin il vitello
card case il portabiglietti
cigarette case il porta-sigarette
cowhide il cuoio
coyote il coyote
dye (v) tingere
eyeglass case il porta-occhiali
fitch la puzzola
fox la volpe
garment bag il portabiti
gloves i guanti
handbag la borsetta
holster la fondina
key case il portachiavi
kidskin il capretto
lamb l'agnello
leather la pelle
leather goods la pelletteria
leather jacket giubbotto di pelle
lizard skin la pelle di lucertola
lynx il lince
makeup case il portatrucco
manicuring kit il completo per la manicure
marmot la marmotta
mink il visone
Moroccan leather il marocchino
nutria il castorino
opossum l'opossum
ostrich skin la pelle di struzzo
otter la lontra
paper holder il portacarta
passport case il porta-passaporto
pigskin la pelle di cinghiale
pocketbook la borsetta
portfolio la cartella
purse la borsa
rabbit il coniglio
raccoon il procione lavoratore
sable lo zibellino
saddle la sella
saddler il sellaio
scissor case il porta forbici
sealskin la pelle di foca
slippers le pantofole
snakeskin la pelle di serpente
suede la pelle scamosciata
suede jacket il giubbotto di renna
suitcase la valigia
tan (v) conciare
tanner il conciatore
tannery la concia
tannin il tannino
trunk il baule
wallet il portafogli
watch strap il cinturino per orologio
whip la frusta

Leather Goods—Italian to English

agnello (m) lamb
astrakan (m) astrakan
baule (m) trunk
borsa (f) purse
borsa documenti briefcase
borsetta (f) handbag, pocketbook
capretto (m) kidskin
cartella (f) attaché case, portfolio
castorino (m) nutria
castoro (m) beaver
cintura (f) belt
cinturino (m) per orologio watch strap
completo (m) per la manicure manicuring kit
concia (f) tannery
conciare tan (v)
conciatore (m) tanner
coniglio (m) rabbit
coyote (m) coyote
cuoio (m) cowhide
fondina (f) holster
frusta (f) whip
giubbotto (m) di pelle leather jacket
giubbotto di renna suede jacket
guanti (m) gloves
lince (m) lynx
lontra (f) otter
marmotta (f) marmot
marocchino (m) Moroccan leather
opossum (m) opossum
pantofole (f) slippers
pelle (f) leather
pelle di cinghiale pigskin
pelle di foca sealskin
pelle di lucertola lizard skin
pelle di serpente snakeskin
pelle di struzzo ostrich skin
pelle scamosciata suede
pelletteria (f) leather goods
portabiti (m) garment bag
portabiglietti (m) card case
portacarta (m) paper holder
portachiavi (m) key case
portaforbici (m) scissor case
portaocchiali (m) eyeglass case
portapassaporto (m) passport case
portasigarette (m) cigarette case
portatrucco (m) makeup case
portafogli (m) billfold, wallet
procione (m) lavoratore raccoon
puzzola (f) fitch
sella (f) saddle
sellaio (m) saddler
stivalaio (m) bootmaker
stivaleria (f) boot shop
stivaletti (m) ankle boots
stivali (m) boots
tampone (m) di carta assorbente (m) blotter
tannino (m) tannin
tingere dye (v)
valigia (f) suitcase
visone (m) mink
vitello (m) calfskin
volpe (f) fox
zibellino (m) sable

Motor Vehicles—English to Italian

air filter il filtro dell'aria
alternator l'alternatore
assembly line la linea di montaggio
automatic gearshift il cambio automatico
automobile l'automobile
automotive worker l'operaio
battery la batteria
belt la cinghia
body il telaio
brake il freno
bumper il paraurti
camshaft l'albero di distribuzione a camme
car la macchina
carburetor il carburatore
chassis la carrozzeria
clutch la frizione
connecting rod la biella
crankshaft l'albero a gomito
cylinder il cilindro
dashboard il cruscotto
defroster lo sbrinatore
designer lo stilista
diesel il diesel
disc il disco
displacement la cilindrata
distributor il distributore
driver l'autista
engine il motore
engineer l'ingegnere
exhaust lo scarico, lo scappamento
fender il parafango
front-wheel drive la trazione anteriore
gas consumption il consumo di benzina
gas pedal l'acceleratore
gasoline la benzina
gasoline tank il serbatoio della benzina
gearshift il cambio
generator il generatore
grille la cuffia del radiatore
horsepower la potenza in cavalli
ignition l'accensione
injector l'iniettore
inspection l'ispezione
mechanic il meccanico
mileage il chilometraggio
model il modello
odometer il contachilometri
oil filter il filtro dell'olio
oil pump la pompa dell'olio
paint la vernice
pinion il pignone, il rocchetto
piston il pistone
power steering il servosterzo
propulsion la propulsione
prototype il prototipo
radial tire il pneumatico radiale
rear axle l'asse posteriore
ring l'anello
robot il robot
seat il sedile
seatbelt la cintura di sicurezza
sedan la berlina
shock absorber gli ammortizzanti
spare tire la ruota di scorta
spark plug la candela
speedometer l'indicatore di velocità
spring la molla
starter il motorino d'avviamento
steering la guida
steering wheel lo sterzo, il volante
suspension la sospensione
tire il pneumatico
torque la forza di torsione
valve la valvola
water pump la pompa dell'acqua
wheel la ruota
windshield il parabrezza

Motor Vehicles—Italian to English

acceleratore (m) gas pedal
accensione (f) ignition
filtro dell'aria (m) air filter
albero (m) a gomito crankshaft
albero di distribuzione a camme camshaft
alternatore (m) alternator
ammortizzatore (m) shock absorber
anello (m) ring
asse (m) posteriore rear axle
autista (m) driver
automobile (f) automobile
batteria (f) battery
benzina (f) gasoline
berlina (f) sedan
biella (f) connecting rod
cambio (m) gearshift
cambio automatico automatic gearshift
candela (f) spark plug
carburatore (m) carburetor
carrozzeria (f) chassis
chilometraggio (m) mileage
modello (m) model
cilindrata displacement
cilindro (m) cylinder
cinghia (f) belt
cintura (f) di sicurezza seatbelt
consumo (m) di benzina gas consumption
contachilometri (m) odometer
cruscotto (m) dashboard
cuffia (f) del radiatore grille
diesel (m) diesel
disco (m) disc
distributore (m) distributor
filtro (m) dell'olio oil filter
forza (f) di torsione torque
freno (m) brake
frizione (f) clutch
generatore (m) generator
guida (f) steering
indicatore (m) di velocità speedometer
ingegnere (m) engineer
iniettore (m) injector
ispezione (f) inspection
linea (f) di montaggio assembly line
macchina (f) car
meccanico (m) mechanic
molla (f) spring
motore (m) engine
motorino (m) d'avviamento starter
operaio/a (m/f) automotive worker
parabrezza (m) windshield
parafango (m) fender
paraurti (m) bumper
pignone (m) pinion
pistone (m) piston
pneumatico (m) tire
pneumatico radiale radial tire
pompa (f) dell'acqua water pump
pompa dell'olio oil pump
potenza (f) in cavalli horsepower
propulsione (f) propulsion
prototipo (m) prototype
robot (m) robot
rocchetto (m) pinion
ruota (f) wheel
ruota di scorta spare tire
sbrinatore (m) defroster
scappamento (m) exhaust
scarico (m) exhaust
sedile (m) seat
serbatoio (m) della benzina gasoline tank
servosterzo (m) power steering
sospensione (f) suspension
sterzo (m) steering wheel
stilista (m) designer
telaio (m) body
trazione (f) anteriore front-wheel drive
valvola (f) valve
vernice (f) paint
volante (m) steering wheel

Pharmaceuticals—English to Italian

alcohol l'alcool
allergy l'allergia
amphetamine l'anfetamina
anaesthetic l'anestetico
analgesic l'analgesico
antacid l'antacido
anti-inflammatory l'antiflogistico
antibiotic l'antibiotico
anticoagulant l'anticoagulante
antidepressant l'antidepressivo
antiseptic l'asettico
aspirin l'aspirina
barbiturates i barbiturici
bleed (v) sanguinare
blood il sangue
botanic botanico
calcium il calcio
capsule la capsula
compounds i composti
content il contenuto
cortisone il cortisone
cough (v) tossire
cough drop la pastiglia per la tosse
cough syrup lo sciroppo per la tosse
crude grezzo
density la densità
diabetes il diabete
digitalis il digitalis
disease la malattia
diuretic il diuretico
dose la dose
drop la goccia
drug il farmaco, la droga
drugstore la farmacia
eyedrop il collirio
hexachlorophene l'esaclorofene
hormone l'ormone
hypertension l'ipertensione
injection l'iniezione, la puntura
insulin l'insulina
iodine lo iodio
iron il ferro
laboratory technician il tecnico del laboratorio
laxative il lassativo, il purgante
medicine la medicina
morphine la morfina
narcotic il narcotico
nitrate il nitrato
nitrite il nitrite
ointment l'unguento
opium l'oppio
organic organico
pellet la pallottolina
penicillin la penicillina
pharmacist il farmacista
phenol il fenolo
physician il medico
pill la pillola
plants le piante
purgative il purgante
remedies i rimedi
saccharin la saccarina
salts i sali
salve l'unguento, la pomata
sedative il calmante
serum il siero
sinus la fistola
sinusitis la sinusite
sleeping pill il sonnifero
sneeze (v) starnutire
starch l'amido
stimulant lo stimolante
sulphamide il sulfamide
synthesis la sintesi
syringe la siringa
tablet la compressa, la pastiglia
thermometer il termometro
toxicology la tossicologia
toxin la tossina
tranquilizer il tranquillante
vaccine il vaccino
vitamin la vitamina
zinc lo zinco

Pharmaceuticals—Italian to English

alcool (m) alcohol
allergia (f) allergy
anfetamina (m) amphetamine
amido (m) starch
analgesico (m) analgesic
anestetico (m) anaesthetic
antacido (m) antacid
antibiotico (m) antibiotic
anticoagulante (m) anticoagulant
antidepressivo (m) antidepressant
antiflogistico (m) anti-inflammatory
asettico (m) antiseptic
aspirina (f) aspirin
barbiturici (m) barbiturates
botanico botanic
calcio (m) calcium
calmante (m) sedative
capsula (f) capsule
collirio (m) eyedrop
composti (m) compounds
compressa (f) tablet
contenuto (m) content
cortisone (m) cortisone
cura (f) medication
densità (f) density
diabete (m) diabetes
digitalis (m) digitalis
diuretico (m) diuretic
dose (f) dose
droga (m) drug
esaclorofene (m/f) hexachlorophene
farmacia (f) drugstore
farmacista (m/f) pharmacist
farmaco (m) drug
fenolo (m) phenol
ferro (m) iron
fistola (f) sinus
goccia (f) drop
grezzo crude
iniezione (f) injection
insulina (f) insulin
iodio (m) iodine
ipertensione (f) hypertension
lassativo (m) laxative
malattia (f) disease
medicina (f) medicine
medico (m) physician
morfina (f) morphine
narcotico (m) narcotic
nitrato (m) nitrate
nitrite (m) nitrite
oppio (m/f) opium
organico organic
ormone (m) hormone
pallottolina (f) pellet
pastiglia (f) tablet
pastiglia per la tosse cough drop
penicillina penicillin
piante (f) plants
pillola (f) pill
pomata (f) salve
puntura (f) injection
purgante (m) laxative, purgative
rimedi (m) remedies
saccarina (f) saccharin
sali (m) salts
sangue (m) blood
sanguinare bleed (v)
sciroppo (m) per la tosse cough syrup
siero (m) serum
sintesi (f) synthesis
sinusite (f) sinusitis
siringa (f) syringe
sonnifero (m) sleeping pill
starnutire sneeze (v)
stimolante (m) stimulant
sulfamide (m) sulphamide
tecnico (m) del laboratorio laboratory technician
tossicologia (f) toxicology
tossina (f) toxin
tossire cough (v)
tranquillante (m) tranquilizer
unguento (m) salve, ointment
vaccino (m) vaccine
vitamina (f) vitamin
zinco (m) zinc

Printing and Publishing— English to Italian

black and white il bianco e nero
bleed la pagina al vivo, smarginato
blowup la gigantografia, l'ingrandimento
boldface il neretto
book il libro
capital il maiuscolo
chapter il capitolo
coated paper la carta patinata
color separation la separazione dei colori
copy il materiale scritto
copyright i diritti d'autore
cover la copertina
crop (v) rifilare
dummy il menabò
edit (v) redigere
edition il numero
editor il redattore
engrave (v) incidere
font la seriecompleta di caratteri
form la forma
format il formato
four colors quattro colori
galley proof la bozza in colonna
glossy lucido
grain la grana
grid la quadrettatura
hardcover la copertina a tela, la legatura cartonata
headline il titolo
illustration l'illustrazione
on press in stampa
inch il pollice
ink l'inchiostro
insert il volantino
introduction la premessa
italic il corsivo
jacket la copertina di libro, la sopraccoperta
justify (v) giustificare
layout la disposizione di una pagina
letterpress la parte stampata
line la linea
line drawing il disegno
lower case il minuscolo
matrix la matrice
matt non lucido, opaco
mechanical il montaggio
negative il negativo
newsprint la carta da giornale
overrun superare la giustezza
packing l'imballo
page la pagina
page makeup la composizione della pagina
pagination l'impaginazione
pamphlet l'opuscolo
paper la carta
paperback in brossura
pigment il colore, il pigmento
plate la lastra
point il punto tipografico
positive il positivo
preface la prefazione
press book l'ultima bozza
printing la stampatura
printing shop la tipografia
proofreading la correzione delle bozza
publisher l'editore
ream la risma
register il registro
scanner l'analizzatore di immagini, il "scanner"
scoring la raschiatura
screen il retino
sewn rilegato
sheet il foglio
signature la firma
size il formato
soft cover la copertina flessibile
spine il dorso
table of contents l'indice
title il titolo
web offset press la macchina da stampa offset a bobina

Printing and Publishing—Italian to English

analizzatore (m) di immagini scanner
bianco e nero (m) black and white
bozza (f) in colonna galley proof
capitolo chapter
carta (f) paper
carta da giornale newsprint
carta patinata coated paper
colore (m) pigment
composizione della pagina page makeup
copertina (f) cover
copertina a tela hardcover
copertina di libro jacket
copertina flessibile soft cover
copiare copy (v)
correzione (f) delle bozza proofreading
corsivo (m) italic
diritti (m) d'autore copyright
disegno (m) line drawing
disposizione (f) di una pagina layout
dorso (m) spine
editore/trice (m/f) publisher
foglio (m) sheet
forma (f) form
formato (m) size, format
gigantografia (f) blowup
giustificare justify (v)
grana (f) grain
illustrazione (f) illustration
imballo (m) packing
impaginazione (f) pagination
in brossura paperback
in stampa on press
inchiostro (m) ink
incidere engrave (v)
indice (m) table of contents
ingrandimento (m) blowup
lastra (f) plate
legatura cartonata (f) hardcover
libro (m) book
linea (f) line
lucido glossy
macchina (f) da stampa offset a bobina web offset press
maiuscolo (m) capital
materiale scritto (m) copy
matrice (f) matrix
menabò (m) dummy
minuscolo (m) lower case
montaggio (m) mechanical
negativo (m) negative
neretto (m) boldface
non lucido matt
numero (m) edition
opaco matt
opuscolo (m) pamphlet
pagina (f) page
pagina al vivo bleed
parte (f) stampata letterpress
pigmento (m) pigment
pollice (m) inch
positivo (m) positive
prefazione (f) preface
premessa (m) introduction
punto (m) tipografico point
quadrettatura (f) grid
quattro colori four colors
raschiatura (f) scoring
redattore (m) editor
redigere edit (v)
registro (m) register
retino (m) screen
rifilare crop (v)
rilegato sewn
risma (f) ream
segnatura (f) signature
separazione (f) dei colore color separation
seriecompleta (f) di caratteri font
smarginato bleed
sopraccoperta (f) jacket
stampatura (f) printing
superare (f) giustezza overrun
tipografia (f) printing shop
titolo (m) headline, title
ultima bozza (f) press book
volantino (m) insert

Winemaking—English to Italian

acid content l'acidità
acre l'acro
aging l'invecchiamento
alcohol l'alcool
alcoholic content il contenuto alcolico
area of origin guaranteed la denominazione di origine controllata (D.O.C.)
blend (v) tagliare
body il corpo
bottle (usually 75 centiliters) la bottiglia
bouquet il naso, il bouquet
case la cassa
cask (225 liters) il barile
centiliter centilitro
climate il clima
cooper il bottaio
cork il tappo
corkscrew il cavatappi
country il paese
dregs i rimasugli
drink la bevanda
dry wine il vino secco
estate (or chateau) la fattoria
estate bottled imbottigliato all'origine
ferment (v) fermentare
fruity fruttato
grape l'uva
grape bunch il grappolo d'uva
grape harvest la vendemmia
hectare l'ettaro
juice il succo
label l'etichetta
liqueur il liquore
liter il litro
magnum (2 bottles in one) il bottiglione da due litri
malolactic fermentation la fermentazione malolattica
must il mosto
neck (of bottle) il collo
pasteurized pastorizzato
production la produzione
ripe maturo
skin la buccia
sour agro
sparkling wine il vino spumante
sugar content il contenuto zuccherino
table wine il vino da tavola
tannin il tannino
tasting (wine tasting) la degustazione
temperature la temperatura
type of vine il vitigno
unfermented grape juice il succo d'uva non fermentato
vat il tino, la tinozza
vine la vigna
vineyard il vigneto
vintage la vendemmia
vintage year l'annata
vintner il vinaio
vintry la cantina
wine il vino
wine cellar la cantina, l'enoteca
wine cooperative la cooperativa vinicola
winegrower il viticultore
winepress il torchio da vino
wine steward l'enologo, il sommelier
wine growing areas le zone di coltivazione delle vigne
yeast il lievito
yield la resa

Winemaking—Italian to English

acidità (f) acid content
acro (m) acre
agro sour
alcool (m) alcohol
annata (f) vintage year
barile (m) cask (225 liters)
bevanda drink
bottaio (m) cooper
bottiglia (f) bottle (usually 75 centiliters)
bottiglione da due litri (m) magnum (2 bottles in one)
bouquet (m) bouquet
buccia (f) skin
cantina (f) wine cellar
cassa (f) case
cavatappi (m) corkscrew
centilitro (m) centiliter
clima (m) climate
collo (m) neck (of bottle)
contenuto (m) alcolico alcoholic content
contenuto zuccherino sugar content
cooperativa (f) vinicola wine cooperative
corpo (m) body
degustazione (f) tasting (wine tasting)
denominazione di origine controllata (D.O.C.) (f) area of origin guaranteed
enologo (m) wine steward
enoteca (f) wine cellar
ettaro (m) hectare
etichetta (f) label
fattoria (f) estate (or chateau)
fermentare ferment (v)
fermentazione malolattica (f) malolactic fermentation
fruttato fruity
grappolo d'uva (m) grape bunch
imbottigliato all'origine estate bottled
invecchiamento (m) aging
lievito (f) yeast
liquore (m) liqueur
litro (m) liter
maturo ripe
mosto (m) must
naso (m) bouquet
paese (m) country
pastorizzato pasteurized
produzione (f) production
resa (f) yield
rimasugli (m) dregs
sommelier (m) wine steward
succo (m) juice
succo d'uva non fermentato unfermented grape juice
tagliare blend (v)
tannino (m) tannin
tappo (m) cork
temperatura (f) temperature
tino (m) vat
tinozza (f) vat
torchio da vino (m) winepress
uva (m) grape
vendemmia (f) grape harvest, vintage
vigna (f) vine
vigneto (m) vineyard
vinaio (m) vintner
vino (m) wine
vino da tavola table wine
vino secco dry wine
vino spumante sparkling wine
viticultore (m) winegrower
vitigno (m) type of vine
zone (f) di coltivazione delle vigne wine growing areas

Agriculture, Industry and Resources

The economic map of Italy will give you a good idea of Italian industrial geography.

MAJOR MINERAL OCCURRENCES

Ab	Asbestos	Mr	Marble
Al	Bauxite	Na	Salt
C	Coal	O	Petroleum
Fe	Iron Ore	Pb	Lead
G	Natural Gas	Py	Pyrites
Hg	Mercury	S	Sulfur
K	Potash	Sb	Antimony
Lg	Lignite	Zn	Zinc
ϟ	Water Power	//////	Major Industrial Areas

Copyright Permission:
Hammond Incorporated,
Maplewood, New Jersey

GENERAL INFORMATION

ABBREVIATIONS

a.a. always afloat
a.a.r. against all risks
a/c account
A/C account current
acct. account
a.c.v. actual cash value
a.d. after date
a.f.b. air freight bill
agcy. agency
agt. agent
a.m.t. air mail transfer
a/o account of
A.P. accounts payable
A/P authority to pay
approx. approximately
A.R. accounts receivable
a/r all risks
A/S, A.S. account sales
a/s at sight
at. wt. atomic weight
av. average
avdp. avoirdupois
a/w actual weight
a.w.b. air waybill

bal. balance
bar. barrel
bbl. barrel
b/d brought down
B/E, b/e bill of exchange
b/f brought forward
B.H. bill of health
bk. bank
bkge. brokerage
B/L bill of lading
b/o brought over
B.P. bills payable
b.p. by procuration
B.R. bills receivable
B/S balance sheet
b.t. berth terms
bu. bushel
B/V book value

ca. circa; centaire
C.A. chartered accountant
c.a. current account
C.A.D. cash against documents
C.B. cash book
C.B.D. cash before delivery
c.c. carbon copy
c/d carried down
c.d. cum dividend
c/f carried forward
cf. compare
c & f cost and freight
C/H clearing house
C.H. custom house
ch. fwd. charges forward
ch. pd. charges paid
ch. ppd. charges prepaid
chq. check, cheque
c.i.f. cost, insurance, freight
c.i.f. & c. cost, insurance, freight, and commission
c.i.f. & e. cost, insurance, freight, and exchange
c.i.f. & i. cost, insurance, freight, and interest
c.l. car load
C/m call of more
C/N credit note
c/o care of
co. company
C.O.D. cash on delivery
comm. commission
corp. corporation
C.O.S. cash on shipment
C.P. carriage paid
C/P charter party
c.p.d. charters pay duties
cpn. corporation
cr. credit; creditor
C/T cable transfer

c.t.l. constructive total loss
c.t.l.o. constructive total loss only
cum. cumulative
cum div. cum dividend
cum. pref. cumulative preference
c/w commercial weight
C.W.O. cash with order
cwt. hundredweight

D/A documents against acceptance; deposit account
DAP documents against payment
db. debenture
DCF discounted cash flow
d/d days after date; delivered
deb. debenture
def. deferred
dept. department
d.f. dead freight
dft. draft
dft/a. draft attached
dft/c. clean draft
disc. discount
div. dividend
DL dayletter
DLT daily letter telegram
D/N debit note
D/O delivery order
do. ditto
doz. dozen
D/P documents against payment
dr. debtor
Dr. doctor
d/s, d.s. days after sight
d.w. deadweight
D/W dock warrant
dwt. pennyweight
dz. dozen

ECU European Currency Unit
E.E.T. East European Time
e.g. for example
encl. enclosure
end. endorsement
E. & O.E. errors and omissions excepted
e.o.m. end of month
e.o.h.p. except otherwise herein provided
esp. especially
Esq. Esquire
est. established
ex out
ex cp. ex coupon
ex div. ex dividend
ex int. ex interest
ex h. ex new (shares)
ex stre. ex store
ex whf. ex wharf

f.a.a. free of all average
f.a.c. fast as can
f.a.k. freight all kinds
f.a.q. fair average quality; free alongside quay
f.a.s. free alongside ship
f/c for cash
f.c. & s. free of capture and seizure
f.c.s.r. & c.c. free of capture, seizure, riots, and civil commotion
F.D. free delivery to dock
f.d. free discharge
ff. following; folios
f.g.a. free of general average
f.i.b. free in bunker
f.i.o. free in and out
f.i.t. free in truck
f.o.b. free on board
f.o.c. free of charge
f.o.d. free of damage
fol. following; folio
f.o.q. free on quay
f.o.r. free on rail
f.o.s. free on steamer
f.o.t. free on truck(s)
f.o.w. free on wagons; free on wharf
F.P. floating policy
f.p. fully paid
f.p.a. free of particular average
frt. freight
frt. pd. freight paid

frt. ppd. freight prepaid
frt. fwd. freight forward
ft. foot
fwd. forward
f.x. foreign exchange

g.a. general average
g.b.o. goods in bad order
g.m.b. good merchantable brand
g.m.q. good merchantable quality
G.M.T. Greenwich Mean Time
GNP gross national product
g.o.b. good ordinary brand
gr. gross
GRT gross register ton
gr. wt. gross weight
GT gross tonnage

h.c. home consumption
hgt. height
hhd. hogshead
H.O. head office
H.P. hire purchase
HP horsepower
ht. height

IDP integrated data processing
i.e. that is
I/F insufficient funds
i.h.p. indicated horsepower
imp. import
Inc. incorporated
incl. inclusive
ins. insurance
int. interest
inv. invoice
I.O.U. I owe you

J/A, j.a. joint account
Jr. junior

KV kilovolt
KW kilowatt
KWh kilowatt hour

L/C, l.c. letter of credit
LCD telegram in the language of the country of destination
LCO telegram in the language of the country of origin
ldg. landing; loading
l.t. long ton
Ltd. limited
l. tn. long ton

m. month
m/a my account
max. maximum
M.D. memorandum of deposit
M/D, m.d. months after date
memo. memorandum
Messrs. plural of Mr.
mfr. manufacturer
min. minimum
MLR minimum lending rate
M.O. money order
m.o. my order
mortg. mortgage
M/P, m.p. months after payment
M/R mate's receipt
M/S, m.s. months' sight
M.T. mail transfer
M/U making-up price

n. name; nominal
n/a no account
N/A no advice
n.c.v. no commercial value
n.d. no date
n.e.s. not elsewhere specified
N/F no funds
NL night letter
N/N no noting
N/O no orders
no. number
n.o.e. not otherwise enumerated
n.o.s. not otherwise stated
nos. numbers
NPV no par value
nr. number
n.r.t. net register ton
N/S not sufficient funds
NSF not sufficient funds
n. wt. net weight

o/a on account
OCP overseas common point
O/D, o/d on demand; overdraft
o.e. omissions excepted
o/h overhead
ono. or nearest offer
O/o order of
O.P. open policy
o.p. out of print; overproof
O/R, o.r. owner's risk
ord. order; ordinary
O.S., o/s out of stock
OT overtime

p. page; per; premium
P.A., p.a. particular average; per annum
P/A power of attorney; private account
PAL phase alternation line
pat. pend. patent pending
PAYE pay as you earn
p/c petty cash
p.c. percent; price current
pcl. parcel
pd. paid
pf. preferred
pfd. preferred
pkg. package
P/L profit and loss
p.l. partial loss
P/N promissory note
P.O. post office; postal order
P.O.B. post office box
P.O.O. post office order
p.o.r. pay on return
pp. pages
p & p postage and packing
p. pro per procuration
ppd. prepaid
ppt. prompt
pref. preference
prox. proximo
P.S. postscript
pt. payment
P.T.O., p.t.o. please turn over
ptly. pd. partly paid
p.v. par value

qlty. quality
qty. quantity

r. & c.c. riot and civil commotions
R/D refer to drawer
R.D.C. running down clause
re in regard to
rec. received; receipt
recd. received
red. redeemable
ref. reference
reg. registered
retd. returned
rev. revenue
R.O.D. refused on delivery
R.P. reply paid
r.p.s. revolutions per second
RSVP please reply
R.S.W.C. right side up with care
Ry railway

s.a.e. stamped addressed envelope
S.A.V. stock at valuation
S/D sea damaged
S/D, s.d. sight draft
s.d. without date
SDR special drawing rights
sgd. signed
s. & h. ex Sundays and holidays excepted
shipt. shipment
sig. signature
S/LC, s. & l.c. sue and labor clause
S/N shipping note
s.o. seller's option
s.o.p. standard operating procedure
spt. spot
Sr. senior
S.S., s.s. steamship
s.t. short ton
ster. sterling
St. Ex. stock exchange
stg. sterling
s.v. sub voce

T.A. telegraphic address

T.B. trial balance
tel. telephone
temp. temporary secretary
T.L., t.l. total loss
T.L.O. total loss only
TM multiple telegram
T.O. turn over
tr. transfer
TR telegram to be called for
TR, T/R trust receipt
TT, T.T. telegraphic transfer (cable)
TX Telex

UGT urgent
u.s.c. under separate cover
U/ws underwriters

v. volt
val. value
v.a.t. value-added tax
v.g. very good
VHF very high frequency
v.h.r. very highly recommended
w. watt
WA with average
W.B. way bill
w.c. without charge
W.E.T. West European Time
wg. weight guaranteed
whse. warehouse
w.o.g. with other goods
W.P. weather permitting; without prejudice
w.p.a. with particular average
W.R. war risk
W/R, wr. warehouse receipt
W.W.D. weather working day
wt. weight

x.c. ex coupon
x.d. ex dividend
x.i. ex interest
x.n. ex new shares

y. year
yd. yard
yr. year
yrly. yearly

WEIGHTS AND MEASURES

U.S. UNIT	METRIC EQUIVALENT
mile	1.609 kilometers
yard	0.914 meters
foot	30.480 centimeters
inch	2.540 centimeters
square mile	2.590 square kilometers
acre	0.405 hectares
square yard	0.836 square meters
square foot	0.093 square meters
square inch	6.451 square centimeters
cubic yard	0.765 cubic meters
cubic foot	0.028 cubic meters
cubic inch	16.387 cubic centimeters
short ton	0.907 metric tons
long ton	1.016 metric tons
short hundredweight	45.359 kilograms
long hundredweight	50.802 kilograms
pound	0.453 kilograms
ounce	28.349 grams

U.S. UNIT	METRIC EQUIVALENT
gallon	3.785 liters
quart	0.946 liters
pint	0.473 liters
fluid ounce	29.573 milliliters
bushel	35.238 liters
peck	8.809 liters
quart	1.101 liters
pint	0.550 liters

TEMPERATURE AND CLIMATE

Temperature Conversion Chart

DEGREES CELSIUS	DEGREES FAHRENHEIT
−5	23
0	32
5	41
10	50
15	59
20	68
25	77
30	86
35	95
40	104

Average Temperatures for Major Cities

	JAN	APR	JULY	OCT
Paris	37°F (3°C)	60°F (15°C)	77°F (15°C)	60°F (15°C)
Bordeaux	45°F (7°C)	61°F (16°C)	77°F (25°C)	63°F (17°C)
Marseille	46°F (8°C)	63°F (17°C)	80°F (27°C)	66°F (18°C)
Geneva	38°F (4°C)	58°F (15°C)	68°F (20°C)	58°F (15°C)
Brussels	38°F (4°C)	55°F (13°C)	72°F (21°C)	58°F (15°C)

Spring	primavera
Summer	estate
Autumn	autunno
Winter	inverno
Hot, warm	caldo
Sunny	sole
Cool	fresco
Wind	vento
Fog	nebbia
It's snowing	nevica
It's raining	piove

COMMUNICATIONS CODES

Telephone

telephone booth	cabina telefonica
public phone	telefono pubblico
telephone directory	elenco telefonico
long-distance call	telefonata in teleselezione
local call	telefonata urbana
person-to-person call	telefonata diretta con preavviso
tokens	gettoni
operator	telefonista
the line is busy	la linea è occupata
dial a number	formare un numero

For most calls from a public booth, you need to use a special 100-lire token *(gettoni)*.

Area Codes in Italy

Florence	055	Rome	06
Genoa	010	Turin	011
Milan	02	Venice	041
Naples	081		

International Country Codes

Algeria	213	Malta	356
Argentina	54	Mexico	52
Australia	61	Morocco	212
Austria	43	Netherlands	31
Belgium	32	New Zealand	64
Brazil	55	Norway	67
Canada	1	Philippines	63
Chile	56	Poland	48
Colombia	57	Portugal	351
Denmark	45	Saudi Arabia	966
Finland	358	Singapore	65
France	33	South Africa	27
Germany (West)	37	South Korea	82
Germany (East)	49	Spain	34
Gibraltar	350	Sri Lanka	94
Greece	30	Sweden	46
Hong Kong	852	Switzerland	41
Hungary	36	Taiwan	886
Iceland	354	Thailand	255
India	91	Tunisia	216
Ireland	353	Turkey	90
Israel	972	United Kingdom	44
Italy	39	USA	1
Japan	81	USSR	7
Kuwait	965	Venezuela	58
Luxembourg	352	Yugoslavia	38

POSTAL SERVICES

In Italy

The Italian postal service is not always reliable and mail is often delayed. For business correspondence, you are advised to use telex and special delivery services. All post offices are open from 8 A.M. to 2 P.M., while in the cities the central post offices are usually open 8 A.M. to 4 P.M. Stamps can also be bought at tobacconists. Central post offices also offer telephone and telegraph services.

In Rome, the main post office (open 24 hours) is at Piazza San Silvestro 00187. In Milan, the main post office (open 8 A.M. to 8 P.M.) is at Piazza Cordusio 20123.

In Switzerland

The postal service is highly efficient and delivery of regular mail ordinarily takes one day. Post offices are open from 7:30 A.M. to noon and 1:30 P.M. to 6:30 P.M., Monday through Friday; 9:30 to 11 A.M. on Saturday. Facilities offer postal, telephone, and telegram service. In Geneva, the office at rue de Lausanne is open from 6:30 A.M. to 11 P.M., every day.

TIME ZONES

Use the following table to know the time difference between where you are and other major cities. Note, however, that during April through September, you will also have to take Daylight Savings Time into account. Since there are four time zones for the United States, eleven zones for the U.S.S.R., and three for Australia, we've listed major cities for these countries.

Note that in most parts of the world, official time is based on the 24-hour clock. Train schedules and other official documents will use 13:00 through 23:00 to express the PM hours.

1PM = 13.00 le tredici (leh trEH-dee-chee)
1.30PM = 13.30 le tredici e trenta (leh trEH-dee-chee ay trEHn-tah)
2PM = 14.00 le quattordici (leh koo-aht-tOHr-dee-chee)
3PM = 15.00 le quindici (leh koo-EEn-dee-chee)
4PM = 16.00 le sedici (leh sAY-dee-chee)
5PM = 17.00 le diciasette (leh dee-chee-ahs-sEHt-teh)
6PM = 18.00 le diciotto (leh dee-chee-OHt-toh)
7PM = 19.00 le diciannove (leh dee-chee-ahn-nOH-veh)
8PM = 20.00 le venti (leh vAYn-tee)
9PM = 21.00 le ventuno (leh vayn-tOO-noh)
10PM = 22.00 le ventidue (leh vayn-tee-dOO-eh)
11PM = 23.00 le ventitrè (leh vayn-tee-trEH)
midnight = mezzanote (meh-tsah-nOHt-teh)

−8 HOURS	−6 HOURS	−5 HOURS	GREEN-WICH MEAN TIME	+1 HOUR	+2 HOURS	+3 HOURS	+ADDITIONAL HOURS
Los Angeles San Francisco	Chicago Dallas Houston	Boston New York Washington, D.C.	Great Britain Iceland Ireland Portugal	Austria Belgium Denmark France Germany Hungary Italy Luxembourg Malta Monaco Netherlands Norway Poland Spain Sweden Switzerland Yugoslavia	Finland Greece Romania South Africa	Turkey Moscow	Sydney (10 hours) New Zealand (12 hours)

MAJOR HOLIDAYS

January 1	New Year's Day	Capodanno
March 31	National Day (Malta)	Festa Nazzionale
April 25	Liberation Day	Festa della Resistenza
May 1	Labor Day	Festa del Lavoro
August 1	National Day (in most Swiss cantons)	Festa Nazzionale
August 15	Assumption Day	Assunzione
November 1	All Saints Day	Ognissanti
December 8	Immaculate Conception	Immacolata Concezione
December 13	Republic Day (Malta)	Festa della Repubblica
December 25	Christmas	Natale
December 26	St. Stephen's Day	Santo Stefano
March–April	Good Friday (Malta)	Venerdi Santo
	Easter Monday	Lunedì dopo Pasqua

The following saints' days are celebrated in these cities:

April 25	San Marco (Venice)
June 24	San Giovanni Battista (Florence, Genoa, Turin)
June 29	Santi Pietro e Paolo (Rome)
September 19	San Gennaro (Naples)
December 17	Sant'Ambrogio (Milan)

CURRENCY INFORMATION

Major Currencies of the World

Andorra	French Franc
Argentina	Argentinian Peso
Austria	Schilling
Belgium	Belgian Franc
Colombia	Colombian Peso
Denmark	Danish Krone
Finland	Finmark
France	Franc
Germany (West)	Mark (DM)
Germany (East)	Mark (M)
Greece	Drachma
Hungary	Forint
Iceland	Krone
Ireland	Punt
Italy	Lira
Liechtenstein	Swiss Franc

Luxembourg	Luxembourg Franc
Malta	Maltese Lira
Monaco	French Franc
Mexico	Mexican Peso
Monaco	French Franc
Netherlands	Guilder
Norway	Norwegian Krone
Peru	Sol
Portugal	Escudo
Puerto Rico	U.S. Dollar
Spain	Peseta
Sweden	Swedish Krone
Switzerland	Swiss Franc
Turkey	Lira
United Kingdom	Pound Sterling
Uruguay	Uruguayan Peso
USSR	Ruble
Venezuela	Bolivar
Yugoslavia	Dinar

Major Commercial Banks

In Italy

Banca Nazionale del Lavoro
Via Vittorio Veneto 119
00187 Rome

Banco di Roma
Via del Corso 307
00186 Rome

Credito Italiano
Piazza Cordusio
20123 Milan

Cariplo
Cassa di Risparmio delle Provincie Lombarde
Via Monte di Pietà 8
20121 Milan

In Switzerland

Union Bank of Switzerland (UBS)
Bahnhofstrasse 45
Postfach
CH-8021 Zurich

Swiss Bank Corporation
Postfach
CH-4002 Basle

Credit Suisse
Paradeplatz 8
Postfach
CH-8021 Zurich

MAJOR PERIODICALS

The *International Herald Tribune* is the leading English-language newspaper sold in Europe. It is available at most hotels and newsstands. The *Journal of Commerce* is also available at some stands.

In Italy

Newspapers

Avanti!
Corriere della Sera
Daily American
Il Giorno
Il Mattino
Il Messaggero

La Nazione
La Notte
L'Osservatore Romano
Paese Sera
Il Popolo
La Repubblica
Il Resto del Carlino
Il Sole - 24 Ore
La Stampa
L'Unità

Magazines

L'Espresso
Panorama

In Switzerland

Newspapers

Neue Zuercher Zeitung
Schweiz. Handelszeitung
Finanz und Wirtschaft
La Tribune de Genève

(All major business newspapers in Switzerland are in German or French.)

ANNUAL TRADE FAIRS

This is a partial list of annual events. Changes may occur from year to year, as well as during the year, and it is advisable to consult local tourist offices and the Government Tourist Offices abroad for up-to-date information.

Rome

January	Presentation: Women's High Fashion Collection
March	International Nuclear Electronics and Aerospace Technology Exhibit
May–June	General Trade Fair
July	Presentation: Women's High Fashion Collection

Bologna

March	International Building and Construction Fair
April	Cosmetics & Perfume Exhibition
	Children's Book Fair
May–June	General Trade Fair
September	Shoe Fair
October	International Building and Construction Fair
November	Farm Machinery Fair

Florence

January	Men's Fashions
	International Footwear, Leathergoods, and Accessories Show
April	International Gift and Handicraft Show
September	International Footwear, Leathergoods, and Accessories Show
November	Leathergoods, Shoes, and Bags Machinery Exhibit

Milan

February	International Housewares Exhibit
	International Tourism Exchange
	International Kitchen Furniture Exhibit*
	Heating, Air Conditioning, and Plumbing International Fair
March	Industrial Automation Exhibit
	Ladies High Fashion Show
	International Shoe Show
April	International Trade Fair
	Gold Italia (jewelry, silverware)
May	International Woodworking Machinery and Tools Exhibit*
June	European Knitwear Fair
September	International Office Furniture Exhibit
	Computers, Telecommunications, and High Technology Electronics Exhibit
	International Hi-Fi, Video, and Consumer Electronics Show
	International Housewares Exhibit
	International Furniture and Lighting Exhibition
October	International Leathergoods Market
	Ladies High Fashion Show
November	International Exhibition of Chemistry, Analysis, Research, and Test Equipment
December	European Knitwear Fair

Turin

February–March	International Vacation, Tourism, and Sports Show
April–May	International Auto Show
October–November	International New Technologies Show

* Biennial

For additional information contact:

Italy-America Chamber of Commerce, Inc.
Empire State Building
350 Fifth Avenue
New York, NY 10118
Tel: 212/279-5520

Italian Trade Commission
499 Park Avenue
New York, NY 10022
Tel: 212/980-1500

Ente Autonomo Fiera di Roma
Via Savoia, 78
00198 Roma
Tel: 2/851 471

Relazioni Pubbliche Informazioni
Via Isonzo, 25
00198 Roma
Tel: 06/868 748

Ente Autonomo Per Le
Fiere di Bologna
Piazza Costituzione, 6
40128 Bologna
Tel: 51/50 30 50

Fiera di Milano
Largo Domodossola, 1
20145 Milano
Tel: 2/34 32 51

Torino Esposizioni
Corso Massino D'Azelio, 5
10126 Torino

TRAVEL TIMES

To Italy

Most international flights go to either Milan or Rome, although there are international flights to other Italian cities less frequently. In Milan, flights arrive at Malpensa, about 40 km from the city. To get into Milan itself, take the airport bus, which leaves the airport every 45 minutes. All domestic flights and flights from other European cities land at Linate Airport, only 7 km from the city and a quick taxi ride into town.

Flights to Rome arrive at Leonardo da Vinci Airport, 35 km from the city. Taxis are very expensive from the airport; better alternative is public transportation.

To Malta

There are some direct flights to Malta from London, but most arrivals are through Rome. The airport is located at Luqa, 5 km from Valletta.

To Switzerland

Flights to Geneva arrive at Cointrin Airport, located about 4 km from the center of the city. Taxis are quick but you can also take the airport bus to the Air Terminal at Gare Cornavin. The airport bus runs every 20 minutes.

Approximate Flying Times to Key Italian Cities

New York–Milan	7½ hours
New York–Rome	8 hours
Chicago–Milan	9 hours
Los Angeles–Milan	12 hours
London–Milan	2 hours
London–Rome	2 hours, 15 minutes
Sydney–Rome	12½ hours

Average Flying Times Between Major Italian Cities

Rome–Milan	1 hour
Rome–Genoa	1 hour

Rome–Venice	1 hour
Rome–Turin	1 hour
Milan–Naples	1 hour, 15 minutes
Milan–Bari	1 hour, 25 minutes
Naples–Bologna	1 hour, 15 minutes
Turin–Pisa	50 minutes

Alitalia and Aero Transport Italiani offer domestic flights to most cities. Alisarda also offers domestic flights, including to Sardinia.

Rail Travel

The major Italian train lines are fast and comfortable, although all service slows a bit during the tourist season. Trains have two classes—first and second—with first class being the advisable one to choose. People often disregard the signs distinguishing the classes, thus you are apt to find second-class passengers sitting in first-class seats. Just politely ask the person to move. Passes that are good for unlimited travel within Italy are available to foreigners. They may be purchased for 8, 15, 21, or 30 days. Consult your travel agent or inquire at any railway terminal. The following is a brief description of the varieties of Italian trains.

R	Rapido	High-speed luxury train between major cities (supplementary fare required)
DD	Direttissimo	Fast train, stopping only at main stations between large cities
D	Diretto	Shorter-distance train, stopping only at major stations
L	Locale	Local train, making all stops (also called an accelerato)
TEE	Trans Europa Express	International luxury train linking Italy and other western European countries (with additional fare and reservations)
TEN	Trans Europa Notte	International overnight train with sleeping cars with berths (cuccette, koo-chEHt-teh), which can be reserved from two months to four hours in advance

In Switzerland, all trains to Geneva arrive at Gare Cornavin, which is conveniently located in the center of the city. There are also link-ups with other major Swiss cities, as well as other European cities.

TRAVEL TIPS

On the Plane

1. Be aware that the engine noise is less noticeable in the front part of the plane. Try to sleep. Some frequent trav-

elers bring along earplugs, eyeshades, and slippers.

2. Wear comfortable, loose-fitting clothing.
3. Walk up and down the aisles, when permitted, at least five minutes every hour to maintain body circulation.
4. Limit alcohol intake—altitude heightens the intoxicating effect.
5. Avoid heavy foods and caffeine, which dehydrates the body.
6. Drink plenty of liquids and eat foods rich in potassium. Pressurized cabins cause dehydration.
7. Take it easy when you arrive. When possible, schedule your first important meeting according to your "at home" peak period.

Jet Lag

Disruption of the body's natural cycles can put a lingering damper on your vacation, so take the following precautions:

1. *Avoid loss of sleep* by taking a flight that will get you to your destination early in the evening, if at all possible. Get a good night's sleep at home the night before your departure.
2. *Rearrange your daily routine* and sleeping schedule to harmonize with a normal body clock at your destination.
3. *Avoid stress and last-minute rush.* You're going to need all your strength.
4. *Rearrange your eating habits.* Start four days early—begin a diet of alternate days of feasting and fasting. "Feast" features high-protein breakfasts and lunches (to increase energy level and wakefulness) and high-carbohydrate dinners (to help induce sleep).

Shopping

Shop hours in Italy change with the season. In the winter shops are generally open 8 A.M. to 7 P.M. with a lunch break between 1 and 3. During the tourist season, shops open and close later in the afternoon (4 to 8). Some remain open on Sundays but most close a half day during the week—often Monday morning or Thursday afternoon. In Switzerland stores are generally open until 6:30 P.M.

Drug Stores

The Italian drugstore doesn't stock the variety of goods available in America. For perfume, cosmetics, etc. you'd go to a *profumeria.* A drugstore has a sign outside—a green or red cross. In the window is a notice telling where the nearest all-night drugstore is.

Clothing Sizes

In Europe, clothing sizes vary from country to country, so be sure to try the garment on. Basically, for men, a suit size is "10" more than the American size; thus, an American 40 is a European or Continental 50. For women, the conversion is the American size plus "28"—thus, an American size 10 is a Continental 38.

Electricity

In most large cities in Italy you'll find voltage for electric lights at 110-127 AC, 50-cycle and voltage for appliances at 220 or 230 AC, 50-cycle. Check the voltage before plugging in your appliance. You may find an adapter plug useful.

Film

Film sizes aren't always indicated the same way in Europe as in America. Check carefully before purchasing.

Telephones

In Italy there are fewer public telephones. Most people use the public phone that can be found in cafes and bars. The cashier supplies tokens (*gettoni*). Dialing is direct and on an inter-city basis. You'll find area codes in the directory. You must order long-distance calls in advance.

If possible avoid making telephone calls from your hotel as the cost is excessively high.

Driving

You'll need the following when driving: passport; international insurance certificate (green card); registration (log) book; and a valid driving license. An international driving permit may save you trouble. A red warning triangle—for display on the road in case of an accident—is compulsory.

Tipping

Tipping, of course, varies with the individual and the situation. The following amounts are typical: In hotels in Italy 5% is included in the bill; in Switzerland, the porter should receive 1 franc per bag; in Italy, the porter should receive 1000 lire; in Switzerland, the tip for the maid is included in the bill, in Italy the maid should be tipped 10–20,000 lire per week. In restaurants, 5% is usually included in the check; lavatory and hatcheck attendants usually expect a few hundred lire in Italy and a few francs in Switzerland. Taxi drivers, barbers, and hairdressers should receive 5%; ushers and guides are tipped lesser amounts.

MAJOR HOTELS

Rome

Aldrovandi Palace Hotel
Via Aldrovandi 15, 00197
Tel: 841091; Telex 616141
Major credit cards accepted

Ambasciatori Palace
Via Vittorio Veneto 70, 00187
Tel: 473831; Telex 610241
Major credit cards accepted
Restaurant

Bernini Bristol
Piazza Barberini 23, 00187
Tel: 463151; Telex 610554
Major credit cards accepted

Cavalieri Hilton
Via Cadlolo 101, 00136
Tel: 3151; Telex 610296
(Outdoor pool)
Major credit cards accepted
Restaurant: La Pergola

Cicerone
Via Cicerone 55, 00193
Tel: 3576; Telex 680514
Major credit cards accepted

D'Inghilterra
Via Bocca di Leone 14, 00187
Tel: 672161; Telex 614552
Major credit cards accepted

Eden
Via Ludovisi 49, 00187
Tel: 4743551; Telex 610567
Restaurant

Excelsior
Via Vittorio Veneto 125, 00187
Tel: 4708; Telex 610232

Grand Hotel de la Ville
Via Sistina 69, 00187
Tel: 6733; Telex 620836

Hassler-Villa Medici
Piazza Trinità dei Monti 6, 00187
Tel: 6792651; Telex 610208
Restaurant

Jolly Leonardo da Vinci
Via dei Gracchi 324; 00192
Tel: 39680; Telex 611182
Major credit cards accepted
Restaurant

Jolly Vittorio Veneto
Corso d'Italia 1, 00198
Tel: 8495; Telex 612293
Major credit cards accepted
Restaurant

Le Grand Hotel
Via Vittorio Emanuele Orlando 3, 00185
Tel: 4709; Telex 610210
Major credit cards accepted

Lord Byron
Via De Notaris 5, 00197
Tel: 3609541; Telex 611217
Major credit cards accepted
Restaurant: Relais le Jardin

Mediterraneo
Via Cavour 15, 00184
Tel: 464051
Major credit cards accepted

Plaza
Via del Corso 126, 00186
Tel: 672101; Telex 624669
Major credit cards accepted

Regina Carlton
Via Vittorio Veneto 72, 00187
Tel: 476851; Telex 620863
Major credit cards accepted

Visconti Palace
Via Cesi 37, 00193
Tel: 3684; Telex 680407
Major credit cards accepted

Florence

Baglioni
Piazza Unità Italiana 6, 50123
Tel: 218441; Telex 570225
Major credit cards accepted
Restaurant

Excelsior
Piazza Ognissanti 3, 50123
Tel: 264201; Telex 570002
Major credit cards accepted
Restaurant

Regency Piazza Massimo D'Azeglio 3, 50121
Tel: 245247; Telex 571058
Major credit cards accepted
Restaurant

Savoy
Piazza della Repubblica 7, 50123
Tel: 283313; Telex 570220
Major credit cards accepted
Restaurant

Villa Medici
Via Il Prato 42, 50123
Tel: 261331; Telex 570179
(Outdoor pool)
American Express, Diner's Club accepted
Restaurant: Lorenzaccio

Milan

Anderson
Piazza Luigi di Savoia 20, 20124
Tel: 6690141; Telex 321018
Major credit cards accepted

Carlton Hotel Senato
Via Senato 5, 20121
Tel: 798583; Telex 331306

Cavour
Via Fatebenefratelli 21, 20121
Tel: 650983; Telex 320498
Major credit cards accepted
Restaurant

Dei Cavalieri
Piazza Missori 1, 20123
Tel: 8857; Telex 312040
Major credit cards accepted

Executive
Viale Luigi Sturzo 45, 20154
Tel: 6294; Telex 310191
Major credit cards accepted
Restaurant

Excelsior Gallia
Piazza Duca d'Aosta 9, 20124
Tel: 6277; Telex 311160
Major credit cards accepted
Restaurant

Galileo
Corso Europa 9, 20122
Tel: 7743; Telex 322095
Major credit cards accepted

Grand H. Brun
Via Caldera, 20153
Tel: 45271; Telex 315370
Major credit cards accepted

Grand H. Duomo
Via San Raffaeli 1, 20121
Tel: 8833; Telex 312086
Major credit cards accepted

Grand Hotel et de Milan
Via Manzoni 29, 20121
Tel: 870757; Telex 334505
Major credit cards accepted

Grand H. Fieramilano
Viale Boezio 20, 20145
Tel: 3105; Telex 331426
Major credit cards accepted
Restaurant

Jolly Touring
Via Tarchetti 2, 20121
Tel: 6335; Telex 320118
Major credit cards accepted
Restaurant

Jolly President
Largo Augusto 10, 20122
Tel: 7746; Telex 312054
Major credit cards accepted
Restaurant

Michelangelo
Via Scarlatti 33, 20124
Tel: 6755; Telex 340330
Major credit cards accepted
Restaurant

Milano Hilton
Via Galvani 12, 20124
Tel: 6983; Telex 330433
Major credit cards accepted
Restaurant

Palace
Piazza della Repubblica 20, 20124
Tel: 6336; Telex 311026
Major credit cards accepted
Restaurant: Casanova

Plaza
Piazza Diaz 3, 20123
Tel: 8058452; Telex 321162
American Express, Diner's Club accepted

Principe e Savoia
Piazza della Repubblica 17, 20124
Tel: 6230; Telex 310052
Major credit cards accepted

Select
Via Baracchini 12, 20123
Tel: 8843; Telex 312256
American Express, Visa accepted

Turin

Jolly Hotel Ligure
Piazza Carlo Felice 85, 10123
Tel: 55641; Telex 220167
Major credit cards accepted
Restaurant

Jolly Principi di Piemonte
Via Gobetti 15, 10123
Tel: 519693; Telex 221120
Major credit cards accepted
Restaurant

Turin Palace Hotel
Via Sacchi 8, 10128
Tel: 515511; Telex 221411
Major credit cards accepted
Restaurant

If you are traveling to cities other than the ones mentioned here, you may wish to call the central reservation office in Milan for either of the two following chains:

Ciga—02-626622
Jolly—02-7703

MAJOR RESTAURANTS

Rome

Alberto Ciarla—one star
Piazza San Cosimato 40, 00153
Tel: 5818668
Major credit cards accepted

El Toulà—one star
Via della Lupa 29, 00186
Tel: 6781196
Major credit cards accepted

Girarrosto Toscano—one star
Via Campania 29, 00187
Tel: 493759
Major credit cards accepted

Hostaria dell'Orso
Via Monte Brianzo 93, 00186
Tel: 6564250

La Rosetta—one star
Via della Rosetta 9, 00187
Tel: 6561002
American Express, Diner's Club accepted

Piperno—one star
Monte de'Cenci 9, 00186
Tel: 6540629

Relais Le Jardin—two stars
Via De Notaris 5, 00197
Tel: 3609541; Telex 611217
Major credit cards accepted

Sans Souci—one star
Via Sicilia 20/24, 00187
Tel: 493504
Major credit cards accepted

Ratings extracted from the *Red Michelin Guide,* 1986

Florence

Da Dante-al Lume di Candela
Via delle Terme 23 r, 50123
Tel: 294566
Major credit cards accepted

Enoteca Pinchiorri—two stars
Via Ghibellina 87, 50122
Tel: 242757
American Express accepted

Harry's Bar
Lungarno Vespucci 22 r, 50123
Tel: 296700
American Express accepted

Sabatini
Via de'Panzani 9/a, 50123
Tel: 282802
Major credit cards accepted

Milan

Alfredo-Gran San Bernardo—one star
Via Borghese 14, 20154
Tel: 3319000

A Riccione—one star
Via Taramelli 70, 20124
Tel: 6086807
Major credit cards accepted

Biffi Scala
Piazza della Scala, 20121
Tel: 876332
Major credit cards accepted

Casa Fontana—one star
Piazza Carbonari 5, 20125
Tel: 6892684
American Express, Visa accepted

El Toulà
Piazza Paolo Ferrari 6, 20121
Tel: 870302
Major credit cards accepted

Giannino—one star
Via Amatore Sciesa 8, 20135
Tel: 5452948
Major credit cards accepted

Gualtiero Marchesi—three stars
Via Bonvesin de la Riva 9, 20129
Tel: 741246
American Express accepted

Turin

St. Andrews
Via Sant'Andrea 23, 20121
Tel: 793132
Major credit cards accepted

Savini—one star
Galleria Vittorio Emanuele II, 20121
Tel: 8058343
Major credit cards accepted

Al Gatto Nero—one star
Corso Filippo Turati 14, 10128
Tel: 590414
American Express, Diner's Club accepted

Del Cambio—one star
Piazza Carignano 2, 10123
Tel: 546690
Major credit cards accepted

Tiffany
Piazza Solferino 16/h, 10121
Tel: 540538
American Express accepted

Vecchia Lanterna—one star
Corso Re Umberto 21, 10128
Tel: 537047
American Express, Visa accepted

Villa Sassi-el Toulà—one star
Strada al Traforo del Pino 47, 10132
Tel: 890556
Major credit cards accepted

USEFUL ADDRESSES

American Chamber of Commerce in Italy
12 Via Agnello
20121 Milan

Unione Italiana delle Camere di Commercio Industria Artigianato e Agricoltura
Piazza Sallustio 21
00187 Rome

Associazione Italiana degli Industriali dell'Abbigliamento
Foro Bonaparte 70
20121 Milan

Camera Nazionale dell'Alta Moda Italiana
Piazza Aracoeli 3
50123 Florence

Unione Industriale Pastai Italiani UN.I.P.I.
Via Po 102
00198 Rome

Federceramica
Piazza del Liberty 8
20121 Milan

Associazione Industrie Dolciarie Italiane A.I.D.I.
Via 6 Oriani 92
00197 Rome

Associazione Italiana Industriali Prodotti Alimentari
Via Pietro Verri 8
20121 Milan

Federazione Italiana
Industriali Produttori
Esportatori ed
Importatori di Vini,
Acquaviti, Liquori,
Sciroppi, Aceti ed Affini
Via Mentana 2-B
00185 Rome

Associazione Italian
Manufatturieri Pelle
Cuoio e Succedanei—
A.I.M.P.E.S.
Viale Beatrice d'Este 43
20122 Milan

Associazione Industria
Marmifera Italiana e delle
Industrie Affini
Via Nizza 59
00198 Rome

Associazione Italiana
Editori A.I.E.
Via della Erba 2
20121 Milan

Borsa Valori
Via del Burro 147
00186 Rome

Confederazione Generale
dell'Industria Italiana
Viale dell'Astronomia 30
Rome

MAPS

The following maps of Europe, Italy and Switzerland, will be useful in doing business in Italian-speaking areas.

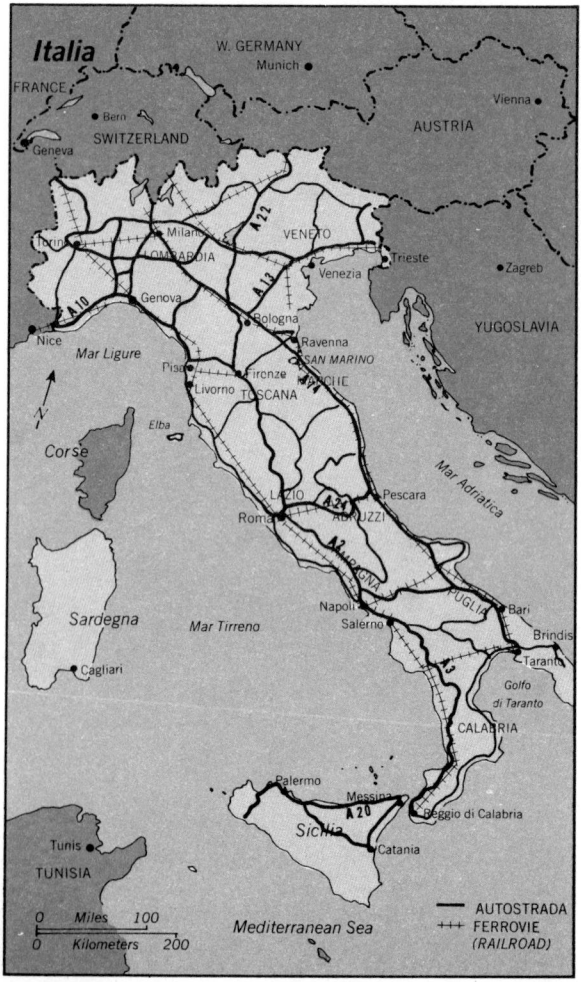

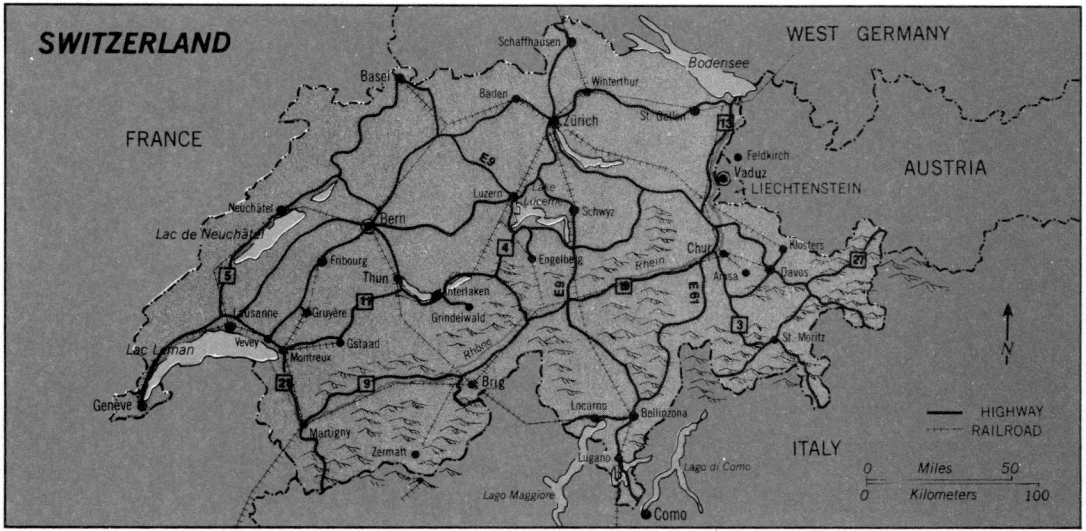
SWITZERLAND
WEST GERMANY
FRANCE
AUSTRIA
ITALY
LIECHTENSTEIN
Bodensee
Schaffhausen
Basel
Baden
Winterthur
Zürich
St. Gallen
Feldkirch
Vaduz
Neuchâtel
Lac de Neuchâtel
Bern
Luzern
Lac de Lucerne
Schwyz
Fribourg
Thun
Interlaken
Engelberg
Grindelwald
Lausanne
Gruyère
Vevey
Lac Léman
Gstaad
Montreux
Genève
Martigny
Zermatt
Brig
Rhône
Rhein
Chur
Arosa
Davos
Klosters
St. Moritz
Locarno
Bellinzona
Lugano
Lago di Como
Lago Maggiore
Como
E9
HIGHWAY
RAILROAD
0 Miles 50
0 Kilometers 100
N

Europe
0
200 miles
0
200
400 Km
Hebrides
Orkney Is.
Sherland Is.
Ber
Stava
SCOTLAND
Aberdeen
Dundee
Glasgow
Edinburgh
North
Sea
UNITED
KINGDOM
Newcastle
Teesside
Hull
Manchester
Sheffield
Stoke
Nottingham
Birmingham
Norwich
Amsterdam
Den Haag
Rotterdam
NETHE
NORTHERN
IRELAND
Belfast
IRISH
REPUBLIC
Dublin
Irish
Sea
Cork
Waterford
WALES
ENGLAND
Swansea
Cardiff
London
Bristol
Southampton
Plymouth
Land's End
English
Channel
ATLANTIC
OCEAN
Lille
Luxemb
Paris
Reims
Brest
Rennes
Le Mans
Nantes
FRANCE
Bay of
Biscay
Limoges
Clermont
Ferrand
Massif
Central
Bordeaux
Toulouse
Nîmes
Marseille
Gulf of
Lions
La Coruña
C. Finisterre
Gijón
San Sebastián
Vigo
Burgos
Pyrenees
ANDORRA
Sabadell
Barcelona
Porto
Coimbra
Valladolid
Zaragoza
Madrid
C. Tortosa
Lisbon
SPAIN
Badajoz
Valencia
Balearic Islands
(Sp.)
Menorca
Palma
Mallorca
Ibiza
C. de
la Nao
Sevilla
Córdoba
Murcia
Alicante
Cartagena
Málaga
Almería
Gulf of
Cadiz
Cádiz
Jérez
C. Trafalgar
GIBRALTAR (Br.)
Tangier
Algier
Medi
terr
55°N
50°N
45°N
40°N
8°W
0°
5°E

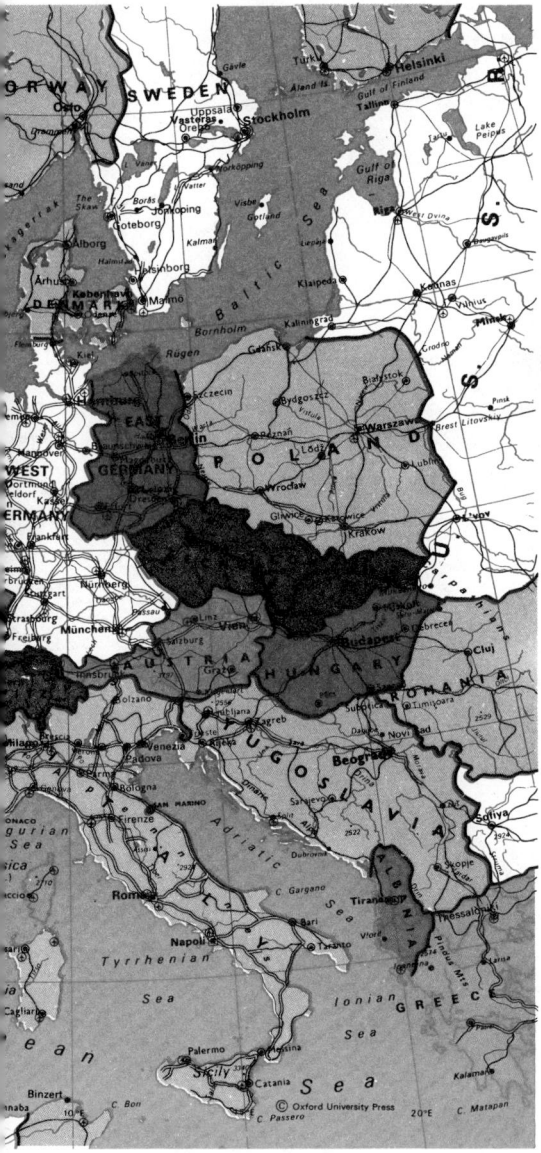
NORWAY
Oslo
SWEDEN
Gävle
Uppsala
Vasteras
Orebro
Stockholm
Turku
Helsinki
Aland Is
Gulf of Finland
Tallinn
Tartu
Lake Peipus
Gulf of Riga
Riga
Norrköping
Vänern
Vättern
Borås
Jönköping
Göteborg
Visby
Gotland
Kalmar
Alborg
Halmstad
Hässleborg
Aarhus
Kobenhavn
DENMARK
Malmö
Baltic Sea
Bornholm
Klaipeda
Kaunas
Vilnius
Minsk
Kaliningrad
Rügen
Gdansk
Bialystok
Pinsk
Brest Litovskiy
Szczecin
Bydgoszcz
Warszawa
EAST
GERMANY
Berlin
POLAND
Poznan
Lodz
Lublin
WEST
GERMANY
Wrocław
Katowice
Krakow
Lvov
Frankfurt
Nurnberg
Stuttgart
München
Passau
Linz
Wien
Bratislava
Budapest
Debrecen
Cluj
AUSTRIA
Graz
HUNGARY
ROMANIA
Bolzano
Ljubljana
Zagreb
Timisoara
Venezia
Padova
Novi Sad
Beograd
Bologna
SAN MARINO
Firenze
Sarajevo
Sofiya
Adriatic
Dubrovnik
Skopje
Roma
C. Gargano
Tirana
Thessaloniki
Napoli
Bari
Taranto
Vlorá
Tyrrhenian
Sea
Ionian
Sea
GREECE
Palermo
Messina
Sicily
Catania
Sea
Kalamata
Binzert
C. Bon
C. Passero
20°E
C. Matapan
© Oxford University Press

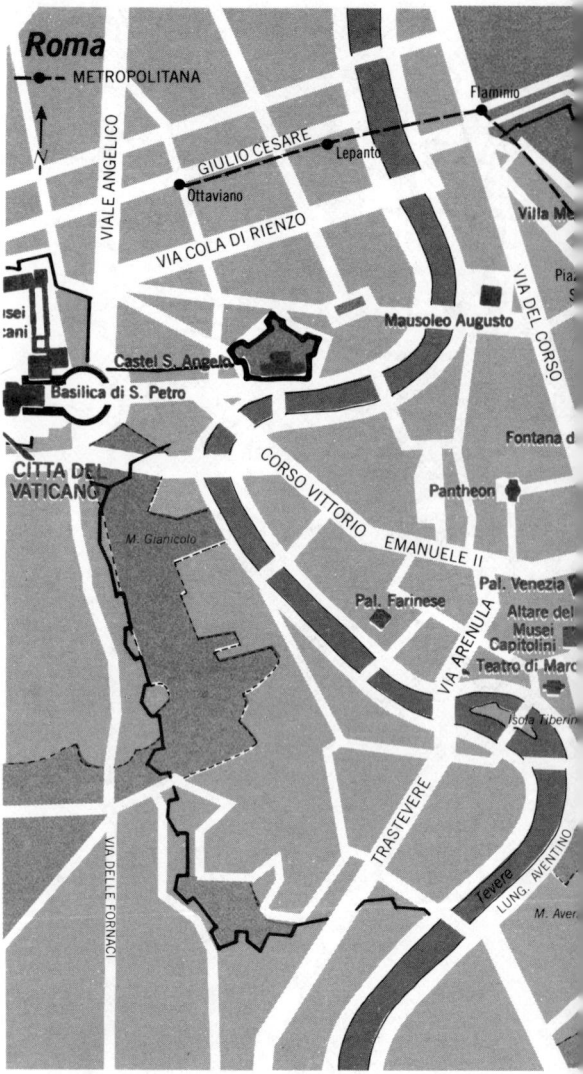
Roma
METROPOLITANA
N
VIALE ANGELICO
GIULIO CESARE
Ottaviano
Lepanto
Flaminio
VIA COLA DI RIENZO
Mausoleo Augusto
VIA DEL CORSO
Castel S. Angelo
Basilica di S. Petro
CITTA DEL VATICANO
M. Gianicolo
CORSO VITTORIO EMANUELE II
Pantheon
Fontana d
Pal. Venezia
Pal. Farinese
Altare del
Musei
Capitolini
Teatro di Marc
VIA ARENULA
TRASTEVERE
Tevere
LUNG. AVENTINO
VIA DELLE FORNACI